THE HELLPIG HUNT

THE HELLPIG HUNT

Humberto Fontova

**A HUNTING AND FISHING
ADVENTURE IN THE WILD
WETLANDS AT THE MOUTH OF
THE MISSISSIPPI RIVER BY
MIDDLE-AGED LUNATICS WHO
REFUSE TO GROW UP**

M. Evans and Company, Inc.

New York

M. Evans and Company, Inc.
216 East 49th Street
New York, New York 10017

Library of Congress Cataloging-in-Publication Data

Fontova, Humberto.
   The Hellpig Hunt: A Hunting and Fishing Adventure in the Wild Wetlands at the Mouth of the Mississippi River by Middle-Aged Lunatics Who Refuse to Grow Up / Humberto Fontova
   p. cm.
   ISBN 1-59077-009-9
   1. Hunting--Louisiana--Mississippi River Delta. I. Title.

SK83.F66 2003
799.29763'37--dc21

Book Design and Typesetting by Evan Johnston

10   9   8   7   6   5   4   3   2   1

DEDICATION

This book is dedicated to James "Tom" Nall. To call Tom a "trooper" hits short. To say he was "good-natured," seems feeble too. To say he was the best hunting-fishing-diving buddy anyone could ever be blessed with is the best I can do.

Malice, acrimony, bitterness—these concepts were alien to Tom Nall. During 17 years of close friendship I simply cannot recall seeing a frown of anger or despair on his face, and God knows he had ample provocation. After all, his hunting, fishing and diving was with the crew you'll read about in the coming pages. You'll see.

On our first scuba-diving trip we "veterans" scoffed at his advice to always carry an extra ten gallon gas tank on the boat.("What a ninny! Knew we shouldn't brought this guy!")

Seven hours later we were frantically bailing the boat with our goggles, empty beer cans—anything!—as five foot waves crashed over the side. We were fifteen miles offshore in a hellacious squall, black skies, horizontal rain, deafening thunder, lighting flashing all around, dead radio, complete hysteria. We'd run out of gas.

On his first duck hunting trip, he suggested (good-naturedly, as always) that we might be overloading a pirogue with so many guns, shellbuckets, etc. "Tom!" we snorted. "We been doin' this crap for twenty years, alright!"

Ten minutes later we were chest deep in frigid slop, groping the muddy bottom of the bayou with our bare hands for our shotguns. The pirogue had sunk, dumping our guns and ammo to the bottom.

I could go on for pages. But you get the picture. He only hung with us for 17 years, so by our standards he was always the newcomer. But we'll treasure those memories of hunting, fishing and diving with Tom as among the fondest of our lives. His ready (and genuine) smile and his relentless (and genuine) good nature became joyful fixtures in our boats, duck-blinds and hunting camps. We'll make a go of it, but I'm afraid those places will never be quite the same without him.

CONTENTS

PROLOGUE

All the planning and shopping for the trip had me pumped. But the *big* day—the day we'd depart for the Delta—was still two days away. No way I could hold off on hunting till then. My blood lust was raging. I had an idea.

I'd been seeing deer almost daily in a little field next to the Wal-Mart. Our bow-season supply of venison had expired long ago and we could sure use some more. So I parked at the Wal-Mart parking lot before dawn, trudged into the woods, and humped up a tree in my climbing stand, shotgun in hand, slugs in pocket.

Ten minutes after daybreak, a fat spike ambled by. I whistled and he stopped, ears erect, looking straight at me. The bead settled on his neck—*squeeeeze*, POW! He collapsed, kicked a little, tried to raise his head once, and was still.

A gorgeous sight. I was trembling spastically, giddy with excitement and glee. Now I'd butcher it and cook up a storm tonight. Shirley (five months pregnant) was on vacation from cooking. The smells "made her sick," so I'd been taking up the slack. I'd rustle up some venison *mignon* for the parting meal tonight, cook a couple of roasts for Shirley to make cold cuts for her office party and for the kids to make sandwiches and stuff while I was gone, maybe make a big pot of venison chili for their tortilla chips and hot dogs, and leave for the camping trip in the warm glow of domestic bliss.

I'm hanging the deer on the swing set, as usual, for skinning and butchering when—

"Oh, Hum-BERTO! Pu-LEAZE!"

I look over and it's our new neighbor, Freddie, wailing from his patio door, his face a mask of horror and disgust.

"Humberto! How could YOU? Why, that's *awful!*"

Freddie moved here recently from San Francisco. People didn't skin deer in their backyards there. Freddie used to open his back door, prance to the fence, and discuss the screen and stage with fellow wine-sniffers.

Now he opens his back door and finds a deer dangling by its hocks from the swing set next door. It's tongue hangs out. Some guy in blood-spattered camo slashes at it with a skinning knife, between swigs from a sixteen-ounce Bud in a crumpled bag.

I looked over after a hearty swig. "How could I?" I belched. "How *could* I? It's easy, Fred." I wiped my bloody finger on my pants, held it aloft, and curled it. "You do *this*." Then I made trigger-pulling motions. "See, Fred? See how easy? Bet even you could do it, Freddie, my boy. You're good with your fingers aren't ya?"

"Oh! You . . . you . . . *you!*" SLAM!

Good riddance. Then the door opens again and Shirley waddles out. "Haven't I told you to do that *someplace else!* My goodness! Can't you . . . oh, why *bother!*" SLAM!

Well, so much for domestic bliss.

Shirley's always having coffee with that dizzy little queen. They get along famously. He's a designer of some kind—designs Mardi Gras floats, in fact. Always happens that way: heterosexual women and gay men get along. Heterosexual men and gay women . . . well, almost never.

But I was in no mood for sociological reflection. I was still giddy from the ego-buzz of a successful hunt, not to mention the fizzy effects of my second Bud Tall Boy.

I shouldn't complain about Freddie, anyway. Like most of his ilk, he's a sharp guy, and a damn friendly one. Two months after moving in, he got free tickets to the Bacchus Ball for Shirley, me, and six of our friends. Great taste in wine, too.

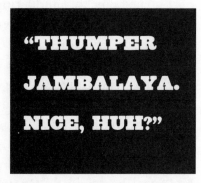

"THUMPER JAMBALAYA. NICE, HUH?"

Watch, he'll bring over an excellent merlot when Shirley invites him over for braised venison mignon tonight. I'll use a little to deglaze the pan I seared the cutlets in, then add a little more butter, chopped fresh mushrooms, and a pinch of diced garlic. Let that gorgeous mess bubble and fill the room with its heavenly aroma, then stir in a little heavy cream to thicken the gravy, then YUMMMM!

Freddie gobbles every smidgen, yumming away while rolling his eyes, almost like he was—never mind.

Sure enough, there's his distinctive knock. Ten minutes early, and each soft little hand holds a bottle of wine. Freddie looked primed to rip into the braised backstrap of the deer he denounced me for assassinating.

He peeked into the kitchen where I slaved over a hot range. "Ummmm!" He exclaimed with an eye-flutter. "Smells *heavenly* in here!"

I gulped deeply from my whiskey, wiped my mouth with my apron, and turned around. "You're in for a treat, Freddie, my boy." I rasped as the whiskey seared my throat. "See here?" I lifted the lid. "Thumper jambalaya. Nice, huh?"

"Oh, yes, certainly looks wonderful, but I . . . . "

"And here!" I banged the spoon on the pot bubbling in the rear. "Donald and Daffy Gumbo Ya-Ya." I pointed toward the microwave. "Bambi's in there, on the serving platter."

"Great!" He smacked his lips and rolled his eyes dreamily. "I can't wait!"

3

I turned quickly, shuddering with revulsion. Shirley balks, but I insist we throw out any silverware he uses when he dines over.

"Monica!" Freddie called to my teen-aged daughter upstairs. "Dinner's served. Hurry before it gets cold." Monica was home from Louisiana State University for the holidays. They get along well. Freddie helped pick her prom dress, did her hair, suggested a restaurant, the whole bit.

"Like your meat warm, do ya, Freddie?" I said, while pouring a hefty glass from his Chateau-something-or-other.

"Sure," he twinkled. "Doesn't everyone?"

"Of course we do!" I said, while raising the wineglass.

"Oh brother," Shirley sighed. "He's starting already Monica! Hurry down, honey. Show's about to start."

"We all like it warm, Freddie, because that's what *fresh* meat tasted like before the discovery of fire. Warm, the temperature of the blood of a living mammal. That's how our primeval ancestors ate it, Freddie, like all predators."

"Oh, Humberto, *please!*" Shirley huffed. "Not *now*. Can't you . . . ."

"Carnivores, especially those lovable cuddly wolves your California buddies get so giddy over, start ingesting prey while it's *still alive*, Fred!" I gulped again, emptying the glass. "They hamstring or disembowel the elk to bring it down. Then they dig in while it's still moaning and writhing in agony. Those big furry puppies daydream about that when Cindy Crawford, Daryl Hannah, and Kim Basinger nuzzle with them for the cameras."

"That's awful." Freddie sighed. "And *must* we really hear all this while . . . ."

"Your cat, too, Freddie." I snapped. The effects of the wine and whiskey were beginning to manifest. "He knows that his claws . . . ."

"It's a *she*, for your information," he corrected.

"Okay, whatever. I watched *her* by the bird feeder the other day. She grabbed a squirrel, Freddie. Shoulda seen *that!*"

"No!" he gasped. "Little Muffin would *never*—"

"The hell she wouldn't, Fred!" I raved. "She knows her claws and fangs weren't made for that mush you give her in a bowl. She craves fresh blood. She longs to feel her fangs sink into a squirrel's throat,

4

to hear the piteous squealing as he scratches and thrashes, to feel the life slowly ooze out of it—then to rip straight into its heart and liver, smacking her lips, and licking her bloody chops in delight. And that's exactly what she did, Freddie. I saw the whole thing. Jesus, and I used to *hate* cats."

"Humberto!" Shirley glared. "That's enough! Come, now. Don't spoil . . . ."

"We're no different, Freddie. Look in your mouth—never mind! Point is, you have incisors, too. And your eyes point *forward*, Freddie, like those of all predators. Behold the hawk or falcon. His eyes point forward, unlike the duck or pigeon, his prey. Their eyes lie on the sides of their heads. Behold the wolf and leopard and, indeed, Muffin. Forward again. The deer, antelope, and squirrel, also on the side of the head. And your eyes are blue, Freddie. Know why?"

"Well," he said sheepishly while fluttering his eyelashes. "They're actually colored contacts. I decided . . . ."

"Never mind! Blue eyes blended better with the snowy landscape inhabited by your Northern European hunter ancestors. They allowed them to sneak closer to prey. . . . Hunting's encoded into your genes, Freddie, give in! Hunting made us what we are!"

I emptied my second helping of wine, then leaped from my chair towards the bookcase, just as Monica entered.

"Oh, NO!" She wailed while rolling her eyes ceilingward. "Not again, Mom! He's grabbing that STUPID book of his again!"

"Stupid book?" I wheeled around and shook the dog-eared copy of José Ortega y Gasset's *Meditations on Hunting*. "A work of genius!" I yelled. "Ortega was the century's most acute philosopher!"

"Yeah, right," Monica huffed. "My philosophy professor says he was a reactionary."

"Figures!" I howled while turning to Shirley. "See? See what we're paying for?"

"She won a scholarship." Shirley said in her best Alice Kramden. "Remember?"

"That's not the point." Then I turned to my multi-earringed (but, mercifully, still untattooed) daughter, "Tell me, Monica. What philosophers *are* they teaching you about up there? Rosie O'Donnell or Courtney Love?"

"Alanis Morissette, actually," she said smugly. "We're discussing her lyrics."

"Heaven help us!" I shrieked, then opened the book and read: "Man's *being* consisted first of being a *hunter.*" I looked up with a Jack Nicholson-type leer. "Hear that folks? That's not some editorialist at the National Rifle Association or Ducks Unlimited. That's the man who wrote *Revolt of the Masses.* I don't suppose they've assigned *that* for philosophy class, huh, Monica?"

"No, *Dad,*" she said with another eye-roll. "But in English they assigned Maya Angelou's . . . ."

"Silence! Before I puke! Now back to Ortega: 'If we imagine our species to have disappeared in the Paleolithic era the word *man* would lack meaning. We would have to call him *hunter.*'"

I pointed a white-knuckle fist inches from Freddie's face. "And you." Then I looked around the room with a lunatic leer, pointing. "And you . . . and you. You're all killers! Every time you buy a hamburger, you're paying for the death of an animal. You're putting a contract, a hit if you will, on a poor stupid cow. Yes! It's called the law of supply and demand—don't suppose they're teaching you anything about *that* up in college, huh, Monica?"

"No, but we learned about Marx and Bakunin and . . . ."

"Figures!" I snarled. "Anyway, folks, I make *my own hits,* like Mikey Corleone. Remember Michael Corleone, Freddie? Remember when he whacked Police Chief McCluskey in that restaurant, huh? BLAM!" I slammed the table with my fist. "Right through the neck!"

"Watch it, you *clod!*" Shirley screeched. " You're spilling the . . . ."

"Oops!"

"And watch the lamp behind you! And the coffee table! And there goes the red wine all over the damn rug!"

"Ooops! Here, I'll get the towel, nothing to it. Well, same with this deer we're eating, folks. Poor sucker was enjoying his meal just like McCluskey, contentedly munching away on acorns. He hears my whistle, looks up—BLAM!" I slammed my fist into my palm inches from Freddie's nose. "Right through his white throat patch. Never knew what hit him."

"Mom, tell Dad to shut up! *Please!*"

"We're all killers!" I turned back to Freddie. "It's encoded into your genes, Freddie! Be true to your human heritage. Stalk the fields and forests, not public toilets!"

"Humberto!" Shirley yelled as Freddie tried to leap to his feet. "Stop IT!"

"Yes! Freddie!" I seized him roughly by the shoulders. "I'm going tomorrow. Come with me and prey on deer and ducks, not Boy Scouts and altar boys!"

"Oh! Oh! Shirley!" Freddie shook free and looked toward her for succor, nearing tears. "He's impossible! This man is so mean! He's simply *impossible!*"

"More wine!" I snarled while holding out my glass.

"Get it yourself!" Monica glowered. "Mom? Don't! You're not his slave!"

"You!" I pointed at Monica. "You stay outta this, before I back-hand ya!"

Monica went apeshit. "Mom, did you hear that? Hear Dad? Ms. Rabinowitz, my sociology professor, says I can sue you for abuse!"

"The hell with that dingbat!" I raved. "Probably a dyke, too! Now get me some more wine!"

"Dad, you're such a fascist!"

"Oh, Monica, hush up." Shirley said. "You know he's never laid a hand on you. He's just showing off in front of Freddie." Then she turned to me and yelled, "Humberto! You *know* Freddie doesn't do those types of things! You apologize *this minute!* And after drinking all his wine. Now you apologize! I *mean* it!"

Freddie ran home in a huff, but I called, feigned contrition, and he returned, amazingly, with more wine. The night improved from that point on, but Elaine, Shirley's sister, never made it in time for the meal.

She finally made her grand entrance—with escorts—just as we turned in. I was bushed, groggy, a headache was already setting in, but my hunting and camping stuff was lovingly packed and stacked.

Shirley hit the remote for Letterman, and I'd just turned over when the door crashed in and the terrified screams erupted.

WHUMP! WHACK! "Oh, *please*, no!"

"Shut up, mutha-fucka! *I said*, shut up!" Thump-thump!

Holy shit! was all I could think, and I sprang for a shotgun. Two were already cased up in the garage, but two were left on the gun rack, about twenty feet away from the bed. I grabbed the pump and started slipping in shells, which I kept on top of the dresser.

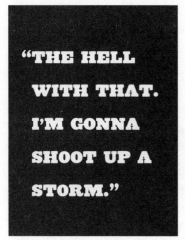

"THE HELL WITH THAT. I'M GONNA SHOOT UP A STORM."

"Don't shoot!" came Elaine's cry from the darkness downstairs. She could hear the loading. She knew me. "Don't shoot, Humberto! Please!"

They'd grabbed her as she was entering through the front door at midnight, rammed a gun to her head, and crashed in.

Jesus, I thought. You rehearse these things all the time in your head, at least in high-crime cities like New Orleans. Now it's *happening!* And I'm sitting here in my underwear with a loaded shotgun, finally facing game that can shoot back. This might be fun . . . .

I swear I wasn't scared at the time (that came later, and in spades). "Don't shoot, Humberto!" my terrified sister-in-law shrieked again.

The hell with that! I thought. *I'm gonna shoot up a storm. Not every day you get the jump on some scumbags and a legal excuse to splatter their guts around. The saps had no idea they were walking into a goddamn armory. Hah! Can't wait to see their eyes when they look down this barrel. I'll scatter their brains all over my den. Hell, we're insured.*

The hallway was dark as I moved toward the stairway. The safety was off and my finger was tense on the trigger. "Under fire a man's powers of life heighten in proportion to the proximity of death," says Philip Caputo in *A Rumor of War*. "He feels an elation as extreme as his dread. His senses quicken."

Phil has a point. This was a far cry from combat, but there was some of that feeling here. I got to the stairs, hit the light switch, and aimed, ready to start blasting away. That would have been very stupid.

At the foot of the stairs stood my sister-in-law, a grimy black hand covering her mouth, and two dreadlocked savages gripping her from each side. One held a revolver to her temple, the other pointed a .44 straight my face. Elaine's eyes looked like cue balls.

My little sweet sixteen pump was aimed at the Rasta-thug who was aiming at me. He was about thirty feet away. The bead covered his ugly, filthy head, everything but the dreadlocks, which came to his shoulders. "Put it down, man!" he snarled. "Put the fucking gun *down*, man!"

I didn't budge. The bead was steady. The safety was off. My finger was tensing. I *swear* I felt no fright, right then. "In combat, he attains an acuity of consciousness at once pleasurable and excruciating—an elevated state of awareness." That's Phil Caputo again. And again, he's right. I simply don't recall being scared at the moment, but I definitely felt that acuity of consciousness.

The same applied to them. They sure as hell didn't look scared either. Elaine? Well, that's a different matter. One of the savages was even starting to smile, displaying some fancy gold bridgework. This confused me.

Jesus, I thought. *It's not supposed to go this way. What now?*

Hell, criminals are always cowards in the movies. Now here's a guy who should be jailed just for his looks, he's got a shotgun pointed at him, and he's *smiling*. In fact, he's walking up toward me!

He took two steps and stopped. He adjusted the grip on his gun for a split second, waving his fingers around the grip just like Lee Marvin as Liberty Valance.

I can't believe this shit, I'm thinking. Just like in the movies. My bead was on his nose now, barely covering from his eyes to his mouth . . . time for a decision. *I know what you're thinking* . . . The Dirty Harry monologue was in my head, only it was directed toward

9

me. *This is your quail-hunting shotgun, right, Humberto? Which means it has the open choke, right? An improved cylinder choke, right? For a good open pattern when a covey explodes from underfoot, right? Did you IN FACT switch barrels from the full to the improved like you'd planned last week? Cause if you did, and you shoot, that pattern will be wide enough to pepper your sister-in-law, too, and probably not tight enough to blast the scumbag's face into black bean chili. You can't take 'em both out with one shot. Either you or Elaine will get it. Elaine for sure . . . so you might ask yourself, "Do I feel lucky today?" Well, do you?*

"Put the fucking gun down, man! Last time!" Then he took another step, as did the other one, shoving Elaine along, up another step, up another. Finally, the first one was five feet in front of me, saying, "Put the fuckin' gun down!"

I did. I lowered it and he jerked it from my grasp. These guys were good. "On the floor," he snarled "You, too!" he said, pointing at my wife in the bed behind me.

"Leave her alone!" I yelled and walked toward her. "She's pregnant." The gun barrel was jammed into the base of my skull.

"Down! *Down* on the floor! *All* of ya! Face down!"

Shirley walked over and lay down on the carpet beside me. We clutched hands. Elaine was shoved down next to her. Thank God the kids were at Maw-Maw's. Yep, execution style, I thought. At least it'll be quick. I lifted my head for a last look around.

"Keep your fuckin' head *down*, I said, or I'll *blow* it off!"

Or? I thought. *Or?* The word caught in my mind. (Here's that "acuity" Caputo was talking about.) Hey, doesn't that imply that they're not gonna blow them off as a matter of routine? Right after they force me to watch them gang-rape and murder my five-months pregnant wife?"

Maybe we'll get out of this thing alive, after all, I thought. I swear, I was thinking that.

"Well lookit there!" one of them whooped.

Wonderful, I thought. Their mood is improving. He sounded genuinely thrilled, almost in a good mood. Then I saw his sneakers walking toward the gun rack. Now the other one walked over. They emptied it. The sneakers walked back toward us. Then one bent down to grab Shirley's hand. I jerked my head up again, but this time he didn't threaten to blow it off.

"The ring," he said, pointing awkwardly with his .44 while cradling his armload of rifles and shotguns. He seemed almost to be asking for it, making no motion to jerk it off himself.

"Oh, yes!" Shirley said while sitting up. "The ring! Why, of course, here!" She started tugging at it herself. "I'm pregnant!" she said, smiling sheepishly. "Five months. See?" She poked out her abdomen triumphantly. "So my fingers are swollen." She held them up. "I can't . . . *just can't*," and she tugged at her finger.

"That's okay, Miss," said the Rasta-thug (I swear he said that). "Don't worry bout it. Now get your heads back down."

We heard them clumping down the stairs. Waited a few seconds, then got up. The front door was open, and they'd booked.

Five minutes later, I was a trembling, stuttering wreck. Elaine and Shirley were—I swear—laughing. The danger was over. The emotional damn had burst. "They were actually kinda nice," Shirley gushed. "To leave me my ring like that."

Then she started cackling crazily. "And there's Dirty Harry!" she laughed, pointing at me. "Mr. Bad-ass Gunslinger at the showdown with his pump shotgun!"

Christ, I thought, *she's flipped—the strain was too much for her.* She was gasping now, red-faced.

"I could see your back through the hall, standing at the top of the stairs, aiming down," Shirley cackled. She was convulsed, dripping drool from her lower lip, leaning on Elaine's shoulder.

"Take it easy, honey." I moved over and put my arm around her shoulder. "Come on now."

"And, and, and!" She kept nodding, eyes shut, but couldn't get the words out of her contorted mouth. She collapsed in Elaine's arms. Both convulsed now. "And your underwear, your *underwear!*" she whooped, catching her breath now. "Your underwear was rolled—up your butt crack!"

This jump-started Elaine. They looked like they were hooked to two hundred volts, doubled over jerking, clutching each other, laughing and drooling. "Like a thong! Looked like a thong. Look!"

Shirley tried to point with her jerking arm.

I felt behind me. Jesus, she was right. I'd slid rather than jumped out of bed. The sliding did the trick. Dirty Harry as American Gigolo.

"I know!" Elaine howled. "I was, I was, I noticed when they shoved you on the floor!" They were rolling on the bed now, in tears. "Whoo-whoo!" Elaine was grabbing the air. "You got a cute butt, honey. Had no idea how cute."

I pulled out the fabric and spread it over my goose-pimpled cheeks, then reached for my robe. Jesus, leave it to women.

When the cops came, we learned of a spate of similar armed robberies in the area—most accompanied by rapes. Good thing I didn't know that. This episode might have ended in a bloodbath. A robbery versus Elaine's life? The decision was fairly easy. But a gang-rape, too? I might have blasted away. Whooo! I still shudder at the memory.

Amazingly, Shirley insisted I go on the trip as planned. She followed the kids and went to Maw-Maw's herself for a few days.

CHAPTER ONE

GIRLS GONE WILD

"Had Dante seen it," wrote Frances Trollope of the place, "he might have drawn images of another hell from its horrors!" Indeed, in Dante's "Upper Hell," "the lustful, gluttonous, and avaricious" are "blown by strong winds, stung by insects, and put to useless labor." Dante described both our trip and us pretty accurately, but he left out: chomped by alligators, menaced by poisonous serpents, pursued by brutal game wardens, blinded and stranded by hellacious fog, stomped by a four-hundred-pound wild boar, chased by a cloud of deadly poison gas, and enticed by exotic dancers.

13

We spent our Christmas vacation in Hell's very gizzard—voluntarily. This book follows the cast of *The Helldivers' Rodeo* on a three-day hunting-fishing-boozing trip to the wild wetlands at the mouth of the Mississippi River, one hundred miles below New Orleans.

Here's a three-day orgy of blood-lust, booze, and lechery; a three-day indulgence of our primal passions in primitive splendor, free from the finger-wagging of pecksniffs, the scowls of moralists and busybodies, the nagging of wives. Three days of shameless boozing, of blasting ducks, of arrowing deer, of chasing (and getting chased by) huge wild boar, of jerking fish from the water, and of drunken campfire reminiscing about the magnificent disco era, our glory years.

"Males have only a brief period of exhilarating liberty between control by their mothers and control by their wives," writes Camille Paglia in *Sex, Art and American Culture*. Indeed! And that was the disco era for us. Just off the nest, in our early college years, no thought of jobs or family—hell, not even a major—just pure partying.

A colorful crew live, work, and play down here in the Mississippi Delta. This area of Louisiana was always a legal limbo, a no-man's land where pirates, smugglers, cutthroats, power-mad political bosses, sleazy politicians, assorted wastrels, and outlaws traditionally fled for cover or carved out little empires, duchies, and hideouts. Convicted murderer Jack Henry Abbott, author of *In the Belly of the Beast* and Norman Mailer's pin-up boy, was finally snared by the authorities down here in 1985 after escaping prison. He'd just returned from a ten-day stint working on an offshore oil platform.

Jean Lafitte started the tradition that continued through the notorious Leander Perez (they even have properly banana-republic sounding names down here), and it is kept alive by scores of drug smugglers and poachers to this day. Plaquemine's parish political boss Leander Perez scoffed at George Wallace as a "softie and a sell-out" and prepared the dungeons in an abandoned Spanish fort at the mouth of the Mississippi, not far from our campsite, for any "Yankee communists and anarchists" who dared set foot in his parish (we have parishes in Louisiana, not counties) during the civil rights struggles. Perez even climbed atop the fort and posed—with a defiant Pattonesque scowl and clutching a shotgun—for the local papers.

In his defiance of the feds, Leander Perez brought even Louisiana Governor Earl Long (Huey's brother) to the edge of apoplexy. "Come on, Leander!" Uncle Earl bellowed at the perpetually scowling Caudillo in 1961 after a particularly stupid outburst. "Whatcha gonna do, man? The feds have the Bomb!"

Some game wardens down here still owe allegiance to the Perez dynasty. Family and friends get away with slaughter, but *woe* to any "outsiders" (us) who try anything cute.

Actually, Frances Trollope didn't know the half of it. She was on her way to New Orleans with lips curled and snoot raised, observing these fetid expanses of tropical brush, squishy mud-flats, and decaying slop from the comfort of a ship. She couldn't see (or feel, or swat, or inhale) the clouds of stinging insects. She never saw the snakes and alligators crawling through the putrid slime. She never got bogged to her waist in its vicious quagmires while stalking a deer with bow and arrow. She never baked, steamed, or sweltered in its foul miasma.

This expanse of prime duck-, deer-, and hog-hunting ground remains surprisingly less than crowded winter long. It's a pain to get here, a pain to travel through, and a bitch to hunt. "Primitive camping," they call it. No roads, RV hook-ups, or even trails in this watery wilderness. The nearest road ends twenty-five miles away. Get home from three days of this camping and don't expect a big hug from the wife. Prepare to hear her screech and flee from the bristly, smelly, mud-spattered apparition.

Primitive, indeed—hence, still pristine. Even better, here's the very tip of the Mississippi Flyway funnel, America's main thoroughfare for migrating waterfowl. For millennia, the Mississippi and its tributaries have served as a network of highways for migrating ducks. A third of North America's wildfowl winter in these marshes every year.

They find the place, to quote Robert Palmer, "simply irresistible," and with good reason. Maps show how Louisiana juts out into the

Gulf below the coasts of Texas and Mississippi. A little sliver of a peninsula bordering the river below New Orleans juts out even further. That was the river's doing, at least until the levees shackled it. For ten thousand years, this "father of all waters," as the Indians called it, whipped back and forth across the landscape like a huge (but somewhat lethargic) water wiggle, depositing its fertile cargo of sediment. The river robs Peter to pay Paul, in a sense. Iowa's loss was our gain, until the levees went up, that is. Most of Louisiana below Interstate 12 thus sprouted. In geological terms, something "sprouts" in ten thousand years.

These fertile mudflats sprout in thick orchards of prime waterfowl fodder every spring, and stay thick and green year-round. According to figures from Ducks Unlimited, Louisiana hunters kill more ducks than those of hunters in the next three states in the rankings *combined*.

The "Birdfoot Delta," they call this area, where the levees that straightjacket the Mississippi finally stop and the main river splits into channels like the toes of a chicken. That fertile cargo of sediment spreads out here to build marsh, or "wetlands" in fashionable lingo. One hundred thousand acres of it are public, open to any hunter for the length of the duck and deer season.

"I never beheld a scene," continues La Trollope, "so utterly desolate as this entrance of the Mississippi River!"

We'll forgive her. After all, "wetlands" weren't much in vogue in 1832 when this English harridan—this nineteenth-century version of Anne Robinson—published her hissyfit of a book entitled: *Domestic Manners of the Americans*. Frances wasn't much of a duck hunter have, a deer hunter, or a fisherperson, or she'd have sung a much different tune.

Even then, this area's natural bounty attracted sportsmen from as far away as Europe. Louisiana owes its license-plate motto as "Sportsman's Paradise" to this "hell" and its "horrors." They also account for the states top position on Fund for Animals' "Cavalcade of Cruelty." This famous animal rights organization ranks states in a "Cavalcade" based on the number of animals killed by hunters as reported by their fish and game agencies. Yep, Louisiana is number one! In the following pages, I'll explain why and how.

The habitat down here is hell on the hunters themselves. Except for the river and the major passes, everything's shallow. The famous Higgins landing craft, the boat that won World War II, as reported by Stephen Ambrose, was actually born down here. The factory was built in New Orleans in the 1930s, when nobody dreamed we'd need such a craft to disgorge soldiers on Omaha Beach or Iwo Jima; the craft was designed for oil exploration crews to navigate the shallow marshes of the Mississippi Delta. Andrew Higgins finally sold the plans to a skeptical Navy in 1942.

I know a lady who actually worked in the Higgins plant, riveting the very craft that carried her fiancé onto an Italian beach resort named Anzio. But this was no vacation; a burst from a German machine gun shattered his legs two weeks later. Almost forty years later, he limped up the church aisle, grimacing slightly with each step, but he smiled when handing me his daughter as a bride. The lady dabbed her eyes in the front row.

"The Greatest Generation," they call these people. You'll get no argument from me.

"See the bullet holes, Tom?" Pelayo tapped Tom on the shoulder from the back seat.

"What?" Tom flinched and looked around. "Bullet holes? *What* bullet holes?"

Poor Tom. He grew up in semi-rural California. Inner-city New Orleans still had him spooked, especially after the episode with the shoeshine boys in the French quarter two nights ago and the winos on the Riverwalk. He swore he'd never return to Bourbon Street. But now he's driving smack through the middle of the city's foulest housing project. There's no other way to get to Venice, where we will launch the boat, get to the mouth of the river, and get our camp-out underway. Fortunately, we're on the elevated Interstate.

"Yeah, Tom." Paul handed me his quart of beer and pointed. "Lookit 'em all. Right there on the roof of the Dome."

We were driving past the Superdome on the freeway and the roof of the place looked like something out of Beirut or Gaza. The holes were clearly visible even at three in the morning. It's one of New Orleans's most interesting sights.

"Huh?" Tom was wide-eyed now. "You mean all those little marks . . . all those holes?"

"Yep, all bullet holes," Paul said as he put both hands back on the wheel.

"But why?" Tom stuttered. "Um, *how?*"

"Look over there, Tom." Pelayo pointed through the opposite window, grabbed the quart I passed, and chugged. "See 'em?" Pelayo was pointing at the high-rise sections of a notorious housing project across the freeway while chugging deeply on the quart.

"See what?" Tom stuttered." "And *you guys.* Isn't it a little early for beer?"

"Not at all—*bu-u-u-r-r-p,*" replied Paul. "The tall buildings over there," he said, pointing. "The windows up there, Tom. *That's* what Pelayo's pointing at. See?"

"Yeah, Tom," I blurted after a hearty chug. "*That's* where the shots come from."

"Yes, sure," Tom nodded. "I see 'em now. I see what ya mean."

"Crack gangs playing army," Pelayo added. "They like to shoot target practice from up there, blowin' off some steam."

"Looks like fun, too," Paul quipped. Then he pursed his lips and frowned, "What's that? A two, three-hundred-yard shot maybe? From that tenth-story window over there? With an AK-47? A breeze."

"Easy to blast out that billboard, too." Pelayo said, pointing. "With one clip, I'd bet. Seems they replace the damn thing every month."

"Damn right," Paul belched. "Remember the fun we had at the dump with Buzzy's AK? That thing was a riot!" Paul chuckled. "Just jam that sucker on full auto, slap that trigger, and hold on tight: BLA-A-A-A-A-A-A-AM!" Paul grabbed the steering wheel with both hands and shook it to mimic the recoil. "Chop a tree down in three seconds flat!"

"And how 'bout that car!" Pelayo cackled. "*Looked* like a junked car anyway . . . .Bunch of 'em lying around. So we opened up on the thing. It's filling with holes, the doors falling off, the windows splat-tering into a million pieces. Only halfway through the clip and the thing was disintegrating, man."

"Then it catches fire!" Paul laughed. "We go, whoops! What's this?"

"Then it blows up!" Pelayo roared. "Starts burning like a huge torch!"

"Then that couple came running out from behind the trees with that blanket!" Paul sprayed the dash with beer as he bobbed his head and cackled at the memories. "Their faces are white, crazy with fright . . . ."

"Yeah," Pelayo laughed. "The chick's boobs are still out too, bouncing all over the place . . . . They thought a freakin' bomb went off!"

"Then they see it's their car! Burning like a bonfire! That poor guy didn't know *what* the hell to do."

"But we sure did!" Paul laughed, "We got the living hell outta there man! Jumped in Buzzy's jeep and boogied on outta there." Paul waved two fingers above his head. "Didn't stop till we hit Thibodaux, fifty miles away!"

"You guys!" Tom nodded with a bent smile. "You guys get into more . . . ."

"It's all bullshit, Tom," I sighed. "I've heard the damn story a million times."

"But it's no bullshit that crack gangs pretty much rule this part of New Orleans, Tom," Pelayo snapped. He was frowning. "We had 323 murders last year here in New Orleans. Per capita, that's double New York's rate."

"Hell," I said. "It ain't just in the city. No way. Look at us last night! In the 'safe' suburbs."

"Yeah, Tom, it's getting bad, man," Paul snorted, shaking his head. "Gettin' so you almost don't wanna come . . . ."

That's when the bass notes drowned out Paul's voice. We were almost to the St. Charles Avenue exit. "Holy shit!" Paul said while letting go of the wheel and covering his right ear with his palm. "Hear that? How can they stand that? What's it sound like in *their* car?"

It wasn't a question of hearing it anymore. You'd have to be in another time zone *not* to. You could feel it, on your chest, on your temples—incredible pounding.

"What the hell's wrong with that asshole anyway?" Paul snarled.

I finally looked over and saw a purple Caddy, 1970s model, with white-rimmed mud-flaps. The window came down as the pounding bass notes almost crippled us, exposing a crazed figure that looked like Coolio. He extended his arm and looked like he was waving at us.

Christ, I thought. Not again.

"Looks like he's rolling down the window!" Pelayo gasped. "Some guy's rolling down . . . what the . . . ? Now he's pointing his arm! Looks like he's aiming a *gun!* Get down!" Pelayo screeched. "Hit the shoulder, On-the-Ball—hit it! Pull over!"

"Dope fiends!" I howled just as Paul hit the brakes and sent Tom face first into the dash. The quart was foaming all over the seat as I came over the seat at the impact and slammed the back of Tom's head with my teeth.

"Crackheads!" Somebody yelled. "Gangstas! They'll open up with their Uzis and AKs! Hit the deck!" I snuck a peek and saw that the purple Caddy had also pulled over on the shoulder and was backing up.

"Oh, goodness! Good Lord," Tom was muttering, huddled under the glove compartment. "Oh, geez," he said while rubbing the back of his head.

I looked up again, rubbing my teeth, looked behind us, and saw a second car pulling up on the shoulder—this one bright green with red bumpers, and a raccoon tail on the antenna.

"It's a whole gang!" I howled. "They've got us surrounded!" Our vehicle was in turmoil. Pelayo was reaching for the shotguns in the back, frantically trying to uncase one. Paul, fumbling under his seat, was reaching for his .357.

Tom was wide-eyed. "Let's take it easy guys," he gasped nervously. "Come on now, we don't know . . . ."

"Call 911! Fast!" I said when I saw the cell phone on Tom's belt. Call it!" I looked behind us and saw the driver getting out by the raccoon tail. He looked like Tupac Shakur.

"Forget that!" Paul yelled as he kept fumbling under him for his big silver magnum. "Too late for that shit! We'll have to shoot it out! They ain't taking me alive! No freakin' way!"

But before we could uncase the shotguns or find Paul's piece, Coolio and Tupac were upon us, with Snoop Dog and Dr. Dre right behind, gold chains and all. But unarmed, and even *smiling?* They pointed behind us, motioning for me to roll down the window, smiling wider now.

I was puzzled. I looked around and Paul nodded. "Go ahead," he said. "Roll it down." Then he hit his own window button.

"Say, brah," Coolio gasped as my window lowered. "Somethin' flew out ya boat back there. Looked like a sack."

"Yeah, man," Tupac giggled. "Almost hit us, then we ran over it . . . . Deyz plastic ducks all over the road back there." Just then we heard a hideous, clattering racket coming down the highway. A truck stormed by dragging a hard plastic decoy, the line of which was tangled in the fender.

"See what I mean?" Tupac pointed.

"Good Lord," I sighed, torn between weeping and guffawing. Then Paul turned around and grimaced weirdly. "Who forgot to bungee-cord the decoy sack?" He glared at Pelayo. We sat there for a second trying to clear our heads. Trying to sort it out. Too early, too much excitement. Your imagination goes wild at that time of the morning. I reached down but the quart was empty, spilled all over the seat.

Then we burst out laughing, everybody, almost on cue. Coolio cackled as his gold teeth gleamed in the headlights. Tupac was doubled over in hysterics, his gold chains swaying. Tears streamed down my cheeks as I guffawed. Tom was convulsed. Pelayo and Paul looked at each other and roared along.

"Thanks, Cooli—oops!" I blurted. "I mean Tupa—oops! I mean . . . *dudes.* Thanks a lot," was all I could blurt. "We thought . . . we thought—never *mind* what we thought." They waved us off and clambered back into their hot rods.

We doubled back and recovered about half the decoys in one piece. We still had a sack of eighteen that stayed in the boat. Plenty enough.

"You guys promised me that this would be an exciting trip!"

Tom laughed as we started up the Mississippi Bridge. "Sure starting out that way!" He chugged on his own quart of beer. "I only drink this early on special occasions! And this certainly qualifies," he said, as we toasted all around.

That's when we saw the fog. It cloaked the frigid river and seeped into the French Quarter. The Riverwalk was somewhere down there, and so was the huge cruise ship at dock. Only the top of the smokestack poked over the eerie white shroud.

"Whooo-boy." Paul pointed with his chin and whistled. "Gonna be fun getting downriver today."

"What?" Tom said. He looked around trying to smile. "Maybe it won't be bad down there, huh? Maybe the wind?"

"It'll be a hundred times *worse*," Pelayo chuckled. "We'll have to follow somebody with radar. A crewboat or something. River's high and full of huge logs right now, too. With this water temperature and currents, we hit one and we're goners. Prepare for excitement, Tom."

Tom capped the quart and stared glumly at the feeble lights of the Riverwalk, barely visible through the fog.

A few minutes later we hit the Belle Chasse Highway and I noticed Pelayo focusing on a car beside us. Good God, I thought. What now? But he was smiling this time, and waving. I looked over and saw a Celica convertible with a hot little momma at the wheel and another in the passenger seat. They were dressed to kill and bopping to some music, their hoop earrings bouncing with the beat. Probably just coming in from some serious partying in the French Quarter. The Sugar Bowl crowds had already turned the place into a madhouse. It was almost like Mardi Gras, complete with the balcony boob-flashing scene. We'd made the scene ourselves, two nights before. The mild weather helped. No bundling up needed to stroll down Bourbon Street when it's 68 degrees, so blouses flapped open like window shutters. T-shirts rose to display all manner of goodies.

Lucky us, we get the live version of "Girls Gone Wild." Problem is, we don't necessarily want to see our own wives featured in it. It's damn easy to get into the spirit of things down in the French Quarter, believe me, especially after a few Pete's Specials. Babes with those glassy eyes and that telltale glow to their cheeks raised their blouses with an abandon that us latter-day Lakefront Casanovas can only marvel at.

"Jesus," Pelayo smirked from a Bourbon Street balcony last Mardi Gras. "I've seen more in ten minutes out here than in five years of backseat pleadings, cajoling, and maneuvering at the Lakefront back in the 70s! Those disco dresses were much easier to lift, too!"

LUCKY US. WE GET THE LIVE VERSION OF "GIRLS GONE WILD"

"And lower!" Chris moaned. "Hell, man, if we'd only known all it took was a pair of beads!" Long beads, mind you—and the pearl ones seem to provoke the most mouth-watering responses. If we'd known this, the money we could have saved! The dinners! The movies! The Gino Vanelli concerts! The bottles of Mateus! And all the sugary lies we could have stifled!

But, ah, it didn't seem to work that way back then. Last Mardi Gras, our wives had gone for a stroll down Bourbon street and to visit some friends at another suite, some old sorority sisters, leaving us free to cut up and drool on the balcony.

An hour later, they hadn't reappeared. So Chris and I wove and stumbled our way down the river of cackling, hooting, whooping, groping humanity known as Bourbon Street to see what the hell was so exciting about *that* party. Something was keeping the girls. We finally made it two blocks down and squeezed our way into the sorority reunion party—and absolute bedlam. "Girls Gone Wild" indeed! But our wives didn't seem to be around, not even on the balcony.

The neighboring balcony was even worse. A huge crowd had massed below it, shrieking and roaring themselves hoarse with progressively lewder requests, then whooping and clapping a thunderous ovation as each was granted. The river of humanity below even stopped flowing as all eyes gawked upwards at the showstoppers next door.

"What the hell's going on next door?" Chris asked a red-cheeked vixen beside him who ignored him. I was wrenching every vertebra in my neck trying to have a look, but to no avail. Too many people in

I WARNED YOU ABOUT MIXING THEM THOSE LONG ISLAND ICE TEAS! DAMN IT, I WARNED YOU!

front of me doing the same as the whoops from below got louder and louder, the crowd bigger and bigger.

"Check it out!" some guy in front of me howled as he finally got a look.

"What?" Chris gasped. "What the hell's going on?" He was trying to climb my shoulders, shoving people rudely aside.

"Get with it, bay-bee!" The guys in front were losing it, whooping like lunatics. "Yeah, yeah, Baby! Whoo-hoo!"

"What?" I pleaded. "Lemme see! What's going on?"

Finally, he turned around, his eyes popping and his faced flushed with merriment. "It's those blonde chicks!" he shouted in my face, his breath heavy on the garlic dip. "The ones who were here earlier, puttin' on that show! The ones with those Helldiver's Rodeo shirts! Now they've got roses in their teeth. They're doing some kind of flamenco dance. And they're . . . ."

"Chris!" I howled. "Let's get over there, fast! I warned you about mixing them those Long Island Ice Teas! Damn it, I warned you!"

Anyway, the babes in the Celica had that "French Quarter partying" look to them. It's unmistakable. It's a little unnerving to see it on our wives, but exciting to see it on "babes." Pelayo was still looking over and waving, adding some sucky-kissy noises while his eyebrows danced. "YEAH!" he yelled suddenly and started rolling down the window frantically. "Show 'em!"

I'd turned away for a second, then jerked back around at Pelayo's outburst, just in time to see the passenger babe face us and lift her shirt.

"Yowza!" Paul yelled, holding a thumbs up. Shake 'em, baby! That's it!" And she did just that, rocking her torso to the frenzied beat bopping from the radio, setting those magnificent white orbs with the cherry tops jiggling deliciously.

"Hey-hey!" Tom's glumness vanished. The fog was ancient history now. He lunged over me for a better look. "Va-va-BOOM! Ve-ry nice! Ve-ry!" These babes were definitely still in the spirit of the evening. She was kneeling on the seat now to face us, jiggling away. We were entranced.

Then came a sound from the road: PACKA—PACKA—PACKA—PACKA—PACKA!

"Watch it!" I said, as Pelayo reached for the wheel. A distracted On-the-Ball had veered out of the lane onto the left shoulder. Good thing for those little bumps that warn you, because a stalled van was right ahead. "Stay on the freakin' road!" Pelayo yelled, before turning back to the titillating action.

The babes were laughing wildly now, and these convulsions added to the mouth-watering motion. Suddenly the driver babe took one hand off the wheel, reached over slowly and pinched her friend's nipple.

"Saw that!" Paul gasped. PACKA—PACKA—PACKA—PACKA! again as we served sharply.

"You're gonna kill us, damn it!" Pelayo snarled. "Keep your eyes on the road!"

"Easy for *you* to say!" Paul shot back, but Pelayo was himself laughing this time. Now the driver babe was back at it, pursing her lips and rolling her head seductively while she lightly pinched her friend, and even added a little rubbing. You see this type of stuff a lot lately—if you watch MTV's *Spring Break*, that is.

We were losing it. This was too much. "You guys *sure* you wanna go huntin'?" Paul whooped just as the babe-car started slowing down. I tore my gaze from the splendor, looked ahead, and saw we were about two hundred yards from a major intersection. The traffic light was yellow. The babe-car was well behind us now when Paul stomped it—VRROOOOM!

Aerosmith's Rock'n Rollcoaster at Disneyworld takes off slow compared to this, but it provides a headrest. My neck bashed backward and my head snapped back like a crash-test dummy's. I give wounded ducks the "coup de grace" on the edge of my 'rogue with the same motion. Tom's eyes were wild as he focused ahead. "You won't make it!" he yelled while tugging Paul's shoulder.

"And look!" Pelayo pointed at two cop cars in the doughnut shop on the corner. "Hit the brakes!"

"Can't!" Paul barked. His lips were tight and gripped the wheel with white knuckles. "We'll jack-knife! That boat and trailer weigh three thousand pounds, man! Got forty gallons of gas! We'll roll, then get hit from both sides, we'll go up like a freakin' bomb! Catch fire and burn alive!"

Made sense. Now I understood. I was confused at first. The stop-light seemed like a perfect chance to take in more boob-flashing, maybe engage in some charming repartee. Problem is, trailering a heavy boat, no way we'd stop in time. I looked over and two pot-bellied cops were coming out of the doughnut shop. Worse, a dump truck and a Suburban were just starting off from the green light at the intersection. I looked up and the light was fifty yards ahead, bright red now. The fat was in the fire. The die was cast. We'd crossed the Rubicon. Whatever.

Paul grimaced, hunched down, and leaned on the horn, which erupted in a ghastly racket. He was bobbing his head, like he'd make his Expedition go faster that way. Speedometer said sixty-five. Well, this is it, I thought. At least it'll be quick.

The dump truck and Suburban slammed on the brakes at the horn racket—and just in time. We blazed past, horn blaring and boat trailer bouncing and clattering over the bumpy road. Good thing for those bungee chords strapping down everything in the boat from ice-chests, to tackle boxes, to decoy sacks, I thought. After the gangsta stop, we'd made sure they were tight, too.

Looking back, I saw one of the cop cars swerving onto the high-way. A second later, the sirens blared and the red lights flashed on. "See!" Pelayo yelled. "Now ya did it!"

Paul pulled over right before the Tunnel and got out even before they were on us. "Sorry, Officer . . . . I know, I know, I'm sure sorry. Just got this Expedition last week, ya unnerstan' . . . . still a little rusty on the cruise control, ya unnerstan'. I promise that I'll be . . . . sure am sorry, sir. An honest mistake," etc., etc., etc.

CHAPTER TWO

FOG FEVER PARTY

At a hundred yards, the hellish roar and rumble from an offshore supply boat rattles the very fillings in your teeth. These huge crafts stretch half a football field long and pack a three thousand horsepower engine with ten massive pistons below the stern. The metal hull does for the engine-racket what a good woofer does for Black Sabbath's bass notes.

Your whole head throbs like an unbalanced washing machine on spin cycle. Your eyeballs rattle in their sockets like maracas. Your chest cavity pounds like when a bass drummer passes you in a parade, and that's while idling past one in plain view during a sunny afternoon, bouncing in its wake as the toothless crew smiles from the railings and the tattooed captain waves from the cabin. These guys are nothing if not friendly. Often they'll add a horn blast to the greetings. If so, woe to the unsuspecting. I've seen people lifted three feet off the deck by this fearsome detonation of sound. I've almost been fished out of the water myself with soiled pants. The freakin' blast seemed to lift me off the deck.

But now it's 4 A.M., pitch dark, and we're virtually blinded by the infamous Mississippi Delta fog—a fog so thick and wet, it's almost a drizzle, so thick we can barely see our own running lights ten feet in front of us, much less the lights on any crewboat that might be bearing down on us through this black smoky gloom at thirty knots like a floating steamroller. And from the sound of it, several qualify right now.

"Turn around!" Paul finally exploded into his brother Pelayo's ear. Paul had been nodding and muttering sullenly for a while now. The tension finally got to him. "We gotta be crazy! Let's go back to the Marina and wait for daylight before we get slammed and dunked!"

We'd been lurching and groping around blindly in the winter-swollen Mississippi River somewhere below Venice for over an hour in Pelayo's eighteen-foot boat, with only the illuminated depth-finder telling us we had a hundred feet of muddy, icy water below us, the compass telling us we're going in about six different directions every five minutes, and the hellish roar of the ghostly ships and crew boats grinding and pounding all around. I was starting to feel like the Flying Dutchman

"I think Paul's ri-right," Tom stammered. "We can always come out later, maybe still get in an afternoon hunt."

"Daylight won't do a freaking thing!" Pelayo snapped back. "Not with this goddamn fog! We're pushing on!"

I found the argument ludicrous. Pushing forth valiantly, or turning around wimpishly? I'd been watching the compass and we'd been doing both, off and on, for about an hour. Fact is, we didn't know where the hell we were going.

Not for us those girly GPS (global positioning system) contraptions, where you punch in coordinates and the thing holds your hand the whole way to your destination.

"That's for pussies," Pelayo snapped at the startled salesman at the outdoor megastore recently. "Takes all the fun outta hunting and fishing. Hell, half the fun of a hunting or fishing trip is getting there, finding your way in. Just gimme a case of the goddamn shotgun shells like I asked. What? Of *course*, magnums!"

JUST GIMME A CASE OF THE GODDAMN SHOTGUN SHELLS LIKE I ASKED.

So, yes, now we're just wallowing in "fun," navigating by sound, and this dreadful dirge of supply-boat engines has taken on a new sense of urgency. Whoever designed these engines had a definite sense of rhythm. Steven Spielberg heard this sound too. It can't be coincidence. It's in the famous tension-mounting soundtrack as the skinny-dipping girl frolics in the water at night, as the barrel floats pop to the surface— ta-dum, ta-dum, ta-dum—as the fin finally breaks the surface, or especially, right before Jaws explodes on the surface and grabs poor Captain Quint. Now the same tune has us badly jangled. There's something universally nerve-wracking about that tempo.

More likely, Spielberg got it from Edgar Allen Poe's "Tell-Tale Heart." Whatever, it's perfectly nerve-wracking.

At least John F. Kennedy and his crew didn't hear the destroyer that crushed them like a floating Popsicle stick. "Without warning, the towering shape of the Japanese destroyer *Amagiri* loomed out of the black night," wrote Robert Donovan. "Frantically, the crew aboard PT 109 tried to steer their boat out of the destroyer's path. But the menace moved steadily forward. Then came the inevitable crash, slicing the eighty-foot torpedo boat in two."

At least they had the brief serenity that comes with a blindfold before a firing squad. We had no blindfold—or we did actually, with the fog. But that infernal sound score of roaring diesel engines keeps blaring that death and doom are all around, and the boats are closing in relentlessly.

On-the-Ball was lying on the deck and screaming something,

but I couldn't make it out from five feet away. This made me very nervous for some reason. It reminded me of those nightmares where you scream but nothing comes out. Was I in one? It all seemed to add up: this blinding darkness, this suffocating fog, these red-eyed faces around me, my hollow, rum-queasy stomach, my quivering bowels. Was this the night of the living dead? Was I an extra in Michael Jackson's *Thriller* video?

And this groaning, pounding soundtrack right out of *The Exorcist* or *The Omen* blaring in the background. "In space, no one can hear you scream," says the ad for *Alien*. Was it actually happening here?

I couldn't hear Paul, but his eyes and frantic movements did hint at a sense of urgency. So I leaned closer and bent my ear.

"Where's the goddamn life jackets?" he bellowed. This jolted me back in a hurry. It was real after all. Then Paul thrust his hand forward and started rummaging under the bow, strewing maps, buckets, a landing net, oil bottles, and flares–many flares–all over the deck in his frenzy.

"The life preservers, man! Where!?" He looked up and his eyeballs seem to jut from his skull. His lips quivered and spittle shot from his lips. I'd never seen him like this. Fact was, the life jackets *did* sound like an excellent idea at the moment but were probably a false hope. They say you don't last long in this icy river water— about as long as the hapless sailors on ships torpedoed by German submarines on the Murmansk run during World War II. This river water was tumbling down from ice-locked Wisconsin. We'd never be plucked out in time. Nobody would see us, much less hear our desperate screams.

But if we're merely swamped by a wake rather than crushed by a crewboat, they say it's a fairly easy way to go. No pain. Not much suffering. You either hit the water, gasp instinctively from the shock of the cold and quickly flood your lungs, or just grow numb, fall asleep, and sink. Then you either settle on the muddy bottom or bounce lifelessly through the ugly swirling currents till your gut contents start to ferment the next day. Then your digestive track bloats and you surface, eventually snagging up against some driftwood, where the raccoons can gnaw your lips, ears, and genitalia off.

Charming thoughts on this, our long-awaited Christmas holiday vacation.

"They're in the *other* one!" Pelayo cupped his hands around his mouth and barked from the helm at his brother Paul. "Life vests are *over here!* But it's too late for *that!*" He had a weird smirk on his face. "Grab those *flares!*" he raved. "Let's start blasting them off like bottle rockets!" He was laughing, always game to ridicule his (to him) overly cautious brother. "It's our only hope! Those boats'll see the freakin' flares and maybe turn or reverse the engines in time. If not?" Now his face changed to a hard grimace. "Were *doomed!*" he roared. "And fellas, it's been good to know ya!" He started laughing to himself—and *by* himself.

We'd heard that obnoxious "Wreck of the Edmund Fitzgerald" on the radio that very morning on the ride down. At our age, the actual merits of the song hardly matter. What matters are the memories it kindles. That's the entire rationale behind classic rock stations. We hated this song passionately, though it hit during some of our fondest youthful memories: the lunacy of pledge week our freshmen year.

I hated it even more now. Then I saw Pelayo's face suddenly harden and he hunched up, buckling his legs slightly. Oh shit, I thought.

The wave smacked us a split second later. I turned around just in time to see the huge wall of water washing over the side as it slammed into us, sending me on top of Tom and him atop a decoy sack with a heavy grunt. Paul was skidding over the bow like a break-dancer and a hundred gallons of river water were sloshing inside the boat soaking everything, including us.

"Whoo-yeah!" Pelayo howled trying to break the tension. Easy for him to say. He'd seen it coming and had time to prepare. Plus, the center console shielded him from the main blast of water. The rest of us were completely soaked. Paul was wedged between a cot and a deerstand on the bow, water dripping from his hair, grimacing heavily and rubbing his knee.

"Whoo-ya!" Tom "The Trooper" Nall gasped from below me. "Really refreshing!" I thrashed around like a turtle on its back, trying to right myself.

31

"Get ready!" Pelayo yelled while jerking the throttle back to idle just as we rolled atop another one. "These wakes always come in threes!" We crashed heavily into the trough, but without taking any more water, thank God. Finally, the last one swelled under us, we rolled out of it, and things calmed down.

Pelayo nudged the gas up again to about ten miles per hour and we continued downstream, or at least "southeast" from what I saw on the compass.

Pelayo suddenly ducked. A half-empty beer can whizzed inches over his head and disappeared into the inky gloom behind the motor. It was Paul's. "Let's turn around!" he shrieked. Saw that goddam log just now. We hit one a dem and we're *history!* Ya hear: history!"

Tom reached down to unlatch the compartment.

Paul swatted his hands aside. "All right, already!" Tom said, nodding as he jerked his arms up. "Geezum. Cool it, will ya?" We were all a little on edge.

New Orleans is America's second busiest port. All that ship traffic comes up the river from the Gulf. So we're bumbling around America's busiest freeway for ocean-going vessels like a blind armadillo on the Interstate at rush hour. And the ocean-liners and tankers aren't the half of it—hell, they're not one-fourth of it.

Thirty-two hundred offshore oil rigs and platforms lie off the Louisiana coast. Massive fleets of huge, powerful, noisy, and ugly boats constantly churn back and forth from this offshore industrial complex, fueling, feeding, and crewing it. These are the ones that throw a wake like a tsunami. Champion surfers would cringe at its approach. In the daytime, you see the watery mountain coming. You have enough time to slow down, grab a handrail, and ride it out. Even then, it can get hairy. In this foggy gloom . . . well, I didn't even want to speculate. At least we'd be going slowly when the wave slammed us.

Don't forget the commercial fishing traffic. One third of America's commercial fish are caught in Louisiana's coastal waters. The fleet of shrimp trawlers and long-liners add to the mad melee of boat traffic. I know boaters who simply refuse to venture into this maritime madhouse known as the Mississippi River, and its "passes" below Venice, in anything under thirty-feet.

Regarding the fog, Pelayo had a point. There's no fog like a south Louisiana fog, and especially like a Mississippi Delta fog. Daylight wouldn't improve things much. It might give us an extra five seconds of screaming time before the hulking steel bow crushes our fiberglass hull like an egg. We'd all be in shock, churning around the maelstrom of frigid water, clawing the air spastically until the huge propellers finally suck us under and dice us into bite-sized nuggets for the alligators and catfish.

Think of fog as clouds that form on the ground instead of up in the sky. Fog consists of the same condensed water vapor you see overhead before and during rain. The water vapor in moist air simply condenses when it meets a temperature that drops below the dew point. When this happens at ground level, you get fog.

Air doesn't get much moister than in south Louisiana. The weather in the Mississippi Delta probably qualifies as "tropical." Most of the plants never wilt, even in December. The mercury might dip below freezing twice a decade, but that river water tumbles down from the ice-locked Midwest, from Lake Itasca on the Canada-Minnesota border to be precise. Up there, you can squat across this same river. Here it's a mile wide, after rumbling and tumbling through 1,880 miles of continent and picking up a huge cargo of sediment along the way. In late winter and spring, 420 billion gallons of silt-rich river water tumble past New Orleans and into the Gulf of Mexico every day.

What a waste. Before the levees went up, this slop slowed down, spread out and built land. Most of south Louisiana is basically a big "alluvial fan," as geologists call it. These fans are simply deposits of soil created by streams. Amazingly, California's Death Valley is another alluvial fan. The streams in the surrounding mountains created it by picking up sediments as they tumbled down and disgorging them at the bottom—not that it has much else in common with tropical south Louisiana. The Death Valley fan is also much older. It took a couple million years for those wimpy mountain streams to puke up enough sediment.

Not so the mighty Mississippi. This big bastard can really pack it away. In this respect, Mother Nature's been very good to

Louisiana. She sees to it that this sloppy lush, this shameless glutton weaves unsteadily across our front yard, staggers through the hall and kitchen, grabs a hold and steadies itself below New Orleans, and finally pukes its guts out below Venice. We would be camping out and hunting on the fertile slop it disgorges down here. Makes for great duck, deer and hog habitat—great fishing too.

Before the levees went up, the River's puking was a more gradual affair. The chunks came out in dribbles, like the dry heaves. This created most of Louisiana below I-12, and only over the last 10,000 years. Nowadays, the Mississippi manages to stumble for another 100 miles past the city, ashen-faced, cold-sweating, frantic, covering it's mouth, bumping the walls, knocking over the lamp and portrait of the family at Disneyworld, stifling the eruption, without even a burp or hiccup—all the way down the hall to Venice. Then it's one huge retch: *BluuuuAAARCH!*

But most of this sediment gets flushed into the deep Gulf, rather than splattering all over everything and crusting itself into brown and yellow "alluvial fans."

Ten thousand years of staggering and puking gave Louisiana its swamps and marshes and the attendant biodiversity, as the greenies call it. Lucky for us, most of this biodiversity goes well in a gumbo, courtboullion, or po-boy.

Temperatures clash down here like no place on the continent. This drastic temperature contrast accounts for all that "condensation" near the ground, or more properly, over the water. This Mississippi River water meets one of those mid-winter warm fronts that back into the Louisiana coast from the muggy Gulf and we're talking some serious condensation. We can get socked in for days at a time, weeks during long warm spells.

The famous Battle of New Orleans was fought thirty miles north of where we were, under identical conditions in 1815. It was a happy coincidence, at least for us. The hellacious fog obscured the defenders in their drab frontier and dark Creole garb, but not the Brits in their bright red coats. History records no battle so lopsided in odds or startling in conclusion. Historians still scratch their heads over it—how did a hodge-podge of pirates and frontier low-lifes so soundly trounce a British Army that outmanned and outgunned them horribly? Even crazier, these were the very British battalions who'd just laid low Europe's most efficient war machine—they soundly stomped Napoleon's Grand Armee in the Peninsular War.

It doesn't add up until you consider the fog. Most historians credit "General Winter" with at least an auxiliary role in stopping Napoleon and Hitler in Russia. "General Fog" did the same to General Packenham below New Orleans, and now it was as big a curse to us as it was to Packenham's Redcoats.

I sided with Pelayo to stay the course, whatever the hell course it was. Daylight might have given us another ten feet of visibility, max. "He's right," I stammered while shrugging at Tom. "Hell, let's push on. It's either that or wave the white flag. Surrender. Abort the whole freakin' trip. I ain't up for that. We've been planning this thing too long."

On another dark, drizzly bayou west of us, another group of seven duck-hunters were on their way to duck blinds this very week. These were high rollers, R.J. Reynolds and Gulf + Western executives, their wives, and three guides. They were guests of Louisiana's toniest hunting club, The Pecan Island Hunting Club. Like us, they'd toasted the morning, but with whiskey. Like us, they'd traveled southbound on a waterway frequented by offshore crewboats. But unlike us, they were warm and comfortable inside the cabin of a twenty-eight foot crewboat themselves, at twenty-five knots, eager only to settle into the blinds.

They were escorted by experienced guides who drove the boats and doubled as footservants when they reached the blinds. From their spacious crewboat these hunters would disembark into smaller twelve-foot "mudboats" for the final few hundred yards to the respective duckblinds, where the decoys were already spread out, the seats were dry, and which perhaps even had heaters added for comfort. Once settled in, they'd slip in the shotgun shells and take in that glorious serenade of whispering wingbeats overhead. They'd watch the silhouettes flapping and dancing slowly over the decoys, maybe hear a soft "splish" as a few set down, then the startled quack and furious wingbeat when the ducks discovered the ruse. Thus would elapse those long minutes till legal shooting time—and bliss.

The guides at the control of the boat had grown up hunting, fishing, and trapping on this very bayou. They could travel it blind-folded. Still, they scanned the shoreline with the spotlight, looking for the reflector that marked the entrance to the smaller canal that led to the interior of the marsh and the duckblinds themselves.

A bit earlier downstream, the offshore crewboat, an *Geerd Tide*, had entered the Gulf and taken an instant and savage pounding from the wind-whipped seas. In a few minutes, it turned back. Too damned rough. Even at 110 feet long, the sturdy steel boat was no match for the angry Gulf that morning. It re-entered Freshwater Bayou and starting making back to port, plowing along at twenty-five knots, just like the *Mallard*. Dark and drizzle be dammed. The big crewboat's radar showed the path clearly. Nothing was in the way.

Minutes later they slammed head-on into the *Mallard*–two craft each traveling at twenty-five knots.

"In Twenty-Five Terrifying Minutes, Capsized Skiff Became Tomb," read the lead in the *Times Picayune* the next day. "Six people who died in a horrific crash when their boat slammed into a one-hundred-foot supply boat on a darkened bayou could be heard screaming and pounding the hull as they tried to escape the sinking ship."

Only one, with a shattered arm and leg, managed to crawl out. The rest drowned. And there, but for the grace of God, went us that morning.

I blame that second cup of Cajun coffee at the marina. We spiked it with rum to toast the occasion. That did it. That little jolt gave us the confidence (or stupidity) that pushed us over the line. We'd been planning this trip for nine months and were raring to go. The elements be damned.

"They all have radar," Pelayo had said while cranking the out-board. "We might not see them. But they'll see us . . . slow down or turn . . . let's go. It'll be light in two hours. I wanna be set up with the decoys out and everything for daybreak." Famous last words.

The dock was lined with boats much like ours. Hunters and fishermen foiled by the weather paced the dock restlessly, sipping coffee and grumbling. Another boat, a bass boat, was approaching the dock right beside us but coming in fast—way too fast.

"Slow down!" bellowed the guy squatting in the bow next to the trolling motor and all heads on the dock turned towards the commotion. The guy had the bow-rope and a beer in one hand and flapped frantically behind him with the other. He was a huge, flabby brute and his massive belly bounced with the arm motion. He looked like Clemenza in *The Godfather*. "Back it up!" he roared at the poor woman at the wheel. She was a looker, in a young Liz Taylor sort of way, with big hoop earrings, a spanking new cap, and a tight blue sweater.

"Reverse, now!" His eyes looked like fried eggs and spittle shot from his blubbery lips. "Come on! Fast!"

You see this a lot down here. A husband and wife team, no doubt. "A peaceful day of fishing with the spouse . . . . How lovely and touching." Yeah, right. Save it for Oprah and Rosie, will ya? We know better. These trips always end up in bitterness, acrimony, and disaster. Hell, they defeat the very purpose of fishing for ninety-eight percent of fishermen.

In turning to roar at his hapless wife, Clemenza flashed the entire dock area with a hideous vista. His tent-like dungarees were riding pretty low in back as he squatted, much like Dan Akroyd as the refrigerator repairman. But his bulk was more like three Belushis.

The poor woman at the wheel was frantic, losing it. "I'm trying!" she sobbed. "But it's stuuuck!" Finally, she let go of the wheel, grabbed the throttle with both hands, and started jerking crazily, her ponytail bobbing and earrings jangling with the motion.

"You're gonna break the goddamn—!" Blubberbutt was still roaring from the bow, shaking his pudgy fist in the air and spilling half his beer, not caring what the dock crowd was thinking. "Listen to me, Becky!" he snarled. "Shut up and listen, will ya! Now just turn!"

"I can't!" The woman was blubbering now; her pretty face, which was strangely familiar, was red and contorted. She pushed and tugged mightily, her sunburned arms straining at the stubborn throttle, her

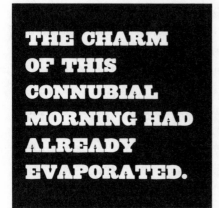

THE CHARM OF THIS CONNUBIAL MORNING HAD ALREADY EVAPORATED.

shoulders rocking and her sweater front bouncing deliciously.

"Ahhhh!" she shrieked. "I can't! It won't." Her frantic jerking finally sent her glasses off her face. She let go of the throttle and grabbed at them awkwardly, flapping her arms around like a drunken belly dancer. Then— *splish*—in they went.

"Hit the throttle!" yelled Blubberbutt. "The hell with the goddamn glasses! Hit the key—the ignition! We're gonna crash here!" Finally he turned around and lunged over the windshield like a crazed sumo wrestler, which he resembled body-wise, just as the hysterical woman jerked the throttle free—but into forward.

WHHRRROOOOM! went the revved up outboard. "AHHH-HH!" went the poor woman.

The crowd scattered from the dock, and I braced for a collision. For a second, it looked like they were heading for us, but she turned the wheel just as Lardbucket slammed the windshield. WHACK!

They slammed the dock hard, mostly with the trolling motor. We hunched up and grimaced involuntarily at the nasty whack of delicate trolling motor against creosote and concrete. The impact sent the guy back over the windshield and rolling onto the bow where he grabbed the shattered trolling motor just in time to halt the momentum of his massive bulk as it rolled and rippled over the carpeted bow like an elephant seal on the Discovery Channel. He stopped just short of joining the sunglasses and his beer, which was bobbing and foaming in the rippled water.

Whoo-boy. The crowd was rushing back now. "Y' alright?" He lay there for a second just staring up, nodding, breathing heavily. The poor woman wept hysterically, her head bent down, her face buried in her hands, her shoulders heaving and her chest area convulsed in massive, heaving, pendulous sobs. The charm of this connubial morning had already evaporated.

"You all right?" Tom was leaning over trying to offer help, as usual.

"Yeah, fine!" gasped Clemenza. "Just fine! Perfect start to the perfect trip!" He rolled over with a mighty grunt and finally managed to stand up, but a little wobbly. He even jerked his pants up in the back. He stood there nodding for a second, then yelled over his shoulder: "Get me a beer willya!"

He rolled his eyes, nodded disgustedly, and looked over at us again. "Helluva day!" he snorted. "Outboard needed a jump at the camp this morning. Yesterday we lost a two-hundred-dollar pole overboard. Then [he held up a bandaged hand] got a treble hook from a crankbait in my hand when she"—he nodded behind him at the snuffling woman with trembling lips, who was dutifully digging in the cooler—"tried to lift a bass into the boat after I told her, I don't know how many times, not to."

She broke back into sobs now, weeping openly as we all looked awkwardly at each other and tried not to notice. "He-here, Cl-Clark," she said, holding out the dripping Bud with one hand and a tissue to her eyes and nose with the other. When she lowered it, Pelayo and I looked at each other wide-eyed, almost on cue. She saw us and quickly looked away, pretending to dig back into the cooler.

She recognized us, too. Yikes! The memories! She'd been a little sister for Doc Fontaine's fraternity at LSU. We're going back over twenty years here, but Becky seemed to be holding up *quite* well. She was still bent over the cooler, and the view was breathtaking. Here was a real woman, not a silicone-sculpted Barbie doll.

She'd always been on the voluptuous side, even as a nineteen-year-old girlfriend of Mitch (now Doc) Fontaine. She was a doll too, the perfect little sister. Planned all the parties. Got along great with everybody, even Pelayo. Looked like her and Mitch were hitched for the long haul, too.

Then that famous LSU/Ole Miss party: whoo-boy. Togas, tequila shots, total debauchery. Toga parties were all the rage that year—that *Animal House* year. Becky's last name was Mansour. So we all requested a belly dance, and boy, did she deliver. Steve Miller's "Fly Like an Eagle" made the perfect sound score for her sensuous tabletop acrobatics. That seductively thumping bass line.

That dreamy synthesizer . . . ."Time keeps on slipping . . . slipping . . . slipping . . . ." Boy, could she *move*. And the tequila shots kept coming, too.

Well, the music, the ambiance, the crowd cheering and clapping, more tequila shots. It was too much for Mitch and he finally left, almost in tears. Becky got carried away and ended up in a back room with a few of his frat brothers.

Some brothers. That ended it.

Now look at her. "Let's head out, boys," Pelayo said with a grimace. "This fog ain't never lifting. Let's get it over with." It was too horrible to see poor Becky that way, our old friend. "Can you believe it?" Pelayo said as we walked out of hearing.

"Who'd a thought it?" I replied sadly. I'd heard from Shirley that she ended up marrying some rich doctor anyway. Well, I guess that's him."

Then a crazy yell turned our heads again. "Help! Goddamnit, goddamnit! No, no! Goddammit!" It came from the direction of the fuel dock, where the big boats docked. "Cut the craaaaaaap, Clem, will YAAAAA-IIIEEAAH!! The booming voice seemed desperate, seemed to be cracking, almost like he was yodeling.

We hustled over, and a few people stood around pointing at something moving steadily along the dock. "Jesus," Pelayo snorted as we jogged over and he ducked down for a look. "What *now?*"

"All right already! Cut the crap, Clem! Come *on!* AY-AY-AY! *Eeeeee*YAAAH! Clem, cut the crap!" The voice was a deep croaking sound, but each wail climaxed with a crazy yodel. Something hairy was going on. Through the legs of the laughing crowd, we saw what looked like a huge pile of camouflage moving along the dock, screaming and yelling.

"What *the . . . ?*" Tom looked over with a flustered expression. We got closer and saw that the screaming pile was actually a person, a rotund chap encased in a massive jumpsuit, groping maniacally with his pudgy hands at anything and everything around him—the boards on the dock, the pilings, the fuel pump, people's legs—trying desperately to stop himself as he moved along the dock on his stomach, but backward, carried by some unseen force while cursing and wailing his desperate entreaty to this "Clem." The crowd around him roared with laughter.

"Gots me a big one, HEE–YAA!" We turned at another crazed yell behind us. It came from the bridge of a massive Hatteras docked about fifty yards away. Now I was really confused, till I spotted the pot-bellied guy with a laughing blonde on his lap up on the bridge. He was cranking away at a huge reel. "New record, HEE-YAAH!" he cackled. "I tells ya, I got me a new record, Hee-YAA!"

The blonde on his lap was helpless with laughter. "Whoo-whoo! Get him in! He's a big one! Somebody get the gaff!" She had one arm around the guy's neck and waved a bottle of champagne around with the other, spilling half. "Mimosas! Mimosas, everyone!"

"Yeah! Right here!" Another curvy blonde with garish make-up and a Hooters shirt was on the deck, waving a champagne glass in one hand and a gaff in the other. "But I'll gaff him first! Come here, honey! You're a record foah shure! But we practice catch and release. Don't worry, honey!"

Just then the yelling camo-blob managed to grab hold of a fuel hose and stopped his slide. Now the back of his jumpsuit started expanding backwards, stretching. A Magnum Rapala gripped the insulated fabric with two of its treble hooks. The lure was attached to some heavy braided line, and following it up, we saw that the line came from the rod held by the pot-bellied reveler on the Hatteras bridge—Clem, apparently.

Now the drag started singing. "W*reeeeeen-wreeeen-wreeeeen-wreeeeEEEEEEN*"—sounded like a huge blender, making a ten-gallon piña colada. But the poor guy in the jumpsuit was still red-faced, yodeling and cursing savagely, gripping the hose with white pudgy knuckles, panting and moaning while pulling himself along the fuel hose on his stomach.

"Real goddamn funny, Clem!"

He panted while pulling the fuel hose with one hand and trying to reach behind him with the other. People formed a circle around him, turning their heads from the Hatteras to their catch and back again, trying to make sense out of the spectacle.

"Ooops, oops, yeah!" laughed Clem from the bridge. "He's a

making another run! Yeah, that's it! Got hisself his second wind! Powerful fish HEE-YAA! Here babe, you fight him a while." He handed the rod to the blonde, exchanging it for the champagne, which he chugged from the bottle as it foamed all over his bejeweled neck. Then he grabbed his radio mike, "We gots us a PARTY over hee-yahh!" he bellowed into the thing. "A real party over hee-yahh! Y'all come down!" The radio was on full blast and responded with a blaze of crackling gibberish, mixed with crazy hoots.

We made out a long "Paaaaaarty!" coming through the static. On-the-Ball tapped my shoulder and pointed left, at some guy bellowing the "party" message into his radio three boats down the dock.

"Fog fever!" the guy next to me laughed. "Up north we call it cabin fever. People get snowed in and go crazy. Down here I guess it's the fog, but it's the same thing. These boats been docked up for two days. Can't get out cause of the weather. I guess they finally lost it. Blowin' off a little steam, that's all."

POP! POP-POP-POP! Suddenly everybody ducked; there were explosions all around. The fog fever guy grabbed me by the sleeve and pulled me down with him. POP! BLAM, BLAM! POP-POP-POP! Tom was face down on the dock. His instincts took over. Pelayo and Paul crouched beside him, wide-eyed, jerking their heads around, looking for the source as people ran down the dock in panic and women shrieked in the background.

POP-POP-PA-PA-PA-PA-PA-PA-PA-POP-POP! PA-PA-POW-BLAM! PA-PA-PA-PA-PA-PA-PA-PA POW-POW-POW! So many explosions, they seemed to go off as one. Some people were shrieking, but through the crazy racket some shrieks sounded like *laughter*–wild laughter. Somebody could barely breathe between his cackles. It sounded like he was choking to death. POP-POP-POP-PAPA-POP . . . POP . . . POP—BLAM! The explosions continued.

I saw Pelayo pointing behind us as the racket intensified. The look on his face was not one of crisis. I quickly saw why. Unreal. Somebody had thrown one of those five-foot-long strings of black cats on the dock. Fog-fever, indeed. The string was dancing and hopping and popping and jerking around in a little ball of smoke, flashes, and fast explosions about thirty yards to our right, until it hopped itself over the side into the water.

BA-LOOOM! BA-LOOM! We ducked again, threw up our arms and jerked our heads around at two tremendous explosions between two cabin cruisers behind us, which looked like mini depth charges going off. The water was still raining on us when I looked up and saw another guy on the bridge of the yacht next to the *Hatteras*. He was doubled over and jerking spastically. He leaned over the railing, eyes shut tightly and mouth wide open, gasping for breath. The guy was convulsed with laughter, cackling crazily in between huge gulps of air. The culprit, no doubt.

Some of the dock crowd was pissed. "Call Security!" yelled one. "Let's get that crazy bastard!" yelled another. His eyes were wild as he looked around baring his teeth. "Come on! He's gonna . . . !" A security guard came running from his little stall, and three people where instantly in front of him, inches from his face, jerking and bobbing their heads while pointing at the yacht, waving their arms frantically. Not everybody caught the joke, apparently. The security guard nodded and shrugged helplessly.

I looked back at the yacht and Mr. Hilarity on the bridge had finally gotten hold of himself and caught his breath. He wiped the drool from his chin, waved to the furious crowd below, and grabbed the brunette walking up the steps to the bridge by the waist, hoisting her up as she wrapped her arms around his shoulders and her legs around his waist. This woman had an ass on her that would not quit. Her back was to us now and her jeans hugged it deliciously. Above it was a tight red turtleneck, matching lipstick, and hoop earrings.

Her curvy derriere faced us as she tightened the grip around the mad bomber with her legs. They went into a long smooch and we could see her hand slide into his pocket and start groping as he rotated his hips in response. The other hand was tight around his neck, with a cigarette between her red fingernails. Some serious sucky-face was going on. They were putting on quite a show, mocking the yo-yos on the dock who couldn't take a joke.

"Mm-*mm!*" Paul smirked. "You guys *sure* you wanna go huntin', right?"

Finally the woman stopped groping, slowly disengaged from his mouth and pulled something from Mr. Hilarity's pocket. She quickly handed it to him and brought her cigarette around to touch it. The thing started sparkling and hissing and someone on the dock started yelling and pointing again. A few were already bolting off. "That crazy bastard! Somebody better . . . . I'm gonna shoot!"

Then the woman quickly grabbed it back and—WHEEEEEE!—threw it over her shoulder like the bride tossing her garter. We scattered on the dock like panicked rats. Another cherry bomb. This one bounced off the hull of a shiny white Sea Ray beside them, hit the water, and BA-LOOM! sent up another geyser.

We were still scurrying around the dock, preparing for the next explosion, while a guy next to me was snarling and cursing in a red rage with balled fists. "I'm gonna . . . ! That's a serious fire hazard! Somebody better!

FRRRRUSH! FRUUUUSH! FRUUUUSH, FRUSH-FRUSH-FRRRUSH! POP—POP!

We hit the deck again. Now came the bottle rockets. I looked around and saw they were launching from empty champagne and Stoli bottles on the Hatteras's bow. The boat crew clapped and whooped at the pretty colors from the explosions above, barely visible through the fog.

"Ce-le-bra-tion time–come on!"

Now Kool and the Gang joined in, blaring from somewhere inside the boat. Two couples immediately picked up the beat and started boogying on the bow. Well, New Year's was three days away. Why not?

Then a crazed yell: "WHOO-OA! OOPS!" Mr. Hilarity had slipped on his way down the ladder from the bridge to get in on the rocket action. Now his feet dangled about three feet from the deck and his arm was snagged awkwardly on the railing. His shirt had jerked up and exposed part of his hairy stomach. The brunette was coming down to help, "My pooooor baby," she pouted. But the Hooter girl on the deck made it over first. She dropped her gaff, gave a gleeful little shriek, and hustled over, clapping. She stopped right in front of him with her face at his stomach level and started smacking and licking her lips. We all stared enviously from the dock. She lifted his shirt higher, stuck one hand up towards his neck and started tonguing his stomach right below his navel, while making slurpy yummy-yummy sounds.

"YEAHH!" The guy whooped. His florid faced contorted in a crazy grin as he wiggled his abdomen and rolled his eyes.

"I'll take my chances with the river," Pelayo snorted. "Think we're safer there. Let's get the hell outta here." We started back to his boat.

> IF IT'S NOT MARDI GRAS, IT'S THE JAZZ FEST. IF IT'S NOT THE SUPER BOWL, IT'S THE SUGAR BOWL.

"Sure about that?" Paul chuckled. "With this crew," he nodded toward the boats, "and this crowd," he pointed behind us, "I'd give it fifteen minutes till the boob-flashing starts, half an hour tops. Remember the Grand Isle Tarpon Rodeo? Reminds me of the same bunch."

"You people are something," Tom laughed as we shuffled back through the cloud of rancid firecracker smoke. "It's always something down here, ain't it? If it's not Mardi Gras, it's the Jazz Fest. If it's not the Super Bowl, it's the Sugar Bowl. If it's not St. Patrick's day, then it's New Year's . . . totally crazy."

"Wait till you see the Grand Isle Tarpon Rodeo," Paul said, "You're comin' with us this year, huh?"

"Oh sure—sure," Tom nodded.

"That thing makes Rio's Carnival look like a Rotary Luncheon."

Funny thing was, those Hatteras revelers didn't sound like locals. They didn't have the right accent. But then, half those "Girls Gone Wild" you see flashing boobs on Bourbon Street aren't locals either. Something happens to normal people when they get down here. Take John James Audubon himself, the patron saint of bird-watchers. Here's what the Audubon Society itself writes about the man who inspired their movement:

"Knowing Audubon's reputation, Grinnell [the Audubon Society's founder] chose his name as the inspiration for the organization's earliest work to protect birds and their habitats. Today, the name Audubon remains synonymous with birds and bird conservation the world over. Audubon was keen observer of birds and nature. He also had a deep appreciation and concern for conservation; in his later writings he sounded the alarm about destruction of birds and habitats. It is fitting that today we carry his name and legacy into the future."

Audubon was a keen observer of birds, all right. How else to blast 144,000 out of the skies in one hunt? I'm serious here.

The proof is in an old book entitled *Migratory Shore and Upland Game Birds*, and it's a quote from J. J. Audubon himself. Fittingly, this massacre took place right here in the Mississippi Delta. They say Audubon was a calm, judicious, mild-mannered man, not given to debauchery, wanton cravings or excess of any type, much less any blood lust. Then he visited Louisiana. Here's what happened on a hunt for plover and snipe outside of New Orleans in 1821. Two hundred gunners took part:

"Several times, I saw flocks of a hundred or more destroyed to the exception of five or six birds," Audubon himself gushes on page 84. "Supposing each man to have killed thirty dozen birds that day, 144,000 must have been destroyed." And notice how J. J. uses the word *destroy*. He obviously relished this avian holocaust. That's 144,000 bagged *in one hunt*, my friends! *Thirty dozen birds per person!* Those were the days! Our limit's a measly six.

This summer would be Tom's first Tarpon Rodeo. He was aping Audubon and taking to Louisiana with a vengeance. I'll never forget one sales meeting we had together. Here's when I realized he'd made it, that he was finally a local.

Our new manager Kevin "Ace" McKee had assembled us in the conference room for a meeting. Ace had only been in New Orleans two weeks and this was the third such meeting. This fetish for herding us into conference rooms for overhead presentations on the slightest provocation was naturally resented most by Chris,

Artie, the other sales reps, and me. We saw valuable hunting and fishing time squandered.

I exaggerate here. Many of us wouldn't otherwise be fishing or hunting. We might be in tittybars, doing our jobs. The overhead presentation hasn't been devised which serves as a better mechanism for closing a deal than four double scotches and a skillful and conscientious lap dancer.

Predictably, Ace was enamored of overheads. He'd transferred down, like so many others had before, with much fanfare to "turn things around." Chris and I had seen them come and go monotonously. But ah! Ace would *surely* whip the office into shape; get those numbers up, etc. Tom was seated next to me for that first meeting, right under a huge, "You make the difference!" banner McKee had put up. Tom had been in New Orleans about a year at the time, after transferring down from the Nashville district himself.

McKee launched the meeting with his usual pep-talk. He fancied himself a top-notch motivational speaker in his own right. He was the crackerjack district manager; the young hotshot who made the numbers soar wherever he took charge. He was tough but fair, always upbeat. He'd worked his magic from Spokane to Atlanta, from Tucson to Buffalo. He entered a demoralized office with numbers in the cellar, and in mere months they'd skyrocket. "Stellar" was a word he loved.

Like Patton taking over the routed U.S. forces after Kasserine Pass in North Africa, like Dick Vermeil lighting that Super Bowl fire under the formerly humdrum Rams, Ace McKee possessed that magic touch. He had that red-hot fire in the belly, and spread that fire magically to all around him. Enter his office and exit electrified with zeal for any mission. Sit through his talks? No way. No one could actually *sit* through his pep talks. Not for long, anyway. In minutes, you'd be cheering and stomping, standing on the very tables, whooping maniacally, ready to grab the banner and charge any barricade. Jimmy Swaggart was a chump compared to Ace; Huey Long a dreadful bore.

Thus his reputation when he walked into the New Orleans office, that chronic screw-up. Nothing seemed to work down here (ask Tom), but Ace had already drawn up an action-plan. Sure enough, it was "proactive" and involved much "empowerment." As a special treat, he'd give us a peek at a few titillating parts that first meeting. He announced it with his booming voice, "Office keys for the entire staff!"

A true egalitarian, that McKee. Here was empowerment with bells on. "This way," he explained excitedly, right after his motivational speech, "any of you, not just top management, will be able to come in the office—after hours, weekends, extra early in the mornings—to get work done! Gosh, gang!" Ace was beaming, his eyes wide. "You'd be amazed at the amount of work you can get done when . . . ." "Sometimes we all do our best when . . . ."

Suddenly, a rude yell from the rear, "BRAAAWWF!"

"What?" Ace lifts his head, looking around.

"PREEEAAWP!" Another outburst.

"HOOO-HAH!" a rude hoot from over by the corner now.

"YAH-YAH!" more laughter from quickly covered mouths.

"Pardon?" Ace's smile was becoming rigid, his eyes hard. "Something wrong back there? Artie? Chris? Would you like to share the joke with the rest of us? Remember, we're a team, here. No secrets among us." McKee's voice trailed off in a nervous little quaver. He'd been hearing rude murmurs all morning.

"YAAAH–YAHHH! HA-HA-HA!" It was Artie, face-down on the conference table, his shoulders heaving. He was out of control. No point hiding it any longer. "WHOO-HOO-HOO-HOO-HOO!" As always, these things are horribly infectious. Even the female reps were losing it. Gina and Cheryl cupped their mouths and doubled over, looking straight down at the desk, shoulders shaking, and chins quivering. A few little gasps leaked from between their fingers. Chris pretended to drop his pen and hid under the table, in hysterics. Tom himself was hiding his face behind the hand-out for the meeting. The paper was shaking and jerking. I peeked behind it, and his eyes and lips were squinched tight, his face crimson and contorted.

Ace McKee didn't have a clue, but entering the office after-hours is *not* a huge issue in the Big Easy. Hell, consider yourself lucky if you get us *during* office hours.

Ace lasted six months. He asked (*pleaded*, we hear) for a transfer out. It was hopeless, he explained. "Never seen anything like it." He was the fourth manager in five years. They all bailed out, except Tom. He had actually arrived as a manager himself two years earlier. Couldn't do a damn thing with the place either, but instead of bailing out, he accepted a demotion and stayed as a rep. He fell in love with the place, the hunting, the fishing, the parties, the people. He recognized the workplace frustrations as the flip side of the same coin. Soon they were "frustrations" no more.

CHAPTER THREE

TOPLESS RED FISHING

{ 🐂 }

One of the hunters on the dock ambled over with us to the boat after Pelayo's remark. He frowned when he heard the boat's engine turn. "Y'all ain't goin' out in *this?*" he asked, while pointing around. "Heck, we're gonna wait till light, see if the fog lifts."

"Then you might as well go back home," Pelayo said while clicking on the running lights. "This fog ain't gonna lift. Not until another front comes down or the wind picks up, and there's no forecast for either. The hell with it, we're heading out. Life's too short."

"That's a good way to put it," the guy chuckled. "We'll probably read about y'all tomorrow, while they're looking for ya."

Tom, Paul, and I looked at each other, shrugged, and hopped into the boat amidst the piles of gear. I grabbed a seat atop a decoy sack, Tom wedged himself between a deer stand and an ice chest, and Paul stood at the helm near Pelayo. He was the lookout.

We were the only boat easing out of the marina. We entered the foggy gloom of Tiger Pass and, just our luck, a crewboat was cruising past. We bounced over his wake and Pelayo got right on his tail. The bilge mist and exhaust fumes were choking us, but there was no denying a certain sense of security.

"We got it made now." "These suckers all have radar, remember, On-the-Ball?" Pelayo was coughing and fanning the air in front of his face as we cleared the mouth of the pass and entered the Mighty Mississippi itself. They'd worked on these boats many a summer during college. "That screen shows you everything, every detail, shoreline, other boats. We'll follow this one down."

What luck. Recently, I'd been helping my daughter with an English project. "That's *your* department," said my wife, Shirley. "Her college textbook uses her dad's own essays for examples."

I fell for it. Married women are champs at this type of stuff. Hell, they've already had one of us (at least) land in their snare. For best results: stroke that male ego. Works every time. They uncork the wine, tune in to *Sex in the City*, and scream at the screen, "No, no, no, Carrie! All wrong!" At least Shirley and her friends do.

Nothing like stroking that male ego for results. She was right. *Model Essays for Composition* was the name of her college English textbook, and dammed if it didn't contain an essay entitled, "Why We Hunt" that I'd written for *Sierra Magazine* years before. "Man is a predator," I concluded in the essay, "has been for millions of years. It's going to take a while to breed it out of us. And thank God I won't be around by then."

I still like that. Anyway, in the course of helping Monica, I steered her toward Edgar Allen Poe and rediscovered his *Complete Stories*. I plunged in and read nothing else for a week. The man was a master. Next to Poe, Stephen King reads like *Chicken Soup for the Soul*.

On this cold, fog-shrouded night, with the menacing rumble

of the huge boats all around, I wish I'd been reading Norman Vincent Peale instead.

Poe's lines kept ricocheting around in my head. They kept flashing up out of the darkness like those witches and goblins at Disneyworld's haunted house ride. I couldn't shake them. "The Maelstrom" seemed particularly poignant.

I CAN FEEL THAT THROBBING TEMPO OF THE PISTONS POUNDING

The sound isn't getting any lower. In a vintage essay entitled "The Police Chief," Hunter S. Thompson wrote about a fictional crowd-control tool called "the Growler, a mobile sound unit that emits such unholy roars that every human being within a radius of ten city blocks is paralyzed with unbearable pain. They collapse in their tracks and curl up like worms, losing all control of their bowels and bleeding from the ears."

A supply-boat engine at close range comes damn close, Hunter. I can feel that throbbing tempo of the pistons pounding on my tympanic membranes, temples, and chest cavity. The boat racket suddenly seems to switch gears. Sounds like they're slowing down. Maybe they see us on their radar? Now the beat's slower, a plodding, haunting, sinister sound, like Led Zeppelin's "Kashmir." Jimmy Page used to jerk that bow across his Les Paul and get a sound more gruesome than anything from a bass cello. Actually, it's the perfect soundtrack for this gig.

But this is louder. It seems impossible that this low-grinding racket can be any more than 100 yards away . . . and closing fast.

Paul crouched and plunged one arm into the slit, feeling around. "Gimme the—!" He snapped while holding up the other hand. Nobody could hear him. "The flashlight, dammit!" His face was red, and the veins looked about to explode.

"Here." Pelayo reached under the console, grabbed the Q-beam, and hit the switch. This light was a monster. It shoots a million candle-power beam that illuminates a rabbit's eyes at a hundred yards on any levee, a deer's at two hundred in any beanfield, and an alligator's at a quarter mile down any bayou.

It also allows you to pick up the green-glowing eyes of a bullfrog through the thickest swamp brush and a flounder through the murky water on the sand flats behind Grand Isle, which is, of course, what we use it for.

This light was also pure hell on the secluded stretch of beach just west of Destin, Florida, during the famous '79 spring break extravaganza. One section was reputed to be a nude beach. We heard this from a reliable source who slurred it to us near midnight while in line at Cash's liquor store while his girlfriend tried to hold him upright by the belt and collar.

Actually, he merely confirmed what we'd heard from slightly more coherent sources on the beach that morning. These friends from back at LSU claimed to have stumbled upon the jiggling, flopping spectacle by accident. They'd gone spear fishing off the beach.

Spear guns are illegal on any public beach in Florida, and that includes even the little chicken-shit "pole spears" or "Hawaiian slings," which are unheard of in Louisiana. When you're lugging a Louisiana-style spear gun that's six feet long, powered by six bands of extra-thick surgical tubing that looks like a goddamn bazooka, the tourists can get a little edgy as you flop past them, rip loose with a long beer-burp, and plunge into the rolling surf.

When the cops arrive they can be extremely conscientious about enforcing the law. We knew this from Spring Break '75 and '76, during which we managed to play dumb and talk our way out of it.

"Why, we had *no idea*, officer, sir, sir!" Pelayo said in wide-eyed amazement.

"Thank you ever so much for informing us sir, sir!" Chris added with an incredulous smile.

"You bet, sir, sir!" Don said with a firm nod. "These things are going right into our car trunks and staying there till we get home to New Orleans, sir. We can't thank y'all enough for giving us this warning."

That very night, right after *Saturday Night Live*, we grabbed the spear guns and some halogen lights and waded back into the surf.

Our spirits were soaring. We were pumped. Joe Cocker had been the musical guest on *SNL*. Surely you remember John Belushi alongside? We were like to *die* laughing! When he opened the beer and poured it on his chest, I almost choked from guffaws.

Anyway, we went spear fishing again, with a serious attitude this time, and much more confidence. Not ten minutes into the dive, Chris, who was holding the light, flashed it on a big dark blur on the very periphery of its range. The blur slowly formed into a bull shark as it closed on us. No one even flinched. That's tequila for ya. The shark was about a five-footer.

Normally, we'd have hauled ass. But like I said, we had an attitude this night. We all kinda looked at each other underwater, nodded, cocked another band, and converged on the hapless shark.

FLUNK! Don shot first. FLUNK! Chris, second. In seconds, we'd turned the toothy swaggering beast into a pincushion. When he finally stopped writhing after Pelayo's headshot, our spear gun cables were hopelessly tangled.

We towed the thing ashore, and while I skinned, cubed and shish-ka-bobbed it for a midnight snack over the driftwood fire, I heard, "Man, saw all dem freakin' stingrays?" from Pelayo. I looked over and he and the rest of the guys were already plunging back out into the gently rolling surf.

They came back about ten minutes later with three stingrays still stuck on the spears. They ripped them off the spear points and in no time the rays had become Frisbees. Somewhat dangerous Frisbees, but everyone seemed to grab them just right and hop out of the way just in time. Cindy came out with another tray of tequila shots and Pelayo finally got nicked on his bicep as he was biting into his lime, but nothing serious.

In 1977 and 1978, we simply left them on the bottom in deep water when we saw the cop Jeep coming over the dunes and said we were sightseeing. "Spear guns? Aren't they illegal out here officer? Yes, of course. That's what we heard, so we left them at home. We come out here for the scenery sir, sir."

Point is, our chums definitely needed a secluded area to spearfish. They weren't taking any chances. That's how they found

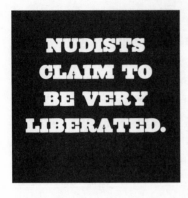

NUDISTS CLAIM TO BE VERY LIBERATED.

the nude beach. Spring Break of 1979, they let us in on it.

That was a famous Spring Break indeed. Mick and Keith's "Shattered" was the theme song on that trip. "*Look at me!*" An excellent mooning song, especially from a speeding jeep on the beach. "*I'm in tatters!*" Wouldn't you know it also served as the perfect theme for the nude-beach infiltration attack.

Nudists claim to be very liberated. Well, we discovered that there are daytime nudists and nighttime nudists, and the nighttime version go temporarily and frantically prudish when caught in the vivid glare of this amazing Q-Beam.

After chatting with the drunkard at Cash's, where we were making a midnight run for more Everclear, we quickly conferred and simply saw no choice but to ice down another couple of cases, hop in Don's Jeep, and attempt to verify this fascinating "human interest" story, as a Sunday supplement might call it, before heading back to our own beach party where the women simply *refused* to part with their bikinis.

If four half-crocked adolescents can have more fun on a clear spring night than piling into a topless Jeep crammed with beer, gunning the thing to a horrendous, valve-threatening roar, and zooming off over the sand dunes in search of a nude beach near midnight on Spring Break with "Shattered" blasting from the tape deck even louder than the engine and wind-scream, I'd like to see it. To this day, we haven't topped it, even at any of our bachelor parties.

But bachelor parties are well planned months in advance. They're planned fun, even forced fun. Everybody pushes it. Bachelor parties can't compete with impromptu fun. That's always the best kind.

Immediately we spotted several fires on the beach, but decided a few ski-jump type runs off a big dune were more important at the moment. Then a half-dozen centrifugal force defying doughnuts at record speed while we clung to the row-bar, to the steering wheel, to the seats, to each other, choking and gasping in hysterics. Then a flurry of fishtailing that sent up gorgeous rooster tails of fine sand, the whole time managing to keep from flying out of the Jeep like a human Frisbee, or flipping the damn thing like something on Cops.

That marvelous sugary sand on Florida's Miracle Strip beaches provides the kind of surface no high school football field or pasture can match. Here in this soft sand, you can really gun it, bore out that baby, and spin around like you'd never manage on the most meticulously manicured golf course, even after a rain.

But now, fifteen years later in the middle of a swollen Mississippi River, that same Q-beam hit Paul's face at five feet. "Aahhh!" he shrieked, turning his head an instant before his pupils fried. "Off! Turn that goddamn thing off! Ya trying to blind me?"

"Just getting ya back," Pelayo laughed, referring to their spat over the last beer last night. Tom and I joined him laughing as he nudged the throttle up a notch. Our unwitting crewboat escort seemed to be speeding up. We didn't want to lose him.

"I can see clearly now, the fog is gone!" We'd just turned into Pass-a-Loutre from the River, when the crewboat escort veered right and Pelayo was suddenly shakin' his bootie, nodding and pointing ahead. The tops of the trees had been visible over the fog for about a mile, and the sun had peeked as a small silver orb through the haze overhead. Now things were getting even better, literally "brightening up." A breeze was starting to stir the willows along the bank, too.

Tom grabbed my shoulder and pointed ahead. On-the-Ball looked over, grinning. Ah yes, just ahead, the fog was finally breaking up. That's the thing about this crazy fog: it tends to form over the water, the frigid river water. Come upon one of the few contiguous landmasses in the Delta, like the one near the "head-of-passes" (our location), and it breaks up or lifts.

A half mile later, we turned left into Dennis Pass, officially entering the Pass-a-Loutre Wildlife Management Area. The sun finally bust through, covering the area in a golden sheen, the dew-laden willows reflecting the glow in every droplet that hung on their leaves. It was almost like an omen. Our spirits surged. "Limit's by noon!" Paul bellowed while pointing overhead. "And only the *drake* of the species!" I looked up and a flock of pintail ducks was just disappearing into the haze behind us.

"They're flying!" I announced while high-fiving all around. "That wind's pickin' up, stirring 'em up. Whoo-yeah!" I was pumped. We were all pumped. Looked like clear sailing for the last couple of miles to our campsite.

We'd set up camp, then for the toughest part: What next? Decisions, decisions. If only all decisions had such sweet options. There's simply no place like the Mississippi Delta for a truly "mixed bag" of outdoor endeavor. It's an outdoor buffet ten miles long. You got nuts choosing among the mouth-watering dishes of this smorgasbord.

Hunt? Fish? Decide, then comes another dilemma: for *what?* Ducks or deer? Hogs or rabbits? Geese or snipe?

You fish? Fine. But here the tantalizing options confound even more. Lets say you're a big-game fisherman. From Australia to Hawaii to Costa Rica, clashing currents and "thermal gradients" make for the best big-game fishing grounds. Off the Louisiana coast, we've got northward flowing Caribbean currents clashing with westward-flowing Gulf currents, clashing with the outflow from the river itself. All this near an undersea precipice called the continental shelf. Even better, river deltas create petroleum deposits. Salt domes often lie near such deposits. Fishermen named the salt domes off the mouth of the Mississippi the "Midnight Lumps." These lumps rise to 200 feet from the surrounding one-thousand-foot depths. And they only lie eighteen miles from the mouth of the river; even small-boaters can reach them.

Throw in these "lumps" or "domes" to make the currents even crazier and the temperature contrasts even more drastic, and we're talking one of the top big-game fishing grounds on the continent. These rips, both horizontal and vertical, concentrate the baitfish, and hence the big pelagic predators, and hence those that prey on the big pelagic predators. So properly outfitted, you might start the day by slugging it out with marlin, wahoo, and tuna. Indeed, the biggest fish ever caught in the Gulf of Mexico was caught right here on May 25, 2003. The monstrosity was a 1,152 pound Bluefin tuna.

Okay, so you battled and landed a big yellowfin and three wahoo by 10 A.M. Now cruise back a short fifteen miles to the dock at Port Eads, celebrate with a toddy, snork down some lunch, then retire for a nap. Awake refreshed, then jerk on the waders, grab the shotgun and decoys. Swarms of ducks will pour into the duck-potato flats as the tides come up in the evening. These are only two miles away. So set out the spread, shove in the shells, and hunker down. Then gape as most of the Mississippi Flyway's pintail and canvasbacks dive-bomb your decoys. But watch it; the limit on pintail's one. And canvasbacks are no-nos. No open season *at all* on them in Louisiana.

No problem, though. The widgeon, gadwall, and teal more than take up the slack. So start blasting them and limit out by dusk. Next morning, you might grab your bow, climb a tree stand along a natural levee and take in a little deer hunting (only bow-hunting is allowed on the state land). Whack a Delta whitetail, grown fat and succulent on the rich vegetation, hang him up behind the houseboat, then head over to the rosseau cane marsh for the best redfish and bass fishing in America—bar none.

Spend a few hours during midday whooping and cranking the reel as musclebound reds strip your spool and strain your rod till it damn near splinters. These Delta redfish grab your jig and take off, barreling through the shallows like crazed torpedoes. Compared to reds, bonefish come away as sorry chumps.

So you land a red on the first cast? After the next cast, your wrist stops in mid crank and a bass erupts from the water, rattling his gills like a tambourine. On the next, your arm jerks violently on the fourth crank. A speck this time, thrashing that big yellow mouth on the surface, trying to throw the lure. Next cast yields a doormat flounder. Then a striper. Then a drum, then another red. An hour later, the ice-chest is filled. Your arm's starting to ache, too . . . . You look up and notice ducks on the wing. Back to the camp for the decoys and shotgun. There's time for another duck hunt before dark.

Except for the tuna trip, none of this requires more than a three-mile boat trip from your headquarters. Unreal, a simply unreal outdoor buffet beckons down here, my friends. For the serious outdoorsman, this place is simply *heaven*. But we weren't outfitted for big-game fishing on this trip. "Inside" fishing for redfish and bass would somehow have to suffice.

"Look!" Suddenly Tom pointed behind us. Looks like . . . .

"Yeah!" Paul waved frantically at a guy in a Boston Whaler behind us. It was our chum, Chris. He'd been down here fishing already with another group of friends, staying in a camp at Pilottown that lies about five miles from our usual camping area. We'd made plans to link up. He wanted to get in some hunting, too, so he planned on linking up with us at the campsite. He was usually along on our camp-outs and knew where we'd be set up.

He came up alongside, motioning us to slow down. He had all his camping gear crammed aboard. "Saw y'all from the dock!" He beamed. "Can't believe you crazy bastards made it! Figured you'd call it off or at least wait for midday, for the fog to lift! No fog yesterday. Made it down with no problem!"

"Time's a wastin', my man!" Pelayo roared back as he pointed ahead. "ADELANTE! Let's go!" He leaned on the gas, and we surged ahead, the boat quickly jumping on a plane. Chris followed just off to the left, then gunned it and raced out ahead of us, one hand on the wheel, the other pointing overhead at another flock of ducks. Then he turned it into a thumb's up and looked back grinning. We all looked up. Things were indeed looking up.

We got to the campsite and unloaded in record time. The three tents went up in minutes. "Can you believe it?" Chris pointed at a little pile of driftwood. "Still here!" Firewood remnants of our last camp-out a month back.

"Wow!" Pelayo was looking at the ground on the edge of the clearing as I unloaded the food ice-chest. "Check these out! Looks like a damn cattle rut!" He pointed at a deer trail on the perimeter of our site. It's easy to get excited over deer sign down here. These marsh deer have oversized hooves to keep from sinking in this slop, and because of the soft clay, the tracks stay fresh for days.

Still, this was one hell of a heavily used deer-trail. Fresh droppings confirmed it. These didn't look like Raisinettes either. These looked more like Milk Duds you left on the car seat in the sun, then sat on. These were from a nice-sized deer.

"Maybe I'll deer-hunt tomorrow morning?" Pelayo nodded. "For now, looks like the tide's still a little low for ducks."

"But it's coming up fast," Chris added.

"Right," Paul said. "Should be dynamite for ducks over in Pintail Alley about one or so this afternoon, ya think?"

"The breeze oughta be up by then, too," Chris said as he grabbed a dripping brewski from Tom and popped it open. "Forecast calls for southeast winds of 20 knots this afternoon."

"Yeah, you right!" I nodded. "That'll get 'em flying. But for now . . . hell, its early, whaddaya y'all say we head on down Johnson Pass and get in a little fishing?"

"Sounds like a winner!" Tom quipped.

"I heard that!" Paul was already walking towards the boat.

"I had my share of fishing yesterday," Chris said. "Wore out the reds right where y'all are heading. Think I'll hang around, tidy up the campsite, sip some suds, and do a little duck scouting." We waved him off and gunned it down Johnson Pass.

Most people consider late summer and fall the best times to fish the Mississippi Delta. That's when you find the crowds down here; the bass tournaments, the redfish tournaments, lines of trailered boats stretching for half a mile from every hoist and launch. The River's at its lowest in the fall and Gulf water creeps up the passes, sometimes as far as New Orleans itself. Gulf fish creep up with it. This makes for some crazy fishing. You'll catch a redfish, followed by a striped bass, followed by a largemouth bass, followed by a channel catfish, followed by a Jack Crevalle, followed by a sheepshead, followed by a bull shark. Not too many places where you can mix it up like that, but with so much clear water around, the fish spread out. Sometimes it takes a while to find a school.

Us, we like the winter and spring for Delta fishing. The high river simplifies things. That dirty water concentrates the fish in the pockets of clear water, typically deep in the rosseau cane marsh and close to the Gulf. The expanses of rosseau cane at the outer edges of this marsh act like a huge natural filter on the silty river water.

Get deep into the cane marsh and you'll find the clear brackish water—and the fish.

"Redfish city" we call the strip of cane marsh dotted with ponds and lagoons that stretches from Main Pass around Redfish Bay, around the mouths of Johnson and Dennis Passes to the South Pass jetties. We'd run for about fifteen minutes down Johnson Pass from the campsite and were about a mile from the Gulf when Paul dipped the anchor thirty feet from the rosseau shoreline. You could see about a foot down through the mild current. Damn clear for these parts, especially for this time of year. "Water looks beautiful," Pelayo rasped while looking over the side. "Shouldn't take long."

Our last trip down here had been in the summer aboard Doc Fontaine's boat. Chris and I brought the wives. Doc Fontaine brought Monique, his girlfriend of the week. She was French, the hostess at a fancy French Quarter restaurant. It's always nice to be shown to your table by a Catherine Deneuve lookalike, even nicer to hear that charming continental accent. Doc fell for her during a bachelor party, of all events. This woman was very easy on the eyes.

That trip had started on a weird note. Chris was rigging and jigging up the poles so as we headed down Southeast Pass, so I'd gallantly offered to apply the suntan lotion to Gina, his lovely wife, who was decked out in an orange bikini under her sheer beach-shirt and fashionable "wrap" around the waist—the kind where you can't see that morsel of white butt-cheek peeking out unless you really concentrate. I did.

Fontaine had one hand on the wheel and the other applying suntan oil to Monique, who shimmied her shoulders and rolled her neck while moaning and sighing deliciously. Both Doc and I made sure to coat the gals evenly, covering every exposed centimeter of skin, kneading it into every crevice.

Suddenly, Doc pointed ahead. Some terns were smacking the water above some sort of feeding frenzy. "Look!" Gina pointed. "What's all that?" Doc pulled back on the throttle, and we idled towards the action. The water's surface was boiling with swirls and splashes. Then a few fish came completely out of the water in their feeding frenzy.

"Spanish mackerel!" I howled. "Hand me that pole, Gina!" She bent waaaaay down, straining to pry it from the rod-holder. Her wrap parted slightly in the back, the bikini bottom slipped up, and I got me an eyefull of sweet meat. "Looks like I missed a spot," I snickered, referring to the sunscreen.

She came up with the rod in one hand and the other hand heading for my head like a trip-hammer. SMAAACK! "Keep your eyes on the fish, buster!" she shrieked.

"OOUUWW!" I roared while turning to Shirley for sympathy. Wrong move.

SMAAACK! now it was Shirley's turn, and I got a stinging swat on the other cheek. "Behave!" she glared. "You're a married man! A father! We're not putting up with that shit this morning!"

"Jesus!" I thought. My face felt like I'd used a jellyfish for a pillow. "What's the matter with these broads?"

They'd gotten up too early on a Saturday, *that* was the matter. But Doc Fontaine had stopped at the Daiquiri Shop the night before, and we had three gallons of piña coladas aboard, along with the wine and beer, and pasta salad, and finger sandwiches, and Camembert and French bread. Leave it to Doc. Always the perfect host.

Within an hour, the gals had mellowed dramatically. Within two, the giggles started, and their cheeks glowed with that telltale pinkish tint. Chris even got his butt pinched while leaning over to net a fish, by my wife Shirley. "Go ahead, Gina," she then instructed her college sorority and dorm-mate. "You put it on." Shirley meant suntan oil, and she was pointing at me. She was "too far away" up in the bow and busy reeling in redfish, you see. Then these wives giggled wickedly at each other. My eyes lit up, and I licked my lips in anticipation.

Soon, the soft hand was working the fragrant oil into my shoulders. I savored the delectable sensation. Amazing what a "strange" female hand does to the nerve endings of a long-married male. Now the neck . . . ummmmm! Now the lower back . . . ummmm! Right down to my shorts' elastic wasitband—Ooops! Under that now!

Another wicked giggle from behind. Shirley herself was looking from the bow and wiggling her eyebrows mischievously at Gina, who softly patted my tensed-up buttock. Then pinched it, gasping a little in the act, followed by more giggles. Then back up to knead the shoulder blades a bit. Now both hands, one on either side of my neck rubbing, kneading, gripping. I could feel something pressing midway up my back. Those must be—oohhh!—Gina's boobs. I was losing it.

I leaned closer to the gunwale lest my aroused condition become obvious. My freaking shorts were poking out like a flagpole in front. I noticed Monique eyeing me and smiling, then looking at the wives and smiling. She knew. Hell, they all knew. The fun was starting.

Then a happy little shriek: "Ohh-eeeh! Got one! Got one here!" Monique was cranking away at her reel as a redfish thrashed the surface off the stern.

"Keep that rod tip high!" instructed Doc, "That's it. Looks like a nice one! A dandy!" Monique's eyes were wide. Her mouth shifted from a smile to a grimace and then back as she battled the fish. "Oh my! Ohhh, yes! Theez eez wonderful!" I couldn't help noticing that the arm-cranking motion had set her bikini top into a pendulous, mouth-watering motion. Her ample cleavage was beaded with sweat too, quite a turn-on.

"One here!" Suddenly Doc reared back on his rod, and the surface exploded. "Yeah, boy!" It was off to the races. His reel was singing as the red took off for Cuba.

"Don't worry, Doc," I motioned. "I'll get it," meaning Monique's fish, which was now thrashing at boat side.

"Hurry! Oh, please, hurry!" She was excited. Her first fish of the day. I leaned over, grabbed the leader, and swung the small red aboard.

"Hummm," I said while prying the jig loose. "Don't think it'll make it, Monique. Gotta be sixteen inches. This one looks about fifteen."

"Vhat?" I looked over and her pretty face had contorted into an angry frown. First time I'd ever seen it like that. "No! No!" She was nodding furiously. Then she turned to Doc for help. "Mitch! Oh, Mitch! He vants to throw my fish back. I vant theeez fish!"

"Too small, honey," he nodded while holding up his bucking rod. "We get caught and it's a big fine. Don't worry. We'll catch plenty more—plenty more. Big ones . . . like *this!* Yeah!" and his rod took off on another spool-sizzling run.

"No! Here! Give me!" And Monique reached over, trying to grab the fish. "It's my fish!"

"Yeah, it's her fish!" Shirley added from the bow.

"Let her keep it!" Gina seconded with an emphatic pat on my back. "That's a stupid law anyway!"

It's always this way. Women are too damn practical for silly abstractions like "catch and release" fishing. Their brains don't work that way. For them, a fish is dinner, period. I've seen it time and again. Like Camille Paglia says in *Sexual Personae*, "Women have a greater realism and wisdom then men." Mencken had their number too: "Women are clear-headed, resourceful, implacable and without qualms . . . any man who is so unfortunate as to have a serious controversy with a woman must inevitably carry away from it a sense of having passed through a dangerous and hair-raising experience. No attack is so desperate that they will not undertake it, no device is so unfair or horrifying that it stays them."

Here was perfect proof. "Okay, okay!" I gasped as Monique started wrenched the fish from my hand, gouging me with her nails in the process. "Let's at least measure it . . . . Geeesh!" I bent down, placing him along the inch markers atop the ice-chest.

Poor red, his fate hung in the balance. He seemed to sense it and was hunching up and curling his tail. No tail! Don't touch that number sixteen! No jaw! Don't touch that zero! Please! He seemed to shrink before our very eyes. But it was close.

"Stretch him!" Gina was leaning over, pressing down on my hand, smashing the poor fish against the ice-chest, trying to get another quarter-inch more. "More! See! He's almost!"

"Yeah!" Shirley added moral support from the bow. "Longer . . . harder! That's it!" Torquemada with a heretic on the rack during the Spanish Inquisition was humane in comparison.

"Okay, okay!" I finally yelled. "We'll KEEP it!"

"Yaaaay!" The gals erupted in cheers and an ovation. "Yippee!" I bent down, opened the ice-chest, and threw him in. I was still bent over, grabbing a handful of bait shrimp from inside the ice chest when I turned my head slightly and almost fainted. Five inches from my nose jiggled Monique's boobs—*bare* boobs.

No tan lines on these babies either. She'd taken off her top.

I tried to act cool. She was French, after all. Topless sunbathing was the norm in her country—bottomless, too, for that matter. I looked over at Chris. He was smiling and wide-eyed, making no attempt to hide his glee. "See Gina? See Shirley?" He pointed at Monique. "Nothing to it. No big deal."

Monique just looked over, smiled, and cast out again. I really liked the motion as she flipped the bail and started popping the cork. I noticed Chris wasn't missing it, either. Doc was busy fighting redfish. For him, this was standard operation procedure.

Oddly, the wives got along fabulously with Monique. Who'd a thought it? They seemed to have nothing in common with her. Usually these match-ups result in an unpleasant outing with constant verbal sniping and dagger eyes. Instead, Monique's company seemed to bring out the old fun-loving sorority sisters in our wives, reminding them of their carefree youth. So we started working on them.

"Hey remember," Chris said while winking over at me. "We'll be on that Caribbean sailboat cruise in two weeks. Lots of nude beaches where we'll be stopping—St. Marten, Martinique. Y'all don't wanna look like unsophisticated yahoos out there, do ya? Monique's gonna show y'all up with her all-over tan . . . so why not?"

"Maybe," Gina and Shirley said, giggling, teasing us mercilessly. "Maybe in a little while . . . we'll see."

Obviously, it wasn't Shirley I was excited about. And Chris wasn't salivating for a peek at his wife. "Y'all ready for another piña colada?" I offered. We were halfway through the supply and had almost limited out on fish when Chris suggested we head over to nearby Breton Isle for a little sunbathing, boozing, and beach frolicking on this secluded barrier island.

Excellent idea, I thought. Indeed, things got really interesting for the rest of the day. Both Chris and I got a super treat.

CHAPTER FOUR

SCREAMING REELS

The delectable memories were swirling in my head when Pelayo ripped off my cap and nearly my scalp with his first cast, jolting me back to reality. "Nice going!" I yelled, while casting myself. My popping cork hit about a foot from the canes. Perfect. I popped it twice while bending down to recover my cap. Tom and Paul cast about twenty feet further along the shoreline. I turned to look at a flock of ducks. "Look like cans," I said, when I felt a tug. Then I looked over, thinking, where's my cork?

"Whooa!" I reared back as a huge swirl marked where my cork had plunged. For a second, it felt like I'd hooked a log. No motion. Then the water erupted in a froth of white foam and a flash of copper. "That's him!" I roared. It was off to the races.

I loosened the drag to let him run, and run he did, heading for the open water like a bull red will. I saw the spool emptying and hauled up a little, tightening the drag. He was making a wild run parallel to the shoreline and I was savoring every sizzling second, pole high overhead, drag screaming, and an idiot grin creasing my face. "Can't beat a shallow water red on light tackle, boys!" I roared.

"Sure can't!" Pelayo yelled while jerking back savagely himself. "Another one here!"

"And here!" said Tom, from the bow.

"And here!" said Paul, right next to him.

We had four of the suckers on at once. It was bedlam. Like I was saying, the few pockets of clear water concentrate the redfish down here this time of year. Pelayo's, fortunately, was streaking for the open water, too. Tom's red was plowing through the canes and Paul's had already crossed my line.

I was running from bow to stern, from aft to starboard, dodging people, poles, and ice chests. So was everyone else. Every man for himself, for now. We'd have to net our own. But every time I horsed the brute near the boat, he'd screech off again and again. He was a monster, ten pounds, I estimated.

Pelayo's was as big. Tom's looked a little bigger, and Paul actually had a chunky puppy drum. Their fight is indistinguishable from a red's in shallow water, ditto their flesh. After a few minutes of stumbling around the boat, I managed to net mine. Then I grabbed On-the-Ball's leader and heaved his drum aboard as he winced, thinking it might fall off. Instead, he flopped on deck. Paul unhooked it and slapped another shrimp.

"Get it out there again, Paul!" Tom yelled as he pumped away at his fish, which was still going strong. Looks like we found a school!" Paul wound up and flung that baby out, catching Pelayo's cap with his jig and sending it overboard like a Frisbee. Paul's cork landed about twenty feet from the boat, a huge bird's nest of mono floating in the water. I was laughing my ass off when . . . "Where's your cork, On-the-Ball? Your cork!" A hatless Pelayo was yelling "Set the hook! Man! Set it!" The reds were everywhere this morning, almost alongside the boat.

Reeengareeengareeengareeenga.
Paul frantically reeled in about twenty
feet of slack. "WHOOAAAA!" He set
the hook. "That's him!" Paul whooped
as the fish lunged and his rod dipped
almost into the water.

"Ride him out, my man!" Pelayo
roared. "Ride him out!" Paul's reel sang
it's sweet music as the brute aimed for
Breton Island. Another bull red, from
the looks of it.

> "PINTAIL ALLEY" WE DUBBED IT ALMOST TEN YEARS BEFORE

"Man, oh, man!" Tom was nodding
from his perch atop an ice-chest as he cranked away at his fish.
"Awesome. Simply *awesome!*" Tom was aglow. "Is the fishing *always*
like this down here?" Then his red hit the surface about fifty yards
out with a breathtaking eruption of foam and a flash of copper
scales. "What—a—fish!" He beamed. "Saw that tail! Looks like a
shovel!"

Now the fish aimed back for the rosseaus with a spirited run.
Then back north. Finally, Tom started gaining on him. Latch a man
onto an eight-pound red in shallow water with light tackle and
you've got a fisherman for life my friends. *For life.* No fishing like it.

"Another one—here!" Pelayo had been bouncing a purple/white
cocahoe along the shoreline and set the hook with the "here."
"Another monster!" he announced. It exploded on the surface and
screeched off, making for open water alongside Tom's.

I cast where Pelayo had been a second before, looked back at
Tom, and then popped the cork. It plunged. "Yes!" I gasped while
jerking back.

Is there a more magnificent sensation, my friends? I felt a solid
WHUMP, then a sharp lunge as the reel started screaming. Give me
a red any day. How many fishermen I've known who've come full
circle. Starting in the marsh with specs and reds as kids, "graduat-
ing" to offshore, to tuna and marlin, then coming back home to
marsh fishing. These people are legion. I know scores of them. Hell,
I'm one myself.

"Another red!" I howled, just as he exploded on the surface about thirty yards out. "A monster!" My line was sizzling out, then it suddenly went flaccid. What the . . . ?

"He's swimming in on ya!" Pelayo howled. "Swimming in! Reel in that slack!"

Indeed, the brute was aiming for the open water, but the boat was in the way. I cranked furiously and tightened it just as it plowed under the boat. Half my rod was underwater as he kept going and I frantically fumbled with the drag. To no avail. I climbed around the bow, somehow passed the pole around Tom and under the anchor rope and breathed a sigh of relief when I felt his bulk on the end of the line. Then he went on another run. I stood on the bow, pole overhead, savoring every sizzling second of the maniac's run. Looking over for applause, I saw Pelayo beaming as he swung in a flounder. We were indeed on 'em!

The action was literally non-stop for the next hour. I mean unbelievable. When we lifted the anchor an hour and a half later, twenty reds from five to twelve pounds crammed the ice chest, along with a smattering of drum, flounder, and sheepshead. A true "box-a-mixed," as we say locally.

Back at the campsite a little after noon, the wind was gusting nicely, the tide inching up. "Oughta see the freakin' ducks over in Pintail Alley!" Chris said as he grabbed the bow rope.

"Oughta see the redfish down Johnson Pass!" Tom replied.

"I did," Chris smirked. "Yesterday. It was unreal. Y'all got on 'em huh?"

"Sure did," Paul said while motioning Chris over to the ice chest on the bow. "Lookit here."

"Nice," Chris nodded. "Yep. Damn nice . . . . Some flounder too, I see. Just like yesterday. Guess they're still there. Y'all fished the place we call professor's cut, huh?"

"Place never fails," Pelayo nodded as he hopped out of the boat. "Now how 'bout dem ducks? I'm about ready for some shootin'. "

We were about fifty feet from the brushy bank when Paul elbowed Pelayo. "Slow down," he hissed. Pelayo nodded, jerked back on the throttle, and we idled toward shore. Suddenly, Paul looked up and pointed. "Pretty, huh?" he smirked. "Watch where they go." He lowered his arm and started pointing straight ahead, moving his finger back and forth. "I bet right in there."

Pretty, indeed. A huge flock of ducks was slowing down and splitting up. They were high, mere specks in the sky. For a moment, they looked uncertain, necks craning back and forth . . . gliding, then flapping again . . . more gliding. Finally, their wings cupped and they started the long descent.

The three of us gaped skyward, entranced.

"Look!" Tom yelled while pointing behind us. "More over here." Another big flock was winging in from the rear. These were flying lower, slowing down at first sight of the bay just ahead, surveying the feast and orgy below.

But not for long. When almost directly overhead, they cupped their wings and started down, mingling with the first flock as it descended from above them.

"Pintail," Pelayo snapped. He pursed his lips and nodded sagely while looking up. "Yep. Same as it ever was . . . same as it ever was . . . same as it ever was." And he started chopping at his forearm à la the Talking Heads' "Once in a Lifetime" video, "*Same as it ever was . . .*"

Pelayo had David Byrne down to a tee, even to the spastic head-bobbing. His wife, Cheryl, *hated* when he started that crap at parties, but it usually slayed everyone else. Especially when he'd kneel down, put the top of his head on the floor, and start spinning and twisting it. Tequila shots usually did the trick.

Tom chuckled as he looked from me to Pelayo to Paul, but he appeared a little confused. "What he means, Tom," Paul said while pointing at the wall of brush straight ahead. Paul had to clear things up for the FNG (Fucking New Guy). "He means Pintail Alley is same as it ever was. It's still packing in the pintail. It's right up ahead. This place never fails. It's *always* fulla ducks. We've hunted it for years."

Tom nodded, but with a blank expression. All he saw in front of us was a wall of willow, rosseau cane, and elephant ear grass, but behind it was a big shallow bay. "Pintail Alley" we dubbed it almost ten years before. Back then, duck limits were on the "point system." A limit was 100 points. Pintail were ten-point ducks, so we could shoot ten a piece. Many a late morning, the three of us paddled out with barely an inch of freeboard around our pirogues. We'd piled up thirty pintail—all drakes.

The flocks poured down on us just like the ones we were watching above. Sometimes we'd have one-hundred ducks decoying at once, all pintail. Picking the drakes was easy. Some people duck hunt their whole lives and never witness such a spectacle. Others go to Argentina. We had it on our doorstep. Those were the days. Hence the name, Pintail Alley.

We hadn't hunted it this season yet, but for almost a decade, this shallow bay had given us some of the best hunts in the Delta. The water was shallow and choked with widgeon grass and milfoil. They always had a standing buffet, even late into the winter. Usually, they winged in during the late morning and dropped down for a late-morning snack, some socializing, a little fanny pinching, and perhaps a nap. The ones above us were following the script perfectly.

As usual, they were winging in from the west. High tides came at night this week, and with a full moon, the ducks had been gorging on duck potato tubers all night on the mud flats off South Pass. Several little deltas (mini alluvial plains) had sprung up in that area lately. The Mississippi had been at flood stage the past two springs. No levees shackle the river as it passes down here in the Delta. The silt-rich tides flood the marsh every year and rejuvenate it like a magic elixir. The river currents pour into the sloughs that poke from the pass and gradually scour these sloughs into channels. The fertile sediments poured through and were carried into the open waters of East Bay. Here the currents slowed down and the silt started accumulating (a miniature version of how all of South Louisiana came into being about ten thousand years ago).

In a month, sandbars rose above the muddy water. A month later, the waters receded and green shoots poked from the tawny muck. By mid-summer, they sprouted into green orchards of prime duck fodder: duck potato, three-cornered grass, and wild millet. By

September, the teal, pintail, and local mottled ducks were pouring in for the feast. By November, the gadwalls, widgeon, blue geese, and most of the Mississippi Flyway's canvasbacks joined in.

For ducks, this natural buffet rivals anything in man's grain fields. Most of the Flyway's pintail—a notorious and picky gourmand—winter down here. They stop to snack in the soybean and rice fields of Arkansas and northern Louisiana, but the allure of the Delta, its balmy climate, it's five-month standing feast, proves irresistible. It's a waterfowl Riviera. One acre of Louisiana marsh yields an annual organic production four times greater than a fertilized cornfield. Seventy-seven percent of the birds known to the American continent have been spotted at one time or another in the Mississippi Delta.

Mallards, the lazy bums, might stop short in Arkansas, Missouri, and southern Illinois, and every year, more of them do. Not the pintail. His sleek physique is that of a long-distance runner anyway. He always finishes the traditional race first, getting to the tip of the Mississippi Delta—North America's last stop—as early as September.

By December, pintail blanket the bay's mudflats and fill the air with their toots and twitters, driving us crazy as we try to figure out how to ambush them. Most Delta duck hunters scoff or scratch their heads when they read the annual duck counts and surveys. For over a decade we've been reading about the low and "troubled" pintail populations. Yet on some days that's all we see—pintails by the thousands, pintails flapping and gliding above us constantly, high and low, hovering over our decoys, splashing amongst them. Easy for us to say. We're lucky. They all winter here.

Twenty years ago, pintail flocked into western Louisiana's rice fields. They rivaled mallards as western Louisiana's premier duck. But in the mid 1970s, as more and more flow diverted into the Atchafalaya River from the Mississippi, a new delta arose along the central Louisiana coast at the mouth of the Atchafalaya River. These sandbars and mud flats sprouted the same lush and nutritious delta plants. This set the same buffet at the mouth of the Atchafalaya that for thousands of years had grown at the mouth of the Mississippi.

Within a year, it started drawing ducks from the rice fields to the west, tuber-eating pintail especially. Within five years it had altered

73

some traditional wintering patterns—to the lament of west Louisiana's hunters. Nowadays, the Atchafalaya Delta gets crammed with pintail from September to February, the same pintail who used to flock into the rice fields further west.

Rice-field hunting is a cinch. After a long night of bouray and Hooter's girls, you drive along the levees to a dry permanent blind in an ATV or truck. The decoys are already out—indeed, they stay out season-long. You climb in, start shooting the breeze, perhaps a nip of brandy if it's chilly, and wait for the ducks to show up. Pretty nice.

Not so Delta duck hunting, which entails setting up in pirogues, brush blinds, or simply squatting in the slop in hip-waders and ambushing the ducks. No permanent blinds or decoys set-ups in the Deltas. Rampaging tides won't allow it. This is hunting with a capital H—hunting in the *genuine* sense of the word.

In Europe, what we call duck "hunting," they call duck "shooting." This makes sense. With most duck hunting, no actual "hunting" takes place, other than "hunting" for a spot to build the blind at the beginning of the season. Ditto for most permanent blind duck "hunting" in Texas, California, and Louisiana. You get there in the morning, and everything's set up. What's to *hunt?* What you do is *shoot.*

In the Delta, you have to *find* them first, and not from a truck or ATV. You locate them from a pirogue or by trudging around in hip boots, the muck sucking stubbornly at your ankles. Every step is a chore, but it's an excellent way to get exercise. It beats hell out of those ankle weights you strap on at the gym, then stagger around the track with. Pelayo loves to mock our hunting chums who buy ATVs, motorized pirogues, etc., etc.—then join a health club. "Shit, man," Pelayo snorts at them. "Hunt like us and you'll get ten times more exercise! Cheaper, too!"

He's right. And here, you're suffering for a purpose. Usually you're so focused on the hunt you forget the muscular agony. Next day, the cramps remind you.

Those pintail overhead had finished their serious nighttime feasting. Now came the loafing and socializing in the deeper sheltered ponds and lagoons of the interior marsh. They were arriving on schedule too. By midday, rafts of pintail and gadwall usually blanketed Pintail Alley's surface.

We hunt the mini-deltas off South Pass too, but they're a royal bitch to hunt, except on a high tide. Just our luck, the high tides came at midnight this week. We'd have to catch the ducks in their midday resting haunts. We'd have no choice but to ambush them in Pintail Alley.

A few feet from the bank, Pelayo finally turned the key and killed the engine. Suddenly, Paul jerked his head around. "Hear *that?*" he gasped. He was wide-eyed and grinning crazily.

Damn right, we heard it. It was almost *too* loud. The dull growl and hum of a crewboat churning up South Pass in the distance muffled it slightly. Slowly the crewboat noise died and the glorious gabfest of ducks replaced it. We looked at each other wide-eyed and gaping. Pelayo simply smirked, trying to look cool, but he was as pumped as anyone.

What we heard was more of a steady roar than any quacking or highballing. "Sure that's ducks?" Tom laughed while cupping his ears, a crazy grin on his face. You couldn't blame him. His duck hunting had been mostly for woodies in swamps or mallards in flooded timber. He'd never been so close to so many ducks. He'd never heard anything like this glorious racket—nothing even *close.*

From two hundred yards, the combined quacks and gabbles of a few thousand ducks merge into a veritable roar, like a steamroller over gravel. A "wall of sound," indeed! But this one had nothing to do with Phil Spector, the Righteous Brothers, or the Ronettes. For the diehard duck-hunter, no sound compares to this din, no symphony so delights.

Finally, we started making out some individual duck sounds from those nearest . . . a few quacks, some chuckles . . . Here the haunting "whew-whew-whew" of a widgeon, there the tooting and twittering of pintail. Now a sharp raspy hail from a hen gadwall calling to her mates above. Paul pointed above us and nodded. "Come on down, she's calling!" We were getting giddy. This place does it every time.

Paul grabbed his call from around his neck and gave a blast—all squeaks and missed notes. He'd been practicing on the damn thing for two days now, driving us crazy. Amazingly, some love-crazed hen answered with a hail of her own from across the spoil bank.

Tom was near the bow. I watched him cock his head and cup his ears again. Those M-60 machine guns he shot from choppers in Nam took a toll on his hearing, but not enough to stifle *this* racket. He mouthed something but I couldn't make it out, just as the bow of the boat hit the bank. The impact slammed Tom headfirst into the side of the fiberglass pirogue with a nasty THUMP.

"OOW!" I looked at him then jerked my head left as a huge splash erupted in the water, followed by a giant muddy swirl and a flurry of bubbles.

"Saw *that?*" Tom yelled. He was still rubbing his head, but his eyes were huge and wild. "What the *hell?*"

"Nutria," Paul said.

"Nutria, my *ass!*" Pelayo laughed while punching his brother's shoulder. "Nutrias don't get five hundred pounds, man. That was an alligator—a *big* one!"

CHAPTER FIVE

GATOR BRAWL

You'd never know it from the media, but alligators topped sharks as killers and maimers of Floridians last summer, as they have for the past twenty years. Sharks killed two people in 2001. Alligators killed three.

Yet the summer of 2001 was billed as the "Summer of the Shark" by *Time* magazine. You couldn't turn on the TV with seeing and hearing of another deadly attack by these vicious toothy brutes. You couldn't pick up a paper or magazine without reading another chilling headline and a horrifying sidebar about some hapless bather or surfer chomped and mangled by "nature's ultimate killing machine." Harvard biologist Edward O. Wilson calls the shark, "the most terrifying creature on Earth," and ever since the movie *Jaws* in 1975, the shark has gotten top billing as man's premier aquatic predator.

The story of seven-year-old Jessie Arbogast was the most heart-rending of that summer. An eight-foot bull shark came stalking into the shallows where little Jessie frolicked on Pensacola Beach, bit him, then swallowed the severed arm and half his thigh. His uncle somehow grabbed the shark, wrestled it ashore, and pulled Jessie's arm from its gullet. Little Jessie lost almost all of the blood in his body and was rushed to a hospital in a coma where his arm was re-attached.

Animal rightists sprung quickly into action. They were frantic. Millions of brainless yokels throughout the land might get the wrong idea and blame the shark, you see. Just like us to overlook "root causes."

"Would you give your right arm to know why sharks attack?" asked a PETA poster last July. "Could it be revenge?"

Damn right it could be revenge. Certainly off Louisiana, where we blast; spear; stab; hook; gaff; blow to smithereens with power-heads, buckshot, and assorted magnums; mangle; pummel; bludgeon; skin; fillet; cube; marinate; skewer; and grill everyone we can get our hands on.

But Florida is different. These enlightened folk dutifully report, capture, and relocate "nuisance" gators. Here in Louisiana we blast, behead, and "barbecue" gators. No "nuisance" at all. Damn tasty in fact.

Florida has an equally progressive approach to "nuisance" sharks. They didn't invite Louisiana's Helldivers, Sea Tigers, and Bayou Bandits over to remedy the problem with their spear guns and grills. This would have cost them a few kegs of beer, at most.

Instead they invited shark "expert" Dr. Erich Ritter to "consult." Ah, that famous word again. Turns out, if you thought little Jessie was "attacked" by that shark, well then you're a tabloid-reading yokel. Dr. Ritter knows better, and unlike you, he has a Ph.D. in "behavioral ecology" from the prestigious University of Zurich. He's part of the Shark Foundation, who's website pleads: "Stop the senseless slaughter of sharks!" and where you can, for a modest fee, actually "adopt a shark" and get photos of the cuddly creature.

They know the Arbogast incident was a regrettable "accident" on the shark's part.

They know that the poor beast was overwhelmed with remorse right after he swallowed Jessie's arm. You see, according to Dr. Ritter, "the shark was not reacting specifically to the

DAMN RIGHT IT COULD BE REVENGE

boy . . . . These animals are very smart, contrary to how many people believe them to be stupid, brute killers. When you lose your fear, you begin to see what a magnificent creature he really is."

Dr. Doolittle has nothing on Dr. Ritter, who explains: "We are trying to develop a body language system to build a bridge to the shark, to try to trigger favorable reactions rather than the wrong ones . . . . We can swim with a pack of hungry sharks and do it safely. There really is nothing to worry about, because you quickly discover that sharks are not mindless monsters."

Except, perhaps, the one who ripped half of Dr. Ritter's leg off a few months later in the Bahamas. Yep, and while the Discovery Channel's very cameras were rolling.

The Discovery Channel was featuring Dr. Ritter in a program about how to properly "interact" with sharks. Indeed, he was right in the middle of demonstrating how he could—by controlling his heartbeat—interact safely with a school of them without triggering any hint of aggressive behavior on their part, when one rushed in, chomped down, and interacted the good doctor's leg right into his gullet. Dr Ritter went into shock from blood loss and quickly into a hospital, like little Jessie.

I prefer my chum Artie's method of interacting with sharks. He prefers a twelve-gauge power-head BA-LOOOOM! My ears are still ringing from his last interaction with a big mako one-hundred feet under the Gulf. I shot my spear in the jerking, twirling monstrosity and hauled him up.

I did a little interaction with the shark myself, on the filet table and with the lemon butter sauce on the grill. Then we tapped the keg, popped open the white wine for the gals, and about 40 hungry guests interacted up a storm. Magnificent creature, indeed! We appreciate sharks too, Dr. Ritter.

PETA even flew airplane banners over yokel-infested beaches in Florida last summer reading: "Dangerous predators in the water . . . you?"

The women all saw it first. Maybe PETA members are different, but while lying on the sand with a brewski on Florida's Miracle Strip, not many of my chums have their eyes focused skyward. The thong bikinis aren't up there, nor the bouncing little tattoos.

My helpful wife jerked the binoculars from my face and redirected my gaze, though, and I can still show you the bruise. After the pain subsided somewhat, I shifted the ice pack, looked up, and said, "Huh?"

That's a shrewd bunch at PETA. I don't think they wanted to compliment us. But flying over a Florida Panhandle beach notoriously infested with beer-swilling rednecks and Cajuns (fanatical hunters all) and calling them "dangerous predators" . . . . that's like me flying a plane banner over Malibu beach or Martha's Vineyard, saying: "Ecologically aware, gender-sensitive, diaper-changing, socially conscious fellows sipping wine on their verandas this evening . . . you?"

Grilled venison sausage, grouper ceviche, and gator-ka-bobs were depleting rapidly on our section of beach. So the response to the plane banner was deafening: "Freakin-ay!" shrieked Pelayo. "You're goddamn right we're dangerous predators!" Chris bellowed while hoisting a beer. "Whoo-hoo!" And so on. Much whooping, beer hoisting, and high-fiving. Then we grabbed the binoculars and resumed the serious business of scanning the beaches, quickly alerting each other to any approaching thong bikinis.

The alligator attack vs. shark attack statistics are in the International Shark Attack File itself. They're put there to say: "See! See what a bad rap sharks keep getting! They're not so bad!"

I guess that's one way of looking at it. Another is that alligators need a bad rap, too. But they were put on the endangered species list with full protection way back in 1962, and thus canonized and Bambified.

In fact, when an alligator attacks a human, he's more likely to actually *kill* him than "nature's ultimate killing machine," which is equipped mainly to kill mackerel. Most shark attacks we can chalk up to mistaken identity. "Oops! Sorry, Mr. Surfer! In this murky water your leg looked like a mullet." "Sorry 'bout that, Mr. Diver. But y'all keep waving all those dead bloody fish in front of my nose. I got a little carried away. Thought your arm was part of one. Don't take it personally."

An alligator is more accustomed than a Gulf shark to make a meal of large prey, so he's equipped for it. Indeed, his equipment is practically identical to his cousin the crocodile, who kills thousands of Africans a year, more than lions, leopards, buffalo, elephants, cobras, gaboon vipers, and, of course, sharks, *combined.* When you're accustomed to tackling, chomping, and swallowing a three-hundred-pound wildebeest or zebra, making a meal of a one-hundred-fifty-pound woman who is pounding clothes on shoreline rocks barely works up a sweat.

And not just in Africa. The salt-water crocodile of the South Pacific (the one Crocodile Dundee hunts in Australia) grows bigger than the Nile crocodile and grabs people with equal gusto. Early in 2002, *Ananova* reported that crocodiles snatched eighteen people in a two-week period along the Ope River in New Guinea. As you might imagine, attacks in such places rarely make it to the wires. These places are too remote, and the attacks too routine, like a car wreck to us.

Fortunately, for whatever reason (probably because he evolved in an environment with smaller prey), the alligator doesn't have near the taste for human flesh as his crocodile kinfolk. That doesn't mean he's completely abstemious. For the past 20 years, alligators have averaged from fifteen to twenty attacks on people per year, mostly in Florida. Alligators are more resourceful than sharks at killing people, too. The stats bear this out. The attack to kill ratio is lower for alligators than for sharks. Simply put, more of their attacks on us are fatal.

This makes sense. It's only a big one who'll attack a human in the first place, and when a big gator chomps down, he's applying

3,000 pounds of pressure per square inch. Here's a recent story from the Associated Press as back up:

> Port Charlotte, Fla.—A woman driving home ran over an alligator, which then *bit through her car's bumper and lifted part of the vehicle off the ground.*
>
> Stephanie Feola, 43, said she first thought she hit an opossum Wednesday night but she saw the tail of an almost seven-foot alligator under her car.

And a measly shark got the moniker "Jaws"? Could Peter Benchley's little pets bite through a bumper and lift a Toyota off the ground?

Makes you wonder why Craig DeArmond is still alive. An alligator grabbed him while he was working under his camp just east of Baton Rouge, Louisiana, back in 1992. It was a lazy afternoon, and 31-year-old Craig was repairing a little wiring and insulation under his trailer, which sat about thirty feet from the shore of the nearby Amite River. The weather was nice. The birds were singing. Except that Craig was still recovering from a water moccasin bite from earlier that month (his second in five years), he was feeling chipper.

The beast came out of the water silently, and stealthily crawled toward Craig, who whistled while tending diligently to his business. Whistling creatures that tower to six feet don't normally constitute an eight-foot alligator's meal, but Craig was lying on the ground at the time, on his back. He didn't look very menacing. Indeed, he probably looked more like an alligator's usual prey.

No hissing, no bellowing, no thrashing around with a gaping maw—none of the usual antics of an angry gator facing a potential enemy with this one. This gator wasn't angry. He wasn't scared. He was *hungry*. His approach was silent, like a leopard stalking the warthog on *Animal Planet*. "An animal appears menacing in order to *avoid* combat," Hemingway tells us in *Death in the Afternoon*. He's hoping to get off with a bluff. Papa referred to those bulls that snort and paw the ground. They're the wimps. The ones who kill you don't advertise.

Female gators often hiss and thrash and snap when guarding a nest. They're telling you, in their own way, that they don't want any trouble. "Scram, will ya?"

An alligator on the hunt for a meal is something entirely different. He can actually run faster than a human for fifty yards. A swat from his muscle-bound tail can snap the legs on full-grown bull like twigs, and as we just read, his jaws can mangle a Toyota.

This creature had zeroed in on Craig DeArmond. This creature figured him for his next meal. Craig didn't hear or see a thing approaching when—CHOMP! Those 3,000 pounds of pressure per square inch clamped down on his thigh.

Let's go back to that AP story for a second: "The car started shaking and the alligator was lifting the front end of the vehicle off the ground," said Ms. Feola. "I thought it was going to come up through the floor!"

Clearly, Craig was in trouble. "Don't let him get you in the water!" was all he could think through the haze of his shock. "Punch him, gouge him, bite him, kick him, yell, scream—do anything and everything to *stay out of the water!*

Craig says that's all he was thinking when he looked down and saw the ugly brute's head, the blood gushing from his leg, and realized the fix he was in. Luckily, Craig's grandfather had been an alligator hunter back in the 1930s and 1940s. Craig's father was also a notorious "river rat," well experienced with alligators and their sometimes ornery ways. The three generations of DeArmonds spent plenty of time together, hunting and fishing. Craig had received invaluable and practical training for mishaps in his favorite haunts—the swamp. Now they were paying off.

Once an alligator (or crocodile) gets you in the water your odds for survival shrink like Spencer's pecker in that cold mud. (You'll see!) Brian knew this from his father and grandad. The alligator knew it, too, and was hell-bent on dragging Craig to a bloody, watery doom—then burp, pick his teeth, and sleep it off.

Once they drag their prey into water, all crocodiles start their classic "death roll." Crocodiles do it on the Zambezi, on the Nile, and in coastal Australia. You see this on the Discovery Channel a lot. Alligators do it in

Florida and Louisiana alike. This you don't see as often.

Alligators have no tongue. They have no molars to chew with. A nutria, a raccoon, a heron, a fawn, a wild piglet, a fifty-pound garfish, another smaller gator—these he can crush in his jaws, mangle to pulp, and swallow whole. An adult deer, a hog, or a Craig DeArmond requires the crushing along with some butchery first. That Amite River gator thought of Craig the way Chef Emeril regards a suckling pig. Looks damn good, but I'll never get the whole thing down in one bite.

That's where the death roll comes in. Alligators' teeth aren't designed for slicing or ripping neatly. They're designed for holding, for gripping tightly. The death roll is where ripping comes in. A gator grabs hold with those sharp conical teeth and 3,000 pounds of pressure, and he'll start twisting his body—he'll start spinning, round and round and round, like a huge and hideous propeller—till enough muscle tears, till enough ligaments snap, till enough bones crack and splinter. Finally, he'll tear it off.

Now perhaps he has a chunk that he can swallow—GULP. Yum! Then CHOMP! He clamps down again and prepares to spin and rip off another fifty-pound morsel.

Craig had seen the procedure often enough, but on other hapless creatures and from the safety of his boat. "No way!" he thought when the big scaly bastard started dragging him toward the river. He wanted no part of it. So he wrapped his arms around one of the pilings that held up his trailer and held on for dear life. *"Don't let him get you in the water"* still screaming in his brain.

A tiger shark's teeth are designed to slice cleanly, like a Ginsu knife. They have serrated edges, and with one shake of his head, a tiger shark might sever your arm, or leg, or head, like a guillotine, which was originally designed as a humane method of execution by the enlightened leaders of the French Revolution. The point was to make it neat and quick.

Nothing neat and quick about perishing in the jaws of an alligator or crocodile, however. Makes you wonder about that "most terrifying creature on earth" title. A shark's teeth slice like a surgeon's scalpel through a leg during an amputation or at worst, like Emeril's butcher knife through a chicken on his cutting board. Either way, it's fairly quick. A lion snags you with his razor-like claws but instantly lunges for your neck, and then those massive canines crush your vertebrae with his first bite. Chomp-snap, and it's over. If a lion gets a good grip, you won't have to worry about gangrene. An alligator or a croc takes his sweet time about it.

One of medieval man's most ingenious tortures was called "drawing and quartering." This was dished out only to top miscreants and wise-asses. You had to really piss off the authorities to get it. This hideous fate befell William Wallace (aka Braveheart) and Sir Walter Raleigh both. In one version, your four appendages were tied to four different horse teams aimed in four different directions. Then giddy-UP! *Ha-ha!*

I'll take the guillotine any day. A human "quarter" is just about what a ten-foot crocodile or alligator can swallow. He does his drawing and quartering in the water, usually with his prey still alive. Like I said, Craig DeArmond had a *tight* grip on that piling that day.

But the alligator had a much tighter one on his thigh, and he was tugging mightily toward the river behind him. Imagine a three-hundred-pound pit bull with three times the teeth and five times the mouth. The only thing missing as Craig grimaced and held on were the growls. Craig could feel his muscles stretching, almost to the breaking point. Would his ligaments hold? How strong is cartilage? What would give first? Parting with a mere leg was starting to sound like a good compromise. He was determined to stay put. *"Don't let him get you in the water!"* kept sounding in his head.

If an alligator grabs an outer appendage—say a forearm—you'll probably make it. He'll just rip it off with a couple of death rolls—okay, let's be precise and call these "appendage-severing rolls." Whatever, this probably saved Kermit George's life back in 1986. Kermit was splashing around in the waist-deep water of a little lake in south Alabama's Conecuh National Forest with his dog on that fateful morning. Finally exhausted, he leaned back into the water for a refreshing plunge—kind of a "Nestea plunge" with arms spread, hitting the water with his back.

"Ah!" he was thinking to himself as the cool water enveloped him. "Delightful!" Suddenly, something grabbed his arm in a bone-crushing grip and jerked him violently. A huge splash erupted beside him. Water was going everywhere, most of it stained crimson. The black of the scaly monster twirling around stood against it vividly. Another violent tug and Kermit's arm was torn off at the shoulder. He stood up in shock and turned to see blood gushing from the stump of his mangled shoulder like from the Black Knight's in *Monty Python and the Holy Grail.* Remember that? Right after King Arthur whacked it off?

"'Tis but a scratch," the knight snorts at Arthur as the blood pours out.

"A scratch?" Arthur responds. "But your arm's gone!"

"I've had worse," says the knight. "Now come on you pansy, fight!"

After Arthur hacks off both his arms and both his legs, the knight finally shouts, "Running away, eh? You yellow bastard, come back here and take what's coming to you. I'll bite your legs off!"

A classic, my friends. Hope you excuse me. Anyway, Kermit was rescued by a nearby boater, rushed to a hospital and patched up. The twelve-foot, five-hundred-and-fifty-pound alligator was "terminated with extreme prejudice" by game authorities the next day. He still had Kermit's arm in his gullet, but unlike in the case of little Jessie Arbogast, it was too late for any surgical reattachment.

Today, Kermit George is happy and healthy and productive. C.C. Lockwood's book *Alligators* has a picture of him smiling while displaying the stump of his arm. He talks about his ordeal and amazing recovery on the lecture circuit. A modern day knight, indeed.

Craig DeArmond's attacker, however, had him by the thigh. A death roll would tear off Craig's leg along with some valuable anatomy. Craig probably wouldn't be smiling for any camera ten years later. And if he ever went on the lecture circuit, he'd have a much higher pitched voice. That's if he somehow survived.

But like Craig's father, Paul DeArmond, told me, "That kid

comes from tough stock. He's a survivor. He wasn't gonna go easy. That alligator had his work cut out for him." Tough, indeed. Craig was half in shock but still thinking clearly, planning his counterattack and escape in between the spasms of horrible pain that wracked his body. "This big bastard's using all his energy on getting me in the river," Craig thought to himself. "That's his priority. Well, I'll give him something else to think about!"

So when the alligator released his grip slightly to try for a better one, Brian retaliated—WHACK! WHACK! WHACK! With his bare fist on the brute's big bony head and snout (his most sensitive spot), trying to smash his eyes. He added a few awkward kicks.

The gator released his leg all right, but then grabbed Craig's shoulder, chomped quickly upward again, and soon included half of Craig's neck in his bone-crushing grip, along with his shoulder. Talk about going from the frying pan into the fire! The beast's jaws were inches from Craig's nose now. The horrid breath gagged him. He was on the point of vomiting.

This was no time to whine. "If he starts tugging now, I've had it. He's much closer to where I'm grabbing on to the pilings now. He pulls me off this piling and I'm a goner. Death-roll time."

Time to distract him again: BASH! BASH—BASH! Craig's right fist rained more blows on the creature's snout. "YAH! YAH! AAR-RGH!" Craig added some sound effects this time, thinking to further distract the brute. The adrenalin had kicked in big time by now. "Fight or flight," psychologists call it. Here's how one describes it:

> Your hypothalamus sends a message to your adrenal glands and within seconds, you can run faster, hit harder, see better, hear more acutely, think faster, and jump higher than you could only seconds earlier. Your heart is pumping at two to three times the normal speed, sending nutrient-rich blood to the major muscles in your arms and legs. The capillaries under the surface of your skin close down (which consequently sends your blood pressure soaring) so you can sustain a surface wound and not bleed to death. Even your eyes dilate so you can see better. All functions of your

body not needed for the struggle about to commence are shut down. Digestion stops, sexual function stops, even your immune system is temporarily turned off. If necessary, excess waste is eliminated to make you light on your feet. Your suddenly supercharged body is designed to help level the odds between you and your attacker.

Nowadays, there's no saber-tooth tiger coming after you. So normally, all these formerly valuable symptoms waste themselves in a panic attack. Some people pay out the wazoo for some psychiatrist (usually much crazier than themselves) to prescribe a pharmacopoeia of drugs to battle Mother Nature's brilliant design—to counteract the very natural responses that kept us alive for ninety-nine percent of our stint as a species.

Not Craig DeArmond. He was making full use of them. Last thing he needed was something to thwart his natural responses. He was employing every ounce of his adrenalin reserves, every ounce of the strength. They were being channeled, not for the flight, but for the *fight!* Like those who know him always say about Craig DeArmond: "When that boy walks by, you can hear the brass clanging." That alligator was learning a serious lesson in "biting off more than he could chew." A more literal interpretation of the phrase was impossible to conjure.

"BASH, BASH! Craig's knuckles were shredded and bleeding by now, but he wouldn't let up. Punching that gator's head was like punching jagged concrete with your bare hands. But Craig had no choice. He was going for the eyes, the only soft part of the powerful creature that gripped him, the only place where he might hurt him.

And finally he did, because the gator finally released his punctured, lacerated, blood-soaked shoulder and clamped his jaws around Craig's arm—his good one, the one attached to the fist recently raining those blows on the gator's rock-like head. Craig picked up where he left off with his other fist. Sure, that forearm was gushing blood, but he had no other weapons left. For a few very dangerous seconds, Craig had lost his life hold on the piling.

This rain of blows was too much for the gator and he released Craig again. In an instant, he was back, jaws agape, but he seemed to know which end was which now. The tugging had gotten him nowhere. "Now I'll have to disable this punk," the gator was thinking. "This time I'm going for the quick kill, to hurry up and be done with this troublesome meal." Craig somehow focused his blood-spattered eyes and saw those Toyota-mangling jaws wide open a foot away—lunging at his head.

"AAAAH!" Craig jerked sideways just as the teeth seemed to reach his nose, but in his condition, he couldn't move fast or far enough. The brute's jaws caught the side of his head. Craig could hear the awful grating from the teeth against his skull, scraping off part of his scalp. "That gator done *really* pissed me off that time!" Craig recalls.

"BASH—BASH, BASH! Both fists were in action now, whacking the gator's head with every ounce of strength, blood spraying with every blow—Craig's blood, not the gator's. It covered his arm, his neck, almost blinded him, still he fought. Still he punched. Still he kicked.

Something told Craig that this couldn't go on much longer. It seemed he'd been at this for a while now. He'd lost track of time, but piecing the story together, he figures he'd been fighting the Alligator for close to half an hour by then. That fight-or-flight response kicks in for a few minutes at most. That little boost was long over. In his delirium, something told Craig that time was running out. Just his luck, too, nobody was at the nearby camps that day to hear his struggle and come lend a hand or, preferably, a twelve-gauge slug.

The alligator moved a bit, and suddenly Craig felt . . . no pressure? Was it . . . ? Yes! He was free! His head cleared for a second and he lunged forward, scrambling on bloody elbows and bloody knees, clawing desperately with his mangled hands, scooting out from under the house with his last reserves of strength. His head had just cleared the edge of the house. The sun hit him. "Now I gotta find somebody to get me to a hospital" he was already thinking when . . . .

CHOMP! Those jaws grabbed him again by the leg, those teeth sunk in, the pain shot to his temples again, and more blood started gushing. The brute wasted no time now. He immediately started dragging him backward—toward the river. Nothing around for Craig to grab this time. He flailed his arms. He clawed the ground desperately. He sunk his bloody fingers into the mud, digging bloody groves as he was jerked backwards. He grabbed a cinder block, but it was loose. No help. He started taking it backward with him—backward towards the river, backward toward the gator's butcher block, backward towards a death roll, backward for a little drawing and quartering.

"Don't let him get you in the water!" blared in Craig's head again, so he started kicking, kicking—KICKING! the living shit out of the gator's head with his free but punctured and shredded leg, landing several blows on the bastard's snout with his foot—as he kept sliding . . . sliding backwards.

Suddenly, one of Craig's kicks hit nothing. His next one hit something softer—the mud. The bone-crushing pressure was off his leg, too. Was he gone . . . ? Craig raised his head and saw the beast's tail as it lumbered back to the river. The alligator finally threw in the towel. "Sheeeesh!" he was probably thinking. "Never again! Ain't worth the trouble! I was looking for a meal, not an ass kickin'! I'll go get me a turtle or a gar! Next time I come out on the bank for a meal, think I'll make it an egret or armadillo! Sheeeesh!"

The battle lasted almost forty minutes. A blood-covered Craig DeArmond managed to hobble—that brass clanging pretty loudly now—into a nearby camp and summon help from his friend Roy Dupree. "He was bloody from the top of his head to the bottom of his feet." Mr. Dupree told the reporter. "I hadn't *ever* seen somebody so scratched and bloody."

Doctors shook their heads while stitching Craig up—from his shoulders, to his neck, to his head, to his legs and torso. Three hundred stitches later, they finished with him.

"That gator was hunting big game that day, that's all," Craig snorts. " I hunt big game, too. We're both predators."

CHAPTER SIX

CAJUN CANNON ATTACK

Back in 1971, country crooner Jerry Reed topped the pop charts with his song about the Cajun alligator hunter, Amos Moses:

> *Now Amos Moses was a Cajun. He lived by hisself in the swamp and hunted alligator for a living. . . . The Louisiana law's gonna getcha, Amos! It ain't legal hunting alligator down in the swamp, boy!*

Well, a year later the Louisiana law had no reason to get ole Amos. It became perfectly legal *to hunt alligator down in the swamp, boy!* The Louisiana Wildlife and Fisheries opened an alligator season in September 1972. It made perfect sense, actually. The alligator, after all, is Louisiana's official state reptile. What's the point of this exalted designation if you can't have any fun with them, like hunting them and especially, *eating* them? We were the first, and still the only state in the Union, to open an alligator season.

The bayou state had become overrun with the beasts by 1972. Some say alligators were never endangered in the first place, nowhere close to it, but that came from people who actually spent time in the bayous, you see. Can't believe those crazy Cajuns.

Every year during this month-long season, from 25,000 to 35,000 alligators grab some morsel—a chicken, a blackbird, a fish, a chunk of cow spleen—hanging enticingly over the water along a bayou shoreline from a bamboo pole. That ain't heartburn! Uh-oh!—they find they've swallowed an enormous hook, too. Tug as he might, there's just no snapping that stout nylon cord from the hook to the stake or tree on the bank. Jerry Reed again:

> *Now the folks around south Louisiana said Amos was a hell of a man. He could trap the biggest, the meanest alligator and just use one hand. That's all he got left 'cause an alligator bit it. Ha, ha, ha!*

Soon the legal version of Amos Moses comes chugging along in his boat, making his rounds. "Aha!" He sees his bait down, then he fishes for the line with a gaff. Snagging it, he grabs it with gloved hands and starts pulling. "Yep. Feels like a big one all right!" *Slowly,* he coaxes the beast to the surface. "Ah, there's his head . . . ."

"BLAM!" He indeed "knocks 'em in the head," but not with a "stump." He uses a bullet or slug. This relocates their tiny brain (the size of a lima bean on an eight-footer) very efficiently, and saves the trapper's hand from becoming a stump à la Amos.

The skins and meat bring about twenty million dollars to the state annually. Not a windfall, but not bad either. More importantly, it takes out "the biggest, the meanest alligators," as Jerry Reed might say. Since the skins are paid for by the foot (usually around twenty-five to thirty dollars per foot) you always want to haul in the biggest ones for the most profit. The meat brings about four dollars and fifty cents a pound, wholesale.

Louisiana has more alligators than Florida, two-and-a-half million by some estimates, yet we have only a tiny fraction of Florida's alligator attacks or "nuisance" encounters. We know why: in Louisiana we've housebroken the brutes. Here they know their place. That place is as "gator on a stick," one of the Jazz Fest's all-time favorite snacks, or alligator pie, or perhaps covered in tomato slices, shredded lettuce and French bread as the stuffing in an alligator sausage po-boy. You see people walking all around the Jazz Fest, yumming away while snorking down these delicious concoctions.

In a French Quarter restaurant, the alligator might have simmered in a rich red sauce and emerged in bowls over steaming rice as "alligator sauce piquante" or been fried golden brown and heaped on a platter with lemon and tartar sauce on the side as the ever popular appetizer, fried alligator.

"Tastes just like chicken," some say, usually to appease the squeamish. Not if you ask me. Tastes much *better* than chicken for anyone with a proper palate. To me, he's more like bigger, thicker, more luscious frog legs.

Let's say you're in hurry; no time to lounge in a restaurant or stroll through the Jazz Fest. No problem, dash into the nearest south Louisiana convenience store, and from right there, next to the Slim Jims, grab a couple of "Alligator Bob's Smoked Alligator Jerky," along with a handful of "Alligator Bob's Hot & Spicy Alligator Sticks."

I could go on for pages with this stuff, but I observe the timekeeper reaching for the gong. I'll close with a recent story from the Newhouse New Service:

The desire for all things alligator has risen in the past decade, spurred by tourists who want to take a bit of Louisiana home to Des Moines or Omaha. Items range from claw key chains to alligator jerky to the most popular seller—preserved heads. "Markets have developed for pretty much anything we can get from the alligator," said Noel Kinler, a biologist with the state Wildlife and Fisheries Department.

Like I said, we've housebroken these creatures. They pretty much know who's on the top of the food chain down here, who perches in that "apex predator" seat. This happens anywhere animals are hunted. Stop hunting them, and they immediately get uppity. Take California, where animal rightists got cougar hunting banned a few years back. Last year, government animal-control officers (supported by hunters license fees) killed more "problem" cougars than hunters themselves ever killed when they were allowed to hunt! In Colorado, the very animal rightist who lobbied to have cougar season banned was attacked and ripped to shreds by one of his big, beloved puddycats while on a jogging trail.

And take the African nation of Botswana, which banned lion hunting recently. Well, animal-control officers in Botswana killed ten times as many lions (because of cattle and human depredations) in the first year of the ban than sport hunters killed the year before. Unreal.

In Florida, as we mentioned earlier, alligators attack fifteen to twenty people a year. In Louisiana, it's one or two a decade.

According to Jerry Reed, Amos Moses lived *"About forty-five minutes southeast of Tippitoe, Louisiana."*

He meant the town of Thibodaux, which is itself about an hour southwest of New Orleans and where the Saints have their training camp. If you travel forty-five minutes southeast of this "Tippitoe," you get to the town of Cut-Off, on the banks of legendary Bayou Lafourche. Here's deepest, darkest Cajun country, and by Scott Bouzigard's account, the home of perhaps the *meanest* if not the *biggest* alligator in those parts. This one would certainly be inclined to chomp down and render Amos's arm into a stump, because he tried it with Scott Bouzigard's head.

Former Saints and Atlanta quarterback Bobby Hebert hailed

from this same town. Indeed, Scott was one of Bobby's star receivers at South Lafourche High School. "Caught the touchdown pass from Bobby for the state championship in 1977," Scott laughs. "Thing was, the pass wasn't intended for me!"

WE'VE HOUSEBROKEN THESE CREATURES.

Details, I say. Mere details. Heck, they won the championship. Bobby left town after high school, but Scott stayed. Today, Scott is principal at the very South Lafourche High where he and Bobby Hebert took the state championship. The hunting, the fishing, the people—Scott couldn't leave them. The place was in his blood. You find this a lot down here. Visit and you'll see why.

Scott was fishing alone in his little twelve-foot pirogue in a canal close to his house last year when he looked around and saw an alligator's head in the dark water just behind him. "No big deal," he thought. "Hell, I grew up in serious alligator country, hunting and fishing. The things had surrounded me all my life. I had a stringer of bass and perch hanging in the water behind the pirogue," Scott continued. "I figured the gator wanted them. But I'll be damned if he was gonna steal my dinner, so I jerked them out and put them in the boat right next to me."

Scott resumed his fishing, leisurely paddling along and casting his bobber and worm toward the bank. Watching it twitch . . . then sink. Then hauling back and reeling in another bluegill, another chinquapin, another small bass as the little spinning reel's drag sang it's sweet music. Scott didn't give the alligator another thought. "Like I said, nothing unusual about seeing an alligator while I'm fishing. I'd be surprised if I *didn't* see one.

"But a few minutes later, I look back and there he is again. Well, there's no fish in the water to attract him *this* time. But you know, lots of people are starting to feed alligators from boats, plenty of those swamp tours, especially, so some alligators are starting to be attracted to boats. I just thought he might think I had a handout for him. They say the same thing's happening with sharks in Florida and the Bahamas. Dive tours are feeding them, so the sharks are starting to associate humans with food. I had nothing to feed him, though. I wasn't about to give him any of my fish. That was dinner, cher. In a few seconds, his head plunged again. Well, that's the end of that, I thought. He knows he ain't gettin' any goodies from this Cajun boy."

Scott turned around and kept fishing. "I'd just cast and was watching the little cork twitching and moving sideways, had another fish on. I was getting ready to set the hook when—KA-BOOOSH—BLOP—SPLAASH!

I hear a *huge* eruption in the water behind me. Man, it sounded like Rosie O'Donnell belly-flopping off a high-dive! I jerk my head around and the gator's in the air. Like a missile man! His tail had cleared the water and everything, and the thing was headed straight for me! Craziest—and scariest—thing you ever saw!"

Columnist Dave Barry knows about airborne alligators. He wrote about it in his travel guidebook. They are the major attraction at Gatorland, right next door to Disney World in Kissimmee, Florida. I'll hand off to him here:

"After entering Gatorland through a giant pair of alligator jaws . . . you witness the Assault on the Dead Chickens, which is technically known as the Gator Jumparoo. The way it works is, a large crowd of tourists gathers around a central pool, over which, suspended from wires, are a number of plucked headless chicken carcasses. As the crowd, encouraged by the Gatorland announcer, cheers wildly, the alligators lunge out of the water and rip the chicken carcasses down with their jaws. Once you witness this impressive event, you will never again wonder how America got to be the country it is today."

Scott Bouzigard was watching a Gator Jumparoo, too, but he had no reason to cheer wildly. This gator wasn't lunging for any headless chicken. He was in mid-air lunging with gaping jaws all right, but zeroed in on Scott's head, which was (for the time being, anyway) still attached to his neck.

"This all happened in a split second, you can imagine, Humberto. In less time than it takes to tell it. But man, if I live to be a million, I'll never forget that sight. The thing was airborne—completely out the water—and coming at me with his mouth wide open. Looked like a million teeth coming at my freakin' face! That *Alien* creature flashed to mind. Remember when the guy looks up and the alien opens his mouth? The only thing missing here was the drool!

"So I ducked, just in time too. Still had those reflexes from high-school football. The gator flew over me like an angry linebacker, but he grabbed my shoulder with his gaping jaws on the way. This slowed him down a bit and he crash-landed in the front of my pirogue, almost sinking it. He was about a six-footer. My pirogue was twelve feet, with a one-hundred-and-eighty-pound man already in it. Not much freeboard. The pirogue was rocking and took in a couple of gallons of water when he crashed in. I figured I'd be tipping over and let me tell you, if there was ever a time I *didn't* wanna tip over in my pirogue—this was it."

After a duck hunt to Louisiana in 1952, legendary outdoor writer Robert Ruark wrote this about the craft Scott fishes from, the same craft that carried Ruark to his duck blind:

"A pirogue is a soapdish of a boat pointed at both ends, and can be poled in an inch of water. It is balanced like the mechanism of a watch, and will capsize if you shave one side of your face."

Locally, we say a pirogue will "ride on a dew." Perfect for traversing our swamps and marshes, but not the most stable craft for deeper water.

"Heck, I'd tipped over in a freezing marsh when duck hunting," Scott continued. "I'll tell ya, it's one thing to have a wet and frozen butt. It's another to have it chomped off by a gator! No man, I didn't wanna go in the water that day—not with that crazy alligator as company."

Kermit George was grabbed in the water, Craig DeArmond under his porch. Scott Bouzigard was *inside* his pirogue. You have to hand it to these gators. They're damn resourceful when hungry. No wonder they've been around virtually unchanged for sixty-five million years.

"Well, he was still going strong when he grabbed my shoulder, Humberto. He ripped it open with his teeth and the momentum kept him going. He hit the front seat of the pirogue and rolled, then rolled right out of the pirogue as fast as he came in. I gripped my shoulder and felt my fingers sliding into holes. The blood was gushing. The thing was over in seconds—*seconds!* But it's in my mind like a slow motion playback, over and over again, complete with freeze-frames. In one, I see the water erupting and the thing launching out like a Polaris missile from a sub. In the next, I see that huge gaping mouth. In another, all those white, pointy teeth. Then that big black scaly thing coming at me, whoooo!"

"Whooo!" indeed, Scott. Amazingly, Scott considers himself lucky. Sure, his shoulder was ripped open. But what are a few score stitches compared to the gut-freezing scenario that might have been?

He continued: "And here's the best, or the worst, part, depending on how you wanna look at it. The day before, I'd been in this same canal, fishin' again—but I had my seven-year-old boy sitting in front of me—sittin' right there where the alligator crash-landed with that gaping mouth! I don't even wanna think what might have been, you know? He'd have pulled him in the water with him or knocked him in with his tail or just his momentum. This gator was hungry, too. So what then?"

Remember Craig DeArmond's mental refrain, the thing that probably saved him: *Don't let him get you in the water!*

The canal Scott was fishing was unusually deep for a coastal Louisiana waterway. It was dug years earlier to provide spoil material for a hurricane protection levee. You couldn't see more than a few inches into the dark water, either. Had that alligator grabbed his son and dragged him down . . . . let's just say any rescue, even by a brave and desperate father, would have been extremely unlikely.

Last summer, any Florida or California surfer who had a toe nipped by a shark found himself surrounded by scribbling reporters while applying the Band-Aid. From every direction, microphones were thrust at his face. A frantic babble of questions followed as tape recorders whirred.

Scott's alligator encounter took place at the same time. It didn't make it past his local newspaper. Considering he lives in Cut-Off, Louisiana, that's pretty local. As they say about the Beltway media: All the News That's Fit to Print.

You betcha.

While a pro quarterback, Bobby Hebert was known as the "Cajun Cannon." "That day fishing," Scott laughs. "I saw another kind of Cajun Cannon."

CHAPTER SEVEN

GATORS, SNAKES, AND QUICKSAND

"Alligator?" Tom said while looking around at Pelayo from the bow. "Wow . . . shouldn't they be hibernating?"

"They don't really *hibernate* down here, Tom," Paul quipped. "They go in their holes and hide out for a while during cold weather, but hell, we have seventy-, seventy-five, degree days in December or January all the time down here." He looked up and waved around. "Like today. So when these gators come out of their holes in the winter, let me tell ya, they're *hungry.*"

"Yeah, but you guys didn't say anything about alligators out here."

"Gators swarm out here," Pelayo snapped. "Why shouldn't they?"

"Huge ones, too," Paul nodded. "They don't do much alligator trapping on this state land, Tom," he continued. "Too many hassles to get the tags and licenses and stuff. So the gators have a chance to grow big. Hell, I've seen some that look like freakin' dragons, man—enormous. Some of their heads are [Paul made a big circle with his arms] yay big around. Remember that stuffed one at the restaurant, in the quarter, Ralph and Kacoos?"

Tom tried to laugh, but it sounded like a cough. His giddy smile turned rigid, and his eyes shifted back and forth between us. "Yeah, I remember."

"Bigger than that bastard," Paul snorted. He pointed behind him to the front of pirogue. "See that?" Paul ran his hand over some holes and scratches near the bow of his pirogue. He looked at Tom and grimaced. "I thought it was all over, man. Thought I'd be twirling around underwater hugging the alligator, like in a Tarzan movie. Sucker musta thought I was a big gar or something. I was paddling up to a little cane island right over there"—he pivoted and pointed towards a lagoon to his left—"ready to set out the decoys. I was looking up at some ducks, as usual, and—WHACK! I felt the pirogue smack into something, almost threw me overboard. I thought I'd hit a stump, but I wasn't going that fast, not for that kinda impact. "Then I look down and almost shit my pants! I see this freakin' monster's *head!*" Paul circled his arms again. "*Yay* big. Then CHOMP! The sucker grabs the bow of the pirogue with his jaws and starts twisting! Water and mud going every which way. He thought he had prey and was going into his death roll, their twisting routine where they rip their prey apart! Man, I started screamin' and yelling, whacking him with the paddle."

Tom looked over at Pelayo, then at me, still pretending to smile, looking for a clue. He looked like a driver's license photo.

"I heard him from clear across the pass!" Pelayo snorted while pointing backwards. "Chris and I were huntin' a good quarter mile away. Didn't know what the hell was going on. Sounded like the crowd at a rassling match."

"Ya think I'm bullshittin' ya?" Paul cocked his head at Tom, whose smile was looking more like a grimace. Then he started rummaging in a side compartment. Finally, Paul found what he was looking for, and he lifted a paddle with the bottom cracked off. "Here! Lookit this! Does this look like I'm bullshittin' ya? Sonofabitch bit the damn thing clean in half!" He held the mangled, punctured, splintered paddle a foot in front of Tom's quivering face. "If I'd a turned over, he'd a bit my dammed head clean off!"

"Crushed it like cantaloupe!" Pelayo added. "Hell, they crush a cow's skull with one chomp!" Pelayo made the motions with his arms, slapping his hands shut with a loud WHACK! "When you see these suckers out in winter they're hungry, Tom. They been lying up for a while with nothing to eat, so they come out and start chomping down on *everything* that freakin' moves! That's why we have so many run-ins with them during duck season, more than we ever have while fishing in the summer."

Tom was silent, nodding slowly. "I just don't remember that y'all said anything. Man . . . ."

I watched Pelayo shift his gaze over Tom shoulders. His eyes lit up and his arms shot up. "There's your nutria, On-the-Ball!" He was pointing behind the outboard.

Tom almost got whiplash jerking his head around. I looked and there he was: the alligator. He had a black, bony head, a good twelve inches between those nostrils and those eyes. *"Ho-ly sh-it!"* Tom labored over every syllable. "That's an alligator all right!" Tom's eyes bugged like Ping-Pong balls.

"Ten-footer, easy!" Pelayo yelled. The brute wasn't thirty feet away.

"Probably a twelve-footer!" Paul snorted. "Probably the same monster that almost turned me over last year!"

Tom seemed entranced. He swallowed hard. "Why is he there? Isn't he afraid? I always read that they feared man? That they avoid all—"

FORGET ALL THAT CRAP YOU SEE ON THE DISCOVERY CHANNEL.

"Forget all that Sierra Club and *Animal Planet* bullshit," Pelayo blurted. "Forget all that crap you see on the Discovery Channel. This ain't Bambi. This sucker ain't afraid of anything out here. He's the apex predator down here. He knows it. Like I said, not much gator trapping out here so he doesn't associate us with danger.

"He associates us with *food*," Paul snapped just as the gator's massive head disappeared under the muddy water. "They're attracted to boats. The sound of an outboard pulls them in for half a mile. Sometimes you'll look down and see four, five cruising around the boat. This one here's probably just the first."

"Shotgun blasts pull 'em in like a dinner bell," Pelayo nodded. "They know it means dead ducks floating around, or nice fat dogs paddling out to get 'em. Lots of gators out here are too damn big to be scared of anything. Hell, you know those cows we see grazing off the passes?"

Tom's lips were tight, his shoulder's slumped. "Yeah, sure," he whispered.

"Goddamn gators grab *them*. Then drag 'em into the water." Pelayo turned to Paul. "Remember, On-the-Ball?"

"Do I remember!" Paul gasped. "You don't forget a sight like that. Looked like something you see on *Animal Planet*. Like on that *National Geographic* special where all the wildebeests started crossing that river, and half got grabbed by crocodiles and ripped to pieces. Ya seen that one, huh?"

Tom nodded quickly, then looked at Pelayo.

"Man, for my video cam that day!" Pelayo wailed. "We were fishing a spillway off South Pass. Hot as hell that day, middle of the summer. We watched three cows come to the bank. They start drinking, then stepped into the water. You see them doing that a lot down here in the summer. There ain't many trees by South Pass. It's the only way for those poor cows to cool off."

"Well, I'm reaching down to net Paul's redfish when I hear this huge SPLASH!" Pelayo waved his arms for effect. "I look over and it looks like a freakin' depth charge went off by the bank! Water and mud going splashing around like crazy! The poor cow's batting her front legs, splashing up a storm, moaning, carrying on." Pelayo is still waving his arms, mimicking the hapless cow.

"We'd never seen anything like *that!*" Paul nodded. "So at first we didn't know what the hell was goin' on. Then we saw the tail come thrashing outta the water, looked like a freakin' dinosaur. The gator was just starting the death rolls as they call them . . . ."

"Wait a minute, now." Tom's smile was like the tenth time of saying "cheese" in a scratchy suit for a family portrait. His eyes kept shifting from Pelayo to me as he chuckled nervously. Nobody else was even smiling. We were all looking straight at him, unblinking.

"Saw one longer than my pirogue, during teal season," Paul said with a nod. "That sucker was laying out on top of some elephant ears. Not too far from that point over there." He pointed behind Tom, who flinched again and jerked his head around. "I could barely make him out at first, just saw the tail. I was paddling my pirogue, so we were at about the same level. I couldn't see down into the grass. I saw about four feet of gator hide and thought that was the whole gator. No big deal. See 'em all the time. So I kept paddling, figured he'd hit the water and scramble away. Well, I got closer and saw another patch of gator though a hole in the elephant ears. This one about six feet in front of the other."

Tom was very attentive now. "When I saw that, I knew it wasn't no four-foot gator, or even a six-foot gator. Hell, we'd gigged some that big while frogging before. Anyway, I says 'Whoa!' and started back-paddling, but couldn't stop in time. I spun the pirogue around and found myself in front of his head, about ten feet away. Like to faint. See *this* gouge?" He pointed toward the other pirogue. "Don't ask me how I got outta that mess. Gator just wasn't hungry, I guess. Probably just had a cow or a coupla dogs."

"Oh yeah," Pelayo whistled. "I remember. That was last season . . . ."

"Season before last," Paul corrected. "Cause Buzzy still had his dog, Barry."

"His dog was named Barry?" Tom chuckled, a hint of a smile now.

"Right," Pelayo nodded sadly. "Beautiful chocolate lab. He was a house dog, too, a pet for the kids, so he'd put on weight between seasons."

"Yeah, he'd get pretty rotund," Paul said. "That's why he named him Barry, after Barry White." Buzzy's wife, Jenny, *loved* Barry White. "Can't get enough of your love," Paul started singing and swaying to the tune. "Jenny put it on during a party after a few daiquiris, and she'd start sucking face with everybody. I mean tongue and everything. Didn't know what to make of it the first time. Anyway, I really liked that dog. Best retriever you ever wanna share a blind with. Obedient as hell, just sat there quivering. Wouldn't move a muscle until Buzz gave the signal. Man, you'd shoot a big pintail and it would glide down wounded two hundred yards away . . . ."

"You really hate to see that, Tom." I sighed. "Cause now, you got a hell of a paddle on your hands. And those damn pintail get with just their beak and eyes above water and start paddling off. Your chasing him in the pirogue, shooting—BLAM! BLAM! Spraying shot all around them. Forget it. He's gone, and you're whipped out. Then you gotta paddle back against the wind. Barry saved the day on many a hunt."

"Never forget the day we lost him." Pelayo nodded. "Wasn't real hot that day, about sixty-five degrees at midday, in the forties at night. So Buzzy kinda figured the gators wouldn't be out much. Poor dog got nailed on the third retrieve."

"Most horrible thing you ever saw." Paul said. "He had to swim a deep canal to get a wounded teal. We saw him climb the far bank."

"Then we heard the howl," Paul sighed. "And we heard the splash."

"Ever hear a dog caught in a coon trap, Tom?" Pelayo asked.

"No, I can't really . . . ."

"Ever hear one hit by a car, or shot with birdshot, or bit by a rattlesnake? That awful yelping and howling?"

"No, nothing like that . . . ."

"You're lucky," I added. "Damn lucky. That sound stays with

you. Poor Buzzy hasn't been duck hunting since that day. Says he can't bear it—the memories. Says hunting would never be the same without Barry."

"I can't blame him, either," Pelayo said. "Heck, he wasn't even our dog, but we were sure bummed out for a long while. We got attached to that Barry."

"Spencer came out a *little* bit better than Barry," Paul said as he reached in the cooler. "But we haven't been able to get his ass out here again, either."

"Spencer?" Tom shot a nervous look around? "Your neighbor? I really liked him, really enjoyed myself at his barbecue."

"Right," Pelayo nodded. "But don't you *ever* mention his Delta duck hunting trip in front of him. Whoooo-boy. You'll notice we never do."

"He wasn't used to this terrain, Tom," Paul said as he rummaged in the ice-chest. "He'd only hunted ducks in California before, in the Central Valley. No alligators or quicksand out there."

"Quicksand?" Tom picked up on the word instantly, looking at each of us and pointing to a mudflat behind us. You mean—?"

"Not *real* quicksand, Tom," Paul said as he popped open a Bud. He gulped deeply, grimaced, and let fly with a thunderous belch. "You won't disappear in it, not past your neck, anyway."

"You usually stop at about your navel," Pelayo added. He stood and marked the spot on his torso with a muddy hand, then moved his palm slowly up towards his neck. "Maybe a little higher if you don't know what you're doing."

"Which Spencer *definitely* didn't," I said, nodding grimly. Tom snapped his head in my direction. His lips seemed tight.

"Spencer's usually a quick learner," Paul expanded. "He's a great guy, a real trooper, a typical yuppie. He's big into physical fitness, belongs to the health club, quick to make friends with his neighbors as he gets relocated around the country, joins clubs, Rotary. You know the type. He's no whiner."

"Has to be something *really* traumatic to faze that guy," I said nodding. "Right after he moved in, he'd always see us coming home from hunts, lugging these big straps of pintail. That's the duck he shot when he hunted California. He loved them, and he begged us to bring him with us."

"We held out for a while, for his own good, ya unnerstan', " Pelayo said. "We explained that this wasn't California yuppie hunting, where you drive up in an SUV, with permanent heated blinds, with hard bottoms to walk on, etc."

"We told it like it was, Tom," Paul added. "Just like we told *you.*"

"Well, I don't remember hearing about alligators." Tom chuckled nervously. "And quicksand . . . "

"Didn't we tell you about the cottonmouths?" Suddenly Paul was standing and pointing behind the boat as Tom stumbled back and jerked his head around. "Look! Right there!" Paul shouted. "There ain't no mistaking a water moccasin, podnuh. See that big ugly head? See how he swims?"

Water moccasins have a distinctive swim, holding their heads high above the water. Just then, the thick, brown, venomous serpent angled close to the boat, no more than twenty feet away. He was still for a second, just floating there, that big evil head with those eyes and mouth set in that perpetual scowl pointed at us, that tongue flicking.

"Wow," Tom hissed slowly, trying to sound calm. "Ne-never seen one that close before." He had the same look Indiana Jones got in the original *Raiders* when he looked down into that pit. "Snakes. Why'd it have to be snakes?"

"They're pit vipers, Tom," I said. "They're attracted to heat. Heat means prey, like a rabbit or nutria. He thinks we might be prey."

"Let's shoot it, then!" Tom said while reaching for a gun case. "I mean, hell . . . ."

"Forget it, Tom," Pelayo said, nodding. "Your shot will spook the ducks away. We don't want that yet. Besides, plenty more cottonmouths where that one came from. Shooting him is like trying to empty the river with a thimble. This warm weather brings them out by the *thousands.*"

"And all as hungry as the alligators," Paul added, as Tom seemed to swallow hard. "So always watch where you sit at the campsite. The campfire and the heat from our bodies attract them. And always zip

106

up your tent. They love to crawl in for the heat, especially into sleeping bags and hip boots."

"And watch where you take a crap," Pelayo continued. "We heard about some guy who got bit while in the very act. He was a deer hunter, huntin' over by Southeast Pass. Got down from the tree, dropped his pants, squatted, YOW!"

"A moccasin won't kill ya, Tom," Paul said. "But there's terrible swelling. When we worked oilfield during the summer, I remember a guy who got bit near the elbow as he bent down to pick up some pipe. Next day his arm looked like a goddamn inner tube." Paul cupped his hands and spread them a foot apart. "They evacuated him in a helicopter. So you can imagine the poor guy who got bit on his ass."

"Remember the Widette family on *Saturday Night Live?*" Pelayo asked. "Dan Akroyd and Jane Curtin were the parents? Had these enormous butts." Pelayo stretched his arms wide behind him for effect. "Only one could sit on a sofa at a time?"

Ha! Yeah!" Tom laughed and coughed. "I used to love that. Belushi was . . . ."

"They say the poor guy looked like that for two weeks. Had to lie on his stomach the whole time in the hospital. Anyway, Spencer said he wasn't worried about moccasins when we were briefing him on hunting down here. He said he'd dealt with rattlesnakes in California and while quail hunting in Georgia when he lived in Atlanta. Maybe so, but he sure wasn't used to poisonous snakes trying to climb in the pirogue with him."

"That's when he tipped over," Pelayo said with a grim look.

"He tipped over the pirogue?" Now Tom was forcing a laugh. "Yeah. That's *easy* to do. Heck, I did that on my first hunt by Pecan Island. Got me a wet butt and like to freeze to death. So I can sure . . . ."

"You probably walked right out of the water, though, right?" Pelayo nodded. "Then emptied the pirogue, right?"

"Yeah, sure. But I got . . . ."

"You won't get off so easy down here," Paul snapped.

"You won't be walking on these bottoms, unless you have webbed feet like a nutria," Pelayo joined in. "Most places we hunt, the bottom's too soft to walk, and the water's to shallow to swim. Your only chance is to *crawl* out, clawing and flapping and trying to shove yourself along like a nutria or otter, hoping you don't end up like a beached whale, or that you attract a gator, thinking you're a wounded animal. Hell, we've all had to do it a couple times by now."

"Poor Spence tried to walk out at first," I added. "Made sense. Heck, the water was only about a foot deep. He said he wasn't too worried. But he immediately sank in." I said this while grabbing the push-pole and jabbing it over the side. "See?" I pushed it easily into the mud, nodding at Tom. "That's why we call it quicksand." Tom leaned over and grabbed the pole with an unsteady hand, moving it up and down like a butter churn, nodding to himself while arching his eyebrows. "Well, in seconds, Spence was past his hip boots in that slop, and stuck *good*. He tried to fight it, tried to walk out instead of slide out on his belly. His boots filled with water and mud, so he couldn't slip out of them. The harder he struggled, the harder the suction and the deeper he sunk. It creates suction. You can't fight it. The poor guy was past his waist in no time. And still sinking . . . ."

"Couldn't he grab his pirogue for leverage?" Tom asked, still struggling to maintain a game face. "I mean . . . to pull himself . . . ."

"His pirogue was thirty feet away," Pelayo cut in. "And drifting further. When he first tipped over, Spence was still worried about the cottonmouth that tried to get in the pirogue with him. He said the damn thing had to be close to four feet long, big around as a two-liter Coke bottle."

"They get big out here," Paul added, "like the alligators. Plenty for 'em to eat year 'round. And they ain't afraid of *nothing*."

"Right," Pelayo nodded. "Anyway, Spence didn't want to shoot a damn hole in the boat, so he had started whacking at the snake with the paddle as it was coming over the side. That's how he lost his balance and went over. Then he *really* got worried about the snake. He was splashing around like a maniac trying to scare it away, in case it was still around."

"That's how the pirogue got away from him," Paul added. "He turned away from it for just a few seconds, and when he looked back, the wind had already carried it out of his reach. The guy was seriously *stuck*. And this was an evening hunt. The sun was almost down when it happened."

"But the water was coming up," Pelayo said, moving his palm up towards his throat. "The high tide's usually at night around here this time of year. They had a two-foot tidal range that day, too. A big tide, from the full moon. Spence didn't know all that. He just knew he was stuck in that mud, hundreds of yards from shore, with no one in sight and nothing to grab. The mosquitoes were coming out in swarms by that time too—vicious marsh mosquitoes, as bloodthirsty as the gators and snakes. Spencer ducked in the water up to his neck, trying to keep 'em off, but they covered his face. Then he covered his face with mud, to foil them."

"An old trick he said he learned when he was in the Marines," Paul added. "Like we told you, Spence ain't no wimp."

"He's a gung-ho guy, all right," Pelayo continued. "But down here, that ain't enough. The mosquitoes started cramming into his eyes and mouth, biting the piss out of him. The poor guy's lips and eyelids swelled up like plums. His eyes were almost closed from the swelling but he could see enough to notice the water getting higher up his chest. At first he though he was still sinking in the mud. But like we said, you usually stop after four feet or so. Finally, he realized it was the tide coming up."

"And that's when he lost it," Paul said whistling softly. "He said he'd tried to keep cool until that time. '*Control the situation. Don't let the situation control you,*' he kept repeating that to himself. More of his Marine crisis training. But now he couldn't control it any longer. He'd run out of handles. He found himself like a victim of the Vikings—remember that movie? Kirk Douglas? Tony Curtis? Remember they'd stake people out on the beach so the tide would come up and drown them slowly? Spence said the movie come up on him like a horrible flashback."

"Hell, we were camped out right over there." Paul pointed to a willow island about a quarter mile to our right. "I could hear something from the campsite, but we thought it was a nutria wailing, or a pack of coyotes, plenty coyotes out here—ya ever hear 'em?"

Tom nodded quickly. "Yeah. Over on Pecan Island, when I went out there with my son-in-law and customers. You're right. It's a weird sound. Not like the howl you hear in western movies. Nothing like that at all. It sounds like a woman screaming, a bunch of women screaming. It's crazy, weird."

"Right, Tom. Hell, to me, it sounds like Yoko Ono sitting on a sea urchin, or Janis Joplin at her booze-addled best. Jesus, the most horrible wailing ya ever heard, like a crazy woman or a hundred babies wailing at once. So we figured that was it, nutrias mating or fighting with coyotes that were trying to eat 'em. Kee-rist, what a racket! Last thing we figured was that it was poor Spence. He was screaming and splashing, first to attract attention, then from the agony of the mosquitoes, finally to scare the alligators away."

"Alligators?" Tom blurted. "Wasn't it cold that day?"

"About like today," Pelayo said. That's why the gators and the snakes were out in droves, why the mosquitoes were so thick, like they'll be this evening—brought your bug spray, didn't ya?'

"No, I sure didn't. I didn't think you needed that in the winter."

"*Especially* in the winter, Tom. But don't worry." Pelayo winked. "I brought plenty of industrial strength Deet. Without it, we might suffocate. They'll cram into your nostrils. Anyway, Spence says the gators showed up right after dark, as usual. It was a full moon and he saw something swimming around him. He couldn't see too good through the little slits of his swollen watery eyes, so he thought it was nutria at first. Then it got closer. Finally he made out the bony head, the hooded eyes."

"He said his heart almost stopped," Paul whispered. "Like he needed that. Like he didn't have *enough* problems. A few seconds later, he noticed another one. Then another. Soon he had three cruising around him. He said his mouth felt like sandpaper, his stomach like a deep freeze. The poor sucker was paralyzed, immobile, gasping. The water was still coming up, too."

"He was damn lucky," Pelayo snorted. "The water, even on a high tide, is only about two feet deep in that lagoon. So no monster gators, no *really* big ones, like the one we just saw, showed up. They like deeper water, like this canal." Tom shot a quick look around him. "No reason to panic now, Tom. But when we paddle over to the blinds? Just keep an eye out."

"And keep one hand on your shotgun," Paul said, winking.

"Hell, we went out to look for Spencer," I said, right after we assured Tom that the thing he was pointing at near the shore behind us was the tip of a submerged log. "But we thought he'd gone deer hunting with his bow in the opposite direction, toward the high levees over by Loomis Pass. We shoulda looked in his tent, 'cause his bow was in there. Well, you know Spence. He hates to be a burden on anyone. He stressed, the whole way down, that he didn't need anyone holding his hand down here. He'd hunt on his own. Fine. Well, we spent half the night looking for the guy, but in the opposite direction. We figured he was tracking a wounded deer or something."

Tom was all ears now. "Man I can't believe I didn't hear this story at his barbeque. I even mentioned to Spence that I was looking forward to coming down here with you guys."

"What did he say?" Pelayo asked.

"Nothing, really," Tom shrugged. "I can't remember that he said anything at all."

"Probably changed the subject," Paul smirked. "He always does when we talk about this place around him. We heard the story *once*, in detail. That was it. We heard it on the ride home from that trip. Spence chugged half a bottle of Bacardi between Boothville and Myrtle Grove."

"*Tried* to chug it," Pelayo corrected. "His lips were still swollen up like balloons from all the mosquito bites. He kept spilling it all over his neck and chest as he blubbered and mumbled the story. I could hardly look at the poor guy. It was a horrible thing to see. He's usually so neat, so well dressed, such a classic preppy. Now he looked like a broken-down wino. At first, the rum seemed to help him. He was describing every gruesome detail, the whole thing, even laughing a little. We picked up on it, trying to help out."

"Yeah," Paul laughed. "We kept asking him: 'Hey Spence, got ya a bellyful of our *wetlands* yet?' Funny, because when he first moved here from California, Spence was big on wetlands. He loved the

111

freakin' word. "You've seen all the *National Geographic* and *Sierra* magazines in his house, right?" Tom nodded while managing a sickly smile. "Well, he never called it the marsh or the swamp—always 'wetlands,' like some greenie narrator on the Discovery Channel. Easy to say when you live just outside the Mojave Desert."

"I guess we went a little too far," Pelayo chuckled. "And how 'bout our biodiversity, Spence? Like that *wetland biodiversity*, Spence? Those magazines and nature shows sure are right about all that *biodiversity* in our *wetlands*, huh, Spence? Did they mention that it bites and stings and slithers? We really rubbed it in."

"Then he got morose on us," I added. "I could see these two" (I nodded towards Pelayo and On-the-Ball) "were pushing it. I could see they were pushin' poor Spence over the line. "Plenty *biodiversity* all around you last night, huh, Spence my boy? They wouldn't let up. He didn't need that shit just then, poor guy. But hell, he did look like he was laughing along with us at first, for a few seconds anyway. Suddenly he got weepy. From laughing to morose to weepy in two minutes flat. The rum shifted gears on him. It was sad.

"Look, guys," he kept blubbering. "Let's keep this between us, okay? I don't want this getting' out there, okay?"

"Remember *Deliverance*?" Paul asked Tom. "Remember towards the end . . . ."

"Do I remember it!" Tom said with a forced laugh. "In fact, it came to mind yesterday when that boatload of hog hunters pulled up next to our tent."

"Right. But you're referring to the bugger*ers*, Tom. Remember the bugger*ee*? The fat guy, Ned Beatty? Remember at the end, he kept saying, 'look guys, I don't want this getting around, okay'? Remember that? Well, that's what Spence sounded like on the way home."

"At least Ned the buggeree had his pants around his knees," On-the-Ball said. "When Spence found himself in that boat with the mullet netters, he had no pants on at all."

Tom flinched, and his forced smile vanished. His jaw muscles seemed bunched.

"Yeah, Tom. About the time Spence had given up hope, and the water was about up to his tits, he hears outboards and sees giant spotlights." Paul swigged from his beer, spat, and resumed. "They were mullet fishermen. They set gill nets in the big shallow bays during the high tides at night, then run around like maniacs scaring the mullet into the net. Finally, they crank the net up with a huge winch. They're gettin' big bucks for the mullet roe in Asia. We'll probably see 'em running around here tonight. Anyway, Spence said he tried to get their attention at first, but couldn't. His throat was burning and swollen from all that terrified screaming already and his lips were swollen from the mosquito bites. He said what came out when he tried to call them was a little wheeze, a low little rasp, something like Brando as the Godfather. No way they'd hear that over their outboards."

"He could barely move, too," I added. "And so covered with mud, when the spotlight hit him a couple times, the mullet guys figured he was a stump, so they made it a point to keep their distance."

"Spence's luck finally turned when they set out the big gill net," Pelayo said. "Turns out, the damn thing drifted right over him. So he flipped out again, figured he'd get tangled up and drown for sure. I mean, what *else* could befall the poor guy, right? You can imagine he wasn't thinking very clearly by that time. But when that nylon mesh went over him, he's sitting there wheezing and grunting with what he figured were his last breaths. He's flailing at the net feebly with his cold, sore, mud-caked arms, and they start cranking it in. He said the mesh got caught under a button on his hunting jacket, and it started pulling him. 'That's it!' he thought. His brain cleared for a split second. Hope returned. Then with the little strength he had left, he wrapped his arms and hands around the mesh. He said he put everything into it. And damned if it didn't start pulling him out."

"Hell, it was like somebody throwing him a life line, when ya think about it," Paul chuckled. "Only it sure didn't seem that way at first. Dammed if they didn't crank him right out. He said he hung on for dear life, and the net tugged and tugged and tugged relentlessly— that's a powerful winch those guys use—finally, it slipped him right out of his hip boots."

"His pants and underwear too," Pelayo quipped. "They were

soaked, full of mud, so they slipped right off. He said when he got close to the boat, the netters felt something heavy, so they put the spotlight on him. They shined it right on his big naked ass. They thought they'd snagged and pulled up a drowned body. A corpse. Hell, you can't blame 'em for thinking that. It was the most logical thing. They find bodies out here all the time. Between boating smash-ups because of the weather, the fog, all the stumps, all the sandbars, then the turf battles and shootouts among shrimpers, commercial netters, recreational fishermen, all the dope smugglers—some DEA guys think there's more of them out here than in the Florida Keys. Hell, it's a wonder they find so *few* bodies out here. Lotsa people just disappear. Closest road is twenty-three miles upriver. This is a great area to dispose of them. Alligators don't talk."

"But back to Spence," Paul said. "They finally pulled him in and he flopped on board like a big catfish, his big white ass in the air. He started moving and trying to talk and now the fishermen *really* freaked. This wasn't no corpse. Finally, they gave him a towel to wrap around his ass and shriveled genitals—you can imagine, all night in that cold mud, scared half-crazy. His nuts were halfway to his throat. His pecker shriveled up like a little pink raisin. He said the mullet guys seemed scared of him at first, backing away, always gripping a gaff. He couldn't understand it. I mean, how dangerous could he be? He could hardly *move!*"

"A little later they finally told him why," Pelayo said. "Turns out they thought he was some kinda hermorphrodite, a goddamn transvestite, because he didn't seem to have anything down *here.*" Pelayo demonstrated by groping himself, Michael Jackson style.

"Spence was damn lucky they didn't throw him back or gaff him," Pelayo huffed. "They figured they had some lunatic sodomite dope smuggler or poacher or something—some freak who'd been gang-buggered by his mates, then made to walk the plank. Finally, he'd drifted in with the tide like a drowned animal. Why didn't he have any pants?"

"Or any pecker?" Paul added.

"Hell, you never know out here," On-the-Ball said, rolling his eyes and sweeping his arms at the wilds around him. "You run across *everything* out here. Finally, they brought him to the camp-site. Musta been about 2 A.M. when he stumbled in, right guys?"

Tom's face was twitching spastically now. The strain was too much. His facial muscles wouldn't behave any more. That forced smile was crumbling; it was taking a toll on his features. His last duck-hunting trip had been the catered kind in western Louisiana with sophisticated business clients. A gentle knock by a footservant announces that a sumptuous breakfast awaits in the main dining area. Then from swanky camp to motorized mudboats to dry heat-ed blind, with cushioned seats and foot rests. Back at nine for a few toddies, some accounts of the morning's hunt, and perhaps a nap before the jazz brunch on white linen with silverware. That was then. Now look at him.

HELLPIG SHOOTING GALLERY

The author, right, with a hunting buddy (left).

Left: Pelayo at a Louisiana animal-rights demonstration.

Above: Chris(on left) shows off the Gumbo fixins'. Duck limits come quickly—often much TOO quickly—in the Miss. Delta.

Right: Stay on that trail, Bambi, PLEASE! Ten more yards and it's your ASS! Perched for wetland deer.

Above: A spool-stripping red.

Pelayo paddling a pirogue—"That gator's getting too close!"

Chris beats alligator to this widgeon.

Hellpig attacks!

CHAPTER EIGHT

SHOOT-OUT AT PINTAIL ALLEY

Tom was good to his clients, but it took him a little while to get the hang of business dealings down here in south Louisiana. This was not like Atlanta, Buffalo, Sacramento—or, hell, like any-place north of the Caribbean or Rio Grande he'd ever been trans-ferred before. I explained to him that we cut more business deals in hunting and fishing camps than on any golf course, but probably just as many in titty bars.

He caught on quick, but I'll never forget our first call together. As always, the good reps refused to take him out. They'd all had an excuse as Dudley, the manager, walked around the office, peering into their cubicles:

"Not today, Dudley," Artie replies coolly as he tries to cover a *Playboy*. "Too busy. I'm trying to close a touchy deal. I don't wanna blow it. Maybe next week."

"Okay, Artie, no problem." Dud is oblivious to the magazine and still cheerful. "How about you, Chris?" he asks, as he peeks next door.

"Not this week, Dud, excuse me," Chris says as he charges out of the office with a grim nod. "I'm on my way to Continental Wireline. They just called. Big doings there, Dud, *big!*" he exclaims, bustling down the hall on his way to the video arcade.

So I took Tom out. At the third "appointment," we finally made it past the receptionist, only to face a lynch mob more vicious than anything Bill Maher later sicked on me on *Politically Incorrect*. ("Tonight's guests include the bloodthirsty author of *Helldiver's Rodeo* and Cuban-American fascist, Humberto Fontova. Sick him!") Apparently everything on the contract had been bungled (by my predecessor, of course).

We had to be quick on our feet that day. I didn't like the drift of the call, excused myself for a second, then scooted through a red-striped exit-door in the lunchroom. Tom would be on his own. "Hands-on" training they call this, I think. Anyway, my escape set off a hair-raising fire alarm—which was just the cover Tom needed to make his move. He caught on quick. He wasn't about to face the horrible wrath alone.

Like a flash, he was off. His tasseled loafers slid dangerously on the waxed floor as he scurried past a water cooler, down the hallway, and pivoted toward the exit sign. His tie flapped furiously over his shoulder as he turned on the afterburners and fled past the receptionist and into the parking lot.

I swooped by just in time. "Over here, Tom!" I yelled, as I came around the corner and opened the car door. Tom cleared the azaleas with a stunning leap and sprung in.

"Fast!" he gasped, while throwing his briefcase in the back. "Gun it! It's that purchasing manager, Bella! She's seriously pissed!"

(Her name was actually Charlene, but she was a ringer for Bella Abzug, so the moniker stuck.)

Then I stomped it for a tire-squealing getaway, á la Charlie Daniels:

When I hit the gas I was really wheelin'/had gravel flying and tires squealin'/and I didn't slow down till I was almost to Arkansas!

Actually, we slowed down at the Gold Club. "That was a close one," Tom sighed with a visible shudder while twirling the ice in a double scotch. A truly skillful and conscientious lap-dancer erased from our rattled minds the ghastly image of Bella, snarling, bellowing threats and muscularly stabbing the air with her letter opener.

Two days later, we were back. Tom had planned this call completely on his own. He'd given up on overhead presentations for his new customers. No more of those long hours on the phone coordinating the presentation so all "decision-makers" might be present. No more compiling of data for all those bullet points. No more rupturing himself lugging that damn overhead around.

He snapped it on with the customer, Bob "T-Boy" Hossbach, grimacing sourly. This continued for the first five minutes. T-Boy nodded vacantly the next five. He rolled his eyes distractedly the next two. Finally, he cut it off with an exasperated snort. "Look," he snarled. "Just tell us what the goddamn thing *costs!*"

I accompanied Tom to the Gold Club for the follow-up call and evinced a dramatic metamorphosis in T-Boy. No sour look, not with twin handfuls of Brandy's butt cheeks. The lap dancer scaled his massive polyester-encased paunch and started tracing little circles around his red, bulbous nose with her perfumed nipples. Low snorting sounds escape from his snout like from a pig rooting in offal. She seemed immune to his putrid breath.

"Show me the overhead presentation that so arrests a customer's attention," Tom chuckled on the way out after inking the deal. As a bonus, he'd been invited repeatedly to hunt at this company's plush camp on Pecan Island.

"Don't get us wrong," I said, and chuckled at Tom, who was still desperate to somehow smile at the ghastly story of Spence. "We love Spencer to death. The guy'll do anything for ya. Mowed half my front lawn last month, while he was mowing his. We just thought it was funny how he shifted gears and vocabulary on his dear wetlands."

"Things got even better when we finally got home," Pelayo said. "His wife, you know his wife. That Megan, she ain't exactly a barrel of laughs to begin with. That freakin' woman . . . let's just say we never did hit it off."

"Calling her "*Mamacita*" every two minutes at her first party probably didn't help," Paul said. "The sucky-kissy sounds and pinching motions weren't exactly called for either."

"That was her *friend*," Pelayo shot back. "The one I called *Mamacita* was her friend. Some chick she went to college with in the Northeast somewhere. I think the same college Hillary went? They were all proud of that, wasn't it?"

"Yeah, that was it," Paul nodded. "Now I remember. Megan went ballistic when you were showing her how to eat crawfish."

"That was Artie," Pelayo corrected again. Then he shrugged. "Besides. What's the big deal? It's a ritual. All newcomers to south Louisiana go through it. She looked like she was having a tough time with them. Kept poking them, even tried to use a fork. Artie thought I was being nice, actually."

"Real nice," Paul snapped. "Lotsa people manage to demonstrate the procedure, even the head sucking, without looking around with a demented leer and bringing up Monica Lewinsky every other sentence."

"And Linda Lovelace on every third," I reminded a nodding Pelayo.

"Yeah, right," Pelayo yelled. "Like that Megan woman is some kinda little angel or something. Hell man. Don't tell *me*! She gets half a bottle of Chablis down, watch out! She starts goosing every man out there. Happened to me plenty of times."

"Pelayo's right." I nodded towards Tom. "Hell, she came in the bathroom when I was taking a leak last party. I didn't think to lock it. Thought it'd be quick. She barged right in. 'Peek-a-boo!' Freaked me out, man. She sat down in that chair in their downstairs bathroom, about five feet away from me and right at crotch level. Well, I shut down right away. Couldn't piss for the life of me. I didn't know what the hell to do. Finally, I started zipping up. 'You know in France they have unisex bathrooms?' she purred. Her eyes were glassy, too, boy, her cheeks good and pink. 'And you mean you're not going to shake it? We can't have you dribbling all over the house. Here, let me.'

"I got the hell outta there! I wasn't exactly sober, but it rattled me. I didn't know the woman that well. Shit, they'd only moved in a month before. I didn't know *what* to make of it. And sure enough—*whooo!* She goosed me on the way out."

"But that kinda stuff happens when she's into the wine," Paul said. "She was cold sober when we pulled into the driveway with Spence that day. She was checking the mail and looking hot in a tight little tennis outfit. Spence smelled like a wino to begin with— we all did, three days in the mud without a shower. Well, add the rum he spilled all over himself—*whooo!* He walked past her all muddy, his face still red, a little swollen, carrying his muddy gun case and duffel bag.

"She took one look at him, got one whiff, and put her hands on her hips. 'Some hunting trip!' she snarled. 'Don't you *dare* walk in my living room like that! Go through the garage!'

"Spence stopped dead in his tracks, halfway to the door. Man, I'll never forget that, huh, Humberto?" Paul looked over wide-eyed. I rolled my eyes and whistled in agreement.

"Shoulda seen Spencer, he dropped everything and just stood there. Finally he turned around, *slowly*. He stood there glaring for a few seconds, breathing heavily. Finally, he exploded. '*Your* living room! Did I hear that right? *Your* goddamn living room?'

"For once, the woman was tongue-tied. Her mouth was half open. Spence was just getting into form, too. He took another step toward her and cocked his head a little. His hair still had a little mud in it, and tufts stood straight up like Don King's. 'And just *who pays* for your living room, Miss Princess?' He hissed through clenched teeth, while staring straight at her from ten feet away. 'I guess those tennis lessons pay for your living room, huh *honey-bunch?*' He took another step toward her, and then looked over at us with a bitter smile. 'Or maybe the maid pays for *your* living room, huh, my little *snookums?*'"

"She had a few friends over, too," Pelayo laughed. "They heard the yells and came out the front door, all in tennis outfits, just in time to hear Spence roar: 'No! I know! Now I got it! It's those weekly pedicures that pay for *your* living room, huh, my *little kitten?*'

"Man, I'd never seen him like this. Never knew he could flare up like that. Spence was in no mood to take any shit just then. He was into the mean drunk stage. He shifted from weepy to mean right around the GNO Bridge, but kept hittin' on that Bacardi."

"Too bad for Megan, too," Paul said.

"Maybe not," I said. "Spence told me later he did quite well that night. Said she even made use of Artie's crawfish eating lessons. I guess he pulled a Rhett Butler on her. Remember when Rhett finally unloaded on Scarlett that night when drunk, then he grabbed her and hauled her upstairs?"

"And funny thing is," Paul added. "We always called Spence pussy-whipped, behind his back, of course. He was that 'sensitive yuppie male,' we always thought. He couldn't do *this* because of his wife, he couldn't do *that* because of his wife, blah, blah, blah. Turns out, we heard the exact same thing about entering through the garage from our wives when *we* got home."

"But we *did* enter through our garages." I laughed harshly. "Then had to sweep it to get the caked mud off where we walked! We wouldn't dare pull any shit like Spencer. Our wives work. When they say '*my* living room,' when they say 'don't dirty up *my* kitchen,' it's literally true! We'd have gotten cold-cocked with a shovel! Been in the dog-house for a goddamn month!"

We exaggerated just a little with Tom about alligators. Those gouges on On-the Ball's pirogue came from a battering by Highway 23, not a fight with an alligator. We were motoring home after a hunt when a truck pulls up beside us, the driver gesturing excitedly and pointing behind us. Finally, he rolled down the window and started yelling.

Pelayo, who was driving, rolled down his window. "Your pirogue!" The guy was mouthing the word carefully and pointing backwards. "Flew out! Back there!"

Good God. Pelayo nodded wearily, hit the brakes, and we rolled onto the shoulder. We got out, looked back, and there's the pirogue, about a hundred yards behind us, fortunately on the shoulder, but unfortunately about ten feet from a state trooper. "Thing looked like a kite," the trooper said when we slinked over and picked it up. "Musta been a hundred feet in the air, spinning around like crazy. Surprised it's in one piece. You're damn lucky there was no traffic behind you. Y'all tie it down better this time, okay?"

"Certainly, officer. Sorry, officer. Thank you, officer."

And that broken paddle Paul shoved in Tom's face? It was Artie's, who'd come home late from the Gold Club and tried to sneak in through the garage. His wife, Joan, had been tipped off and ambushed him. "Come on!" Artie mumbled. "Though you said it was okay if I worked up my appetite out there—as long as I ate at home!"

The paddle was the nearest thing Joan could reach. "WHACK!" he ducked and it hit the brick wall.

Despite the alligator, we'd hit upon a duck feast and orgy here at Pintail Alley. From the sounds of it, they had quite a crowd in attendance. By late December, ducks start pairing up on their southern wintering grounds. The actual orgy was a couple months away—ducks do the "wild thang" back up north, on the nesting grounds.

This was the preliminary. The bay was a huge disco. All that gabbling and quacking was easy to decipher:

"If ya think I'm sexy, and *ya want my body,* come *on*

sugar, let me know!"

The Gadwall were chuckling, quacking, and hailing. The hens (surprise!) do most of the yakking. The hen Gadwall has a distinctive hail, shorter, sharper, and higher-pitched than a mallard hen's. I could just imagine how they grate on the drakes's nerves. Several were yakking out in the bay. Actually, they were probably *laughing* at the drakes.

I'll quote here from a scientific journal of ornithology and maybe you'll agree:

> Female ducks attract the males by swimming in front of the desired mate. The males' behaviors intended to attract unpaired females include preen-behind-wing, preen-dorsally, belly-preen, preen-back-behind-wing, turning back of head, and head-dip. Then he engages in head-bobbing.

Sounds like us, polyester-clad, during our glory days at Fat City. And there's no mistaking those widgeon. A few must have been close to the bank, because their "whew-whew-whews" came through loud and clear. Pintail were out there too, tooting and trilling away, but from a distance. No doubt they were bunched up far out in the open water. They might be "puddle ducks," but pintail like their puddles *big* and they like to get smack in the middle of them, where they thumb their noses at us hunters. Their shrill little toots always sound like snickers to me.

"Today, you'll be whistling out of the other side of your beaks!" I thought to myself. I was giddy, pumped. Hell, we were *all* pumped, even Tom. Looked like we were in for a dynamite duck-hunt.

We sat there for a second, taking it in. Suddenly, Pelayo looked up and motioned with his chin again. He mouthed something like "check it out!"

Ah yes, a huge flock was just starting to cup up overhead. Mere specks in the sky, but to me they looked like pintail—the masters of aerial ballet, of elegance on the wing. Must be a flock of about a hundred. Here's the royalty among ducks. Can't be too skinny or too rich they say in New York and Hollywood. Pintail agree. Even at three hundred yards, there's no mistaking that sleek profile of theirs: the long wings, the slender elongated neck—longer than Iman's even—and the same color, a rich mahogany.

HEMINGWAY THRILLED TO THIS SIGHT, TOO.

Their wings were barely flapping now and there was another flock right behind them. Tom was pointing skyward at more winging in from the east. Seemed he'd forgotten all about alligators. Those flocks look down, see the crowd, and that's it. "Looks like a happenin' scene down there," the lead duck says over his shoulder. "Let's get in on the action!"

Those wings lock up and the long descent commences. Sometimes the pattern's like a corkscrew, circling, circling, circling, each circle constricting on the way down. Then a few back-flaps to slow down right above the water. Then SPLISH!

Others get impatient. They "wing-wag" almost straight down, pivoting their bodies from one side to the other, stretching one wing and cupping in the other. Either way, it's a magnificent sight, a gorgeous thing to watch. We'd hit upon a hot spot. They were pouring in from three directions. We were gazing at a bay that was simply a duck magnet. Even better, we hadn't heard any shots. Looked like we'd have the place to all ourselves today. Guess the fog had kept most hunters in port. Now it had cleared and we were set for what looked like a superb hunt.

Hemingway thrilled to this sight, too. He was a duck fanatic, like us. He'd hunted practically every animal worth hunting on any continent. He'd looked down the barrel at charging lions and buffalo, stalked kudu with Kilimanjaro as a backdrop, and climbed after wild sheep through the clouds at the summit of the Rockies. Descending a bit, he'd stalked mule deer and bugled up elk.

He chronicled these hunts in some of the most enduring prose of the century. But if you ask me, his most heartfelt writing was inspired by decoying mallards and twisting squadrons of teal. Hemingway hunted ducks, even on safari. He wrote about it in *Green Hills of Africa*. Even on the Serengeti, surrounded by the biggest concentrations of game animals on earth, the bug wouldn't leave him. Any duck-hunter would understand why: for the afflicted, there is no cure.

Our fraternity has some of the most grueling and expensive initiation rites of any in the outdoors, but the dues serve for a lifetime membership.

Finally, Tom couldn't control himself and clambered clumsily on the bow for a look. He'd already pulled on his hip boots. I was eager for a better look myself, so I jumped atop an ice chest and tried to steady myself by leaning on Pelayo's shoulder. He looked up for a second, started to frown, but said nothing. No point in spoiling the moment.

I stretched and could just barely see over the top of the brush into the bay beyond. "Wow," was all I could manage. "Wait till you see this."

Tom started nodding from the bow. He raised his head, craning and stretching, struggling to see over the willows on the bank. Soon he was looking back, smiling wickedly, and waving a fist, thumbs up. Those alligators were a distant memory. I decided not to point out one whose head just popped up about fifty yards down the bank, a big one, too. Tom had enough.

The ducks Tom was watching were really whooping it up. Had to be hundreds out there—*thousands*, perhaps! I cupped my mouth, looked around, and whistled, but no one heard it over the avian gabfest. By now the fog had long parted in this area, the sun had broken through and revealed the wetland panorama in all its glory. The scenery, I'm convinced, makes up a big part of waterfowling's appeal.

Think about it. Hunter and non-hunter alike, we all love to gaze over the water. "Water is everywhere a protection," writes anthropologist Lionel Tiger, trying to explain the lure. "Like a moat, it serves as protection. As a species we love it." Hell, why else is waterfront property always the most expensive?

Stands of rosseau cane wrapped around the far shore. Willows and elephant ear grass bracketed the bay on all sides, all green and shimmering, even now in December. The sun was out. The fog had long cleared. The breeze was stirring. We were pumped. "Well?" Paul finally shouted. "Let's get after 'em!"

Pelayo and I paddled in one fourteen-foot pirogue, and Tom and On-the-Ball followed in the other with the decoys. We'd all hunt from one pirogue, though. This sounds crazy to some, but we put a board from one seat to the other and sit down comfortably side by side. We like this set-up, because it lengthens the hunting experience. This way we get to watch four limits decoying into our faces. And ain't that half the fun? With the masses of ducks that winter down here in the Delta, hunt alone or with one partner, and often the hunt is over in no time.

One man might down his five ducks in twenty minutes. Two people might limit out with their ten in one hour. Like the Pointer Sisters say: *"I want a lover who can spend some time, not come and go in a heated rush."* Well, we fancy ourselves these ducks' lovers, and we're not going to "come and go in a heated rush" ourselves. No way. We want to savor the glorious experience of blasting them outta the skies. Hence, our four-man blind set-up.

"No way!" Pelayo gasped as we rounded a stand of cane. He was in the front seat paddling and looked around with his eyes wide. "Gotta be hyacinths, huh?" He pointed ahead with an upraised paddle. "Maybe some pouldeau?"

A haze hung over the water in this area, so I couldn't be sure. "Lotta *something* out there," I quipped. Then he looked over again and let out a low whistle. "I *can't* believe—!"

The roar of a thousand wings drowned the rest of his phrase. I turned my gaze at the source in the big open bay. The bay's cover was lifting, straight into the air. We could only gape. Behind us we heard Paul let fly with a crazed whoop. Tom followed up with another. I looked around, and they were waving their paddles in the air crazily.

The ducks ahead leapt straight into the air and started flapping off, their long wings propelling them skyward in seconds. None of that running, then flapping off parallel to the water, of diving ducks. These were all puddlers. They peeled off in huge bands from the middle and in little bands from the edges, those closest to us first, each band triggering another and another.

Now some mottled ducks (known as summer mallards down here) take off from the edge. Now a huge band of greenwings take off from the far side. The teal, as usual, can't make up their minds, careening over the bay in that crazy zig-zag of theirs, looking like overgrown snipe. The Gadwall seems to regroup in the air and flap off in ragged groups, peppering the skies with their glorious multitudes. The pintail take off first and fly off fastest.

We were wide-eyed. We were speechless. We shouldn't have been. It's twenty years we've been hunting down here at the very tip of the Mississippi Flyway funnel, and these sights are downright commonplace. The river and its tributaries act as migrating thoroughfares for North America's ducks and geese. They finally get down here—down to the mouth of this "father of all waters," as the Indians called the Mississippi—and stop. One third of North America's wildfowl winter here. Another third visit, then head further south. Teddy Roosevelt, Black Jack Pershing, and Huey Long all hunted down here, and they all thrilled to these same sights in their day.

Now it was our turn. I thought back to our first hunt down here over twenty years ago. Nobody could sleep the night before, and we were set up a half hour before legal shooting time, like most duck hunters. The concert of whistling and quacking and gabbling was worth it. The roar of rushing wings was heavenly. We trembled spastically with anticipation, like a lab ready to pounce, like my wife anticipating a sale. The sky lightened, and ducky silhouettes peppered the sky, gliding around, landing all around us. We could hear the splashes. We were giddy from the show, laughing to ourselves, punching each other's shoulders. We were pumped like we'd never been pumped for a duck hunt before.

"Okay!" Chris finally gasped. "Legal shooting time!" We'd been hearing shots for five minutes already. "And look! Here they come."

He jerked down my shoulder. A big flock of pintail had locked up and was circling it's way down . . . almost in range . . . another circle . . . a little further from range now . . . a little further, then SPLISH, right in the open water, a good two hundred yards away.

That was the story for the next three hours. In effect, we were bird watching. By 10:30 A.M., we'd seen more ducks than we'd seen in all the hunts of our lives.

And we'd shot three of them: two greenwing teal and a stray gray that blundered into range. Ducks had been in constant action, lifting, landing, and buzzing, within two hundred yards of us all morning. They might as well have been in Arkansas. They wouldn't even buzz the decoys, wouldn't acknowledge a call, *nothing*. So naturally we started snarling at each other.

"Who wanted to set up here?"

"Not me!"

"Not me!"

You know how *that* goes. Like JFK said about the Bay of Pigs, "Success has a thousand parents, but failure is an orphan." Our first Delta duck hunt was an orphan with bells on.

By now we'd wised up, setting up mid-day on a high tide after studying flight patterns. It's the only way to hunt down here. The ducks simply have too much open water crammed with food to land in, so you'd better get the flyways *just* right. And set up *just* right. Successful set-ups down here come only after scouting, the kind of thing most people associate with deer hunting. Down here, you'd better associate it with duck hunting, too. In our case, we simply started hunting later in the day, never setting up before eight o'clock or so. This gives us time to scout. When we lift those huge flocks from the open water, we sit tight and watch them. We stick around for twenty minutes or so and watch their flight paths and where they come down.

It might seem haphazard at first, but after a while, you'll notice patterns. These big lagoons and open bays all have certain areas, sometimes close to shore, that puddle ducks favor. Invariably, we find a fairly shallow area clogged with food when we paddle to them.

Some were already settling back in as I tossed out the last decoy. I paddled over and helped shove the pirogues into the little cane island, then started bending down the canes in front for our natural blind. You can't beat these for concealment. Takes a little work, though.

We'd just arranged the seating board and were settling in, jamming shells into the guns, when Pelayo rasped: "On the left!" He let fly with a loud hail: "QUACK! QUACK! QUACK! QUACK! QUACK!" The flock was flying low but moving away from us at an angle.

Paul followed up with his whistle. "WHEW–whew–whew . . . WHEW–whew–whew," doing the widgeon call. I mouthed my own call and added a few quacks and chuckles, and damn if the flock didn't turn on a dime. Then they saw the decoys. "Looks like a feast over there, gang!" the lead duck announces. "And an orgy! Let's go!"

Soon they were boring in, and the faces on either side of me glowed with rapture. Dogs get this look when you pour their food. Cats, too, when eyeing that cardinal at the bird feeder. Business clients get it at the Gold Club, just as the lap dancer straddles them. Shooting—fast frantic shooting at the prince of wildfowl—was seconds away.

"They're grays!" Pelayo gasped. Ah, not pintail as I thought. "And they're *coming*. Get low! And hide your face!" as he jammed down his cap and shoved Tom down by the shoulder.

What a sight. They were winging right in, cupping their wings, swerving slightly while slowing down. My jaw quivered. My trigger finger tapped the safety spastically. Tom had the look of a leopard about to pounce. Pelayo's eyes bulged; he panted.

But how to explain this thrill to the non-hunter? I'll take the easy route and toss the ball back in your court. "How can you *not* hunt?" I ask. Hunting's not a hobby. It's not a pastime; it's an *instinct*.

"Man evolved as a hunter," says Chicago University anthropologist W. S. Laughlin. "He spent over ninety-nine percent of his species's history as a hunter, and he spread over the entire habitable globe as a hunter."

How'd you get it out of your system so fast? How'd you shake it? I have a theory. The instinct's still down there somewhere, but latent. The embers have cooled after millennia of inactivity. I specialize in rekindling them for friends. I hear of the poor saps mowing the lawn on weekends, grocery shopping, vegetating in front of the TV, or worst of all, plodding through a golf course. I hear these things and choke back the sobs. My rambunctious college buddies have mutated into slaves, drones, pansies, and eunuchs!

So I spring to the rescue. I'll take a dedicated golfer hunting. He wallops a high-flying pintail, and his eyes light up! Next week, he's clamoring to go again. A month later, he's selling his clubs

HE RETURNS FROM THE CHASE DIRTY, BEDRAGGLED, BUT ALWAYS WITH A CAR-NAL GLEAM IN HIS EYE.

for a shotgun, then the cart for a boat. Fifteen patterns of camo soon cram his closet. The embers have ignited a raging inferno by now. By the end of his first season, he makes my chum Ted Nugent look like Phil Donahue.

Invariably, his wife, once tolerably civil, starts to loathe me openly. She addresses me exclusively in snarls and curses. She hangs up on me, erases my messages. She becomes my bitter foe. I can't blame her. Sure, her husband used to spend time at the golf course, but it was a harmless hobby. This hunting stuff, however, is a *passion*, an *obsession*. "That's *all* he talks about!" she wails. "I never see him anymore! He pays more attention to that stupid shotgun than to me! We can't go out anymore cause he's always gone on weekends, and that damn racket from that damn duck call! Night and day!"

The ducks and deer now compete seriously for her time. She resents it, but this always fades. By Christmas she's smiling, thanking me. "Humberto!" she beams. "So nice to see you! Can I get you a beer? Hey, aren't y'all goin' hunting this weekend again? Wonderful! Here, and in a nice frosty mug!"

Always happens this way. Her hubby's new passion brings her benefits in the boudoir, you see. Conquest afield is usually followed by conquest at home. He returns from the chase dirty, bedraggled, but always with a carnal gleam in his eye. It was so for our Paleolithic ancestors. It remains the case today. Ask around.

"Then why don't more men hunt?" you ask.

"Lack of opportunity," I answer. "They turn to golf for the same reason men turn to sodomy in prisons and Arabic countries."

"This guy's a raving loon!" you snort. "A complete nutcase!"

"Perhaps," I answer. "Can't help, it though. Hunting season always does this to me. It's a serious jones, my friends, and me and my chums are wallowing in it right now, after six months of withdrawal. Compared to this, Keith Richards and John Belushi had it easy.

Yes, the ducks were still winging in and they were almost in range, almost . . . gliding a little closer now. Finally, they started dropping the landing gear.

"Now!" Pelayo yelled. We rose and the flock scattered and rocketed skyward. A wild flurry of furiously flapping wings and startled quacks filled the air. I swung left—BLAM! One folded and hit the water. I swung higher . . . .

BLAM! Tom nailed him before I slapped the trigger. A puff of feathers and the duck staggered in flight. "*Sha-wuck*" goes Tom's pump and—BLAM! again. The duck's neck sagged like a noodle. His wings folded . . . SPLISH! he went, into the decoys.

I started following another one, high overhead by now. The bead past his beak—BLAM! My shoulder bucked, and he folded. What a pretty sight! Then THUMP, into the mud bank on the left.

BLAM! I was startled by a final shot. It was Paul. He nailed one with a gorgeous going-away shot. The duck twirled down like that kamikaze with one wing blasted off you always see on the History Channel. We sat there trembling with idiot grins, looking around. Finally, we erupted in wild whoops and rebel yells. Then the high-fives. Finally, I started getting out to retrieve them, but Tom yanked my sleeve as I stepped into the other pirogue. Instinctively, I hunched up and started looking around, slowly, trying to shield my face from the sun's glare. Ah yes, those four were high. The kind that appear *way* up there, but with the slow wing beat and craning neck movement that signals "ducks looking for company. Ducks that might decoy."

Sure enough, they slowed and banked at Pelayo's first hail. We chimed in with more quacks and whistles, and they cupped. Down they came, almost straight down. It was amazing. Cupped wings are one thing. These ducks cupped their wings in, almost to the body, for a rapid descent. Usually, you start calling at ducks at that altitude and they'll circle three or four times. Not these. These were probably here earlier. They were probably among those we spooked. They wanted back in now. We watched the wind rustling their wing feathers, and what a heavenly sound. In seconds, they were almost on top of us.

My heart was in my throat as we rose to greet them at point-blank range. BLAM! Pelayo beat me to the draw, and I saw one fold on the left. BLAM! BLAM! Tom and Paul shot almost as one, and two more cartwheeled into the dekes. I was drawing a bead on the last one but held off. He looked out of range.

More high-fives. More whoops. "Whatcha think, Tom?" Pelayo poked him.

"You guys weren't kidding!" He beamed as he slapped Pelayo's hand. "Slap my hand, black soul man!" He chuckled á la Steve Martin as the Wild and Crazy Guy. "Nope, you guys sure weren't kiddin'!" Alligators and water moccasins and quicksand had vanished from Tom's mind. Pintail Alley was coming through again. Pelayo turned, pointed left, and started slowly hunching down, motioning for us to follow.

Good move. There's no mistaking pintail in flight. Those long wings and sleek profiles can only belong to the prince of wildfowl—his majesty, indeed. Here was a whole flock, young ones, no doubt, young and stupid. Good. Two toots from Paul's whistle and they'd locked in on the decoys.

In seconds, those long slim wings, more reminiscent of shore-birds or gulls than ducks, were barely flapping; they were cupping. Those longs necks were craning back and forth, but at seventy yards the three in the lead started veering off.

My own pintail whistle came up and I tooted softly, twitting my tongue against the roof of my mouth. Paul kept up his tooting.

Pelayo added a quick hail and a few chuckles. It worked. They swung back on course, their wings started gliding again, barely moving. The landing gear started to go down, but they were still fifty yards out. A little too far, but still a dizzying sight. Pintail landing, actually landing! Doesn't happen very often (except during teal season, of course), even down here in the Delta.

A jet-like roar of wings from behind and a flock of greenwings rushed in over the rosseaus, practically knocking our caps off. They swerved just in front of the pintail, blazed out into the bay, and started turning back for another buzz at the decoys. Pelayo, Tom, and I looked at each other, trying to stifle guffaws, but it was shooting time. Four of the pintail hovered a bit closer. They glided over the decoys. We rose.

BLAM! BLAM! BLAM! Three shots and two big drakes crumpled. A third staggered off to my left. I followed him with the bead, lead him about two feet (this steel shot in the wind), and touched the trigger—BLAM! His neck sagged and he splashed down, clobbering the furthest decoy.

BLAM! I hear a shot. "That's *it*, man!" I howled. "Three down! That's three limits!"

"Chill out!" Paul snorts. "One on the water was swimming off. Got him."

Tom was sounding off in another loud whoop when Paul startled him by cupping his mouth with his muddy palm and yanking him down. I saw Pelayo pointing with his chin as he ducked his head and plastered it against the rosseau cane. Ah yes, a pair almost directly overhead, too high to shoot but cupped and looking down. I gave a short hail: four quick, sharp notes—the way ducks do it, not mariachi trumpeters—and they started spiraling down.

I mean almost *straight* down. I watched this time. They were widgeon, drake and hen, looking snazzy in their late winter plumage, the colors gleaming in the sun. They cupped while directly over, banked, and set a gliding course for their bogus brethren below. In seconds, they were hovering over the decoys—not landing, just hovering like they weren't sure. They decided they didn't like what they saw and started drifting off—too late.

Tom and Paul rose—BLAM! BLAM! Both ducks folded—SPLISH, SPLISH—into the decoys! "Way to go!" Tom was jubilant, high-fiving all around. "Never seen duck shooting like this!" he beamed. "Wow!"

Paul was already pointing right and squinting. "Shorebirds?" he asked. "Or teal?"

"Teal!" Pelayo gasped. "Down!" He started tugging at his brother's elbow.

"Naw, man," Paul snorted. "Too many to be teal. Gotta be forty or fifty of 'em!"

"Teal! I'm telling ya," Pelayo hissed through gritted teeth. "Get yer freakin' ass *down!*" He yanked him again.

Pelayo was right. They were greenwings. These tasty little ducks bunch up in huge flocks this time of year down here. They're not much bigger than snipe, so they can be deceptive, but their flight pattern—those fast little wingbeats and erratic course—gave them away. They were too fat to be shorebirds. Their wings moved too fast.

"Looks like they're coming, too!" Tom said as he hunched down and looked over, his eyes wide, a giddy grin creasing his face. Oops, then the teal turned—oops, then they turned *back*. That's the thing with these huge flocks of greenwings, they turn on a dime, at the slightest whim. You never know if they've seen the decoys are not, or if they're interested. These veered off three more times till they were about a hundred yards out. Then I blasted out a raspy hail, figuring I had nothing to lose.

That did it; now they saw the decoys for sure. They were blazing in like a swarm of little kamikazes. I looked over and had to stifle another guffaw. Those *faces!* Grown men here, too. We all looked at each other, laughing silently, our torsos heaving. In they came . . . closer . . . closer. They started cupping their wings, weaving crazily back and forth—*now!*

We rose and they rocketed skyward. BLAM! BLAM! Nothing falling. I swung right. I swung left. Flapping targets everywhere, then flapping targets *nowhere*. I almost fell backward following another one. That's the thing with these huge flocks—you go crazy aiming from one to the other, never picking one out.

Finally—BLAM! BLAM! BLAM! Three quick shots from around me.

Then—POW! POW!—I get two off into the flock and POW! one last one as they flapped off. We sat there, looking around.

"What the—? No! *Impossible!*"

Tom was roaring, "Can't believe I missed!"

"Hell," Pelayo laughed. "I think we *all* missed!" Actually, two teal floated in the water, one wounded. We'd sent *twelve* shots, each packing three hundred pellets and a lethal zone three feet across, raking through that mass of fifty-odd teal, and *two* teal fell! Nice shooting!

Never fails with these huge flocks, but now the flock had broken up. Now came some easier shooting as smaller groups started winging back in for seconds. I was reloading frantically when BLAM! Tom tumbled one to my left. Then BLAM! Paul folded the second one. "That's better," I said, nodding.

We hunched down again. Another five were blazing straight in, somehow oblivious to the shooting. I rose and drew a bead on the first one. He shot upward. The bead just cleared his beak. BLAM! Feathers flew and he folded.

Yeah, you right!" I howled. "Got his ass!"

BLA—AM! Pelayo got a double on my left. "Now we're gettin' somewhere!" Paul yelled. We'd vindicated ourselves, somewhat.

Then a flock of four big ducks appeared from behind, heading straight for us. We crouched, turning our faces to watch their approach. These were big-bodied ducks with a deliberate wing beat. They looked like mottled ducks, a mallard kissing cousin that lives year-round along the Gulf coast and looks almost identical to a black duck. He acts like a black duck, too— exasperatingly wary. Makes sense; mottled ducks live down here year round. They know the lay of the land down to the last cattail. Any blind pops up, they notice.

These passed about eighty yards to the left, and I gave a short (three-note) hail. One cupped immediately and started banking. The others flew on. I called again, and again. Now Pelayo chimed in. After another hundred yards of flight, the remaining trio decided to join the first.

What a picture. We had that first one circling directly behind us. He'd probably appear in range over the dekes in seconds, and we had three others gliding in from the front, still 150 yards out. Quite a dilemma. "A bird in the hand," they say. A mottled in the hand, however, is worth about *fifty* in the bush. Hunkering down we traded looks; we couldn't even risk a whisper. Our eyes and grimaces said it all: "Do we blast this one that's almost on top of us? Or wait for the trio?"

The first one glided in from the left, almost skimming the water near the furthest decoy, and landed! The remaining trio kept closing the distance on alternately cupped and gently flapping wings. This was rare for mottled ducks, almost as rare as that first one landing. But these weren't landing, just looking. I noticed one was a greenhead. They often hang out together, mallards and mottled ducks. They even interbreed at times; we once shot one with the curly tail feathers of a greenhead but the body of a mottled duck.

They were well within range as we rose. BLAM! BLAM! BLAM!! The greenhead and the duck to his left folded. The other mottled duck faltered but regained his altitude. BLAM—BLAM!! Now he crumpled. We forgot about the one that landed.

"Somebody better make a retrieval run," Pelayo said while standing and shucking a spent shell. "We gotta be close to half a limit. Hey, wait a minute." He pointed left toward the bank. "Weren't three ducks floating against those rosseaus a few minutes ago?"

"Right." Paul stood and looked over. "I'd been looking at them, two pintail and a gray. Ya think a raccoon or something?"

"No raccoon," I said, pointing over Pelayo's shoulder. "There's your duck thief." An alligator's head poked above the water next to a little clump of water hyacinths.

"That sonofabitch!" Paul snarled. That's our dinner—duck gumbo, man! I even bought the roux pre-made, the onions and celery and stuff pre-chopped. He ain't gettin' way with it!" He lifted his shotgun.

"Are you crazy?" Tom gasped. "You're not gonna shoot?"

"Just wanna scare him off." Paul said while sighting down the barrel. "I'll shoot next to him. We can't have this sort of shit goin' on, man." Before I could mount a protest myself, BLAM! Paul slapped the trigger and the water exploded.

"You crazy sucker!" Pelayo yelled. "Lookit, now ya did it!" The alligator was going crazy, twirling around, his tail in the air, going nuts.

"You scared him all right!" Tom said half-laughing.

"Dammit!" Paul snarled. He looked over with a worried look. "Forgot about this steel shot, much tighter pattern. I was aiming next to him thinking to pepper him, to dust him a little. Get his ass away from here."

"Looks like you did more than that," Pelayo snorted. "Probably the steel pellets entered through his eye and hit the brain. "Better hope Ratso doesn't have the binoculars on us. That's a heavy rap, man—an endangered species rap."

"I love alligator," Tom suddenly blurted. "I eat it at the Jazz Fest every year. I'd hate to see all that good meat go to waste."

CHAPTER NINE

DISCO
BULL-EYEING

"Sneaky bastard, huh?" Pelayo snorted. He drew back on the throttle and pointed toward the bank. I peered and saw nothing.

It was after dark and we approached the campsite from the backside. The tide was up now. At daybreak, this canal had been an oozing mudbank with fiddler crabs scampering along its edges and nutria tracks stitched across. Now it provided access to our island campsite from the rear and cut the distance to the duck blinds by half a mile. The crabs were on higher ground now and the nutrias swam across. One was chugging along right ahead of us, his wake rippling in the moonlight. He finally dove when almost under our bow.

Pelayo kept pointing, but all I saw was a big shaggy willow leaning over the water. "He's out to get us one way or the other," Pelayo said. He bashed the steering wheel with a muddy fist and looked over disgustedly.

Chris stood up behind me, handed me his Bacardi flask, and peered toward the brambles on the bank, nodding and shrugging. He'd been hunting about a quarter mile from us in Pintail Alley, set up by himself, and came over to help us pick up decoys and retrieve ducks when we limited out. Hunting alone, he'd limited out much earlier.

"Took me all of fifteen minutes," he laughed. "And I held off on the teal. Or I'd have limited out in three minutes."

Now Chris was shrugging along with me. "Pelayo's hallucinating again," he laughed while poking my ribs. "Last trip down here he saw a deer on the bank and went nuts scrambling for his crossbow—did he tell ya? Hah! Didn't think so. Well, he nearly broke my leg and Paul's neck when he rammed the boat up on the bank with no warning. He jumped out and started slithering through the slop, stalking the deer almost on his belly. Paul and I watched, confused at first, then almost popped a gut to keep from laughing out loud. We didn't want to ruin his stalk. At twenty yards, Pelayo finally sneaked into position. Tense finger on the trigger, he peered around the rosseau cane—at a rusted oil drum. Paul and I liked to die laughing. Guess he sees another one now."

"All right already," Pelayo grunted. "The story's funnier the first hundred times." His face was still grim.

I'll be dammed if I could tell why. I peered closer, but still saw only a mass of branches clogged with water hyacinths and swaying with the muddy current. Chris shrugged again and handed me the rum.

"Okay, come on," I said to Pelayo after a throat-searing gulp. "End the suspense. What ya see?" I figured he saw a raccoon huddled up in the branches, or maybe a deer, frozen up, hiding and waiting for us to pass, or perhaps a hog, rooting around. But why would that enrage him?

"Still don't see it, huh?" Pelayo rasped while reaching under the console. "No wonder y'all never see the damn ducks until they're on top of us. No wonder you never see a deer, until he's bounding off with that white flag waving." He came up with the spotlight, snapped it on, and shot the beam into the shoreline brambles. "There, satisfied?"

Red reflectors glared back. Yep. Pelayo's eyes were keen this time. He'd redeemed himself from the deer-oil drum gaffe. It was a big green skiff. "Hey isn't that . . . ?" Chris asked as Pelayo played the beam along the side and stopped on the Louisiana Wildlife and Fisheries Enforcement Division emblem. "Holy shit!" Chris gasped from behind me. "Sure is." He'd just taken another hit from his rum and went into a violent coughing-hacking fit. My own stomach felt an icy jolt.

We can't help it. It's an instinct. The law, the "heat," still manages to unnerve us. Some things never change. That little emblem had sent so many shivers up our spines, provoked so many wild runs through the marsh, mad dashes through the woods, wild Jeep-runs crashing through the briars, over ditches, through canebrakes—sometimes laughing wildly, other times scared shitless—but always exciting, always with the adrenalin pumping big-time, all in our misspent youth.

Not that we were ever big-time outlaws. We never really plundered the game stocks, always kept within the limits. Problem was the hours we kept. Like so many young males, we had a passion for "bull-eyeing"—night hunting, if you will.

"*After midnight*," wailed Eric Clapton, "*We gonna let it all hang out . . . .we gonna chug-a-lug and shout.*"

We did plenty of both, but Eric didn't know the half of it. Sure, barrooms and nightclubs and discos were fun. But so was Chris's red Jeep with "The Midnight Rider" painted on the side, with a cooler of

Bud between the seats, with a scoped .22 in the rack, and with four shaggy nineteen-year-olds inside, bouncing over levees, pastures, and golf courses, occasionally stopping. "There's one! Hold the light steady, dammit." The crosshairs hung behind the shining eye. POP! The rabbit somersaulted and went into convulsions.

Chris was at the wheel the night I popped one on a rural golf course just west of New Orleans. I hit the rabbit a little low in the head, and the thing started flipping, running in circles, squealing, and wailing. Nothing unnerves like the squeals of a wounded rabbit. It's a mini version of a wounded hog. Only the racket in a circumcision ward (or the first Plastic Ono Band album) comes close. Hell, any sound that provokes pity from a gun-totin' nineteen-year-old male with a buzz has to be pretty damn piteous.

I jumped out and was stumbling around trying to grab the poor screaming thing, then trying to bash it with the gun butt, then trying to kick it. "Whoa!" I kicked mightily, finally connected with the creature, and sent it off like Tom Dempsey's field goal, but— "Whoooops!"—slipped back on my ass in the dew-covered grass. The horrible wailing continued.

Pelayo, Perry, and Chris stayed in the Jeep, doubled over cackling, pointing, occasionally catching enough breaths to lend guidance and moral support. "Sounds like Vanessa in passion!" Chris yelled. "Did she ever get your name right?"

"Shut the hell up!" I snarled back. Damn if they weren't right, though. Vanessa—that TKE little sister—did have a squeaky little voice. She was a passionate little vixen, and she always had a tough time with my name, but I was in no mood for that shit right then. The terrible squealing was getting to me.

"Yeah, Vanessa after the Ole Miss Game!" Perry yelled. "Whoo-boy! We were listening from the kitchen!"

"Will you bastards shut the hell up?" I was getting frantic. "And come gimme—"

"Yeah, at Eddie's party!" Pelayo whooped. "Remember we had that tape recorder behind the dresser. Ooh-hoo, Horatio! Eeh, Eeh, EEEEEHH! Yes! Yes! Ah! Ah! Faster, Horatio! What ever happened to that tape anyway?"

"Come gimme a *freakin' hand!*" I sputtered. My charming friends answered with more pointing and hooting.

"Perry says she always likes it doggie style!" Pelayo laughed. "That true? That why she was squealing? Hunh, *Horatio?*"

"Okay, that's it!" I said, and I rushed the Jeep. Chris stomped it, and the Jeep started spinning and swerving off, the huge "gumbo-mudder" tires throwing up big wads of mud and dewy grass that splattered all over me as I ran behind them, panting, red-faced, enraged. "You goddam, freakin'—!"

By now, they could barely breathe. The tires started digging in and they started losing me. Finally, I gave up and they spun off over the levee, their howls and cackles ringing in my ears. I sat there mud-splattered, with my lungs aching, catching my breath and cursing. Then it hit me: no more squealing? The poor rabbit had finally expired. Thank God. I walked back towards the putting green, and there he lay, sprawled.

Twenty minutes later, I heard the slashing riff of "Jumpin' Jack Flash" from afar. In seconds the Midnight Rider came rumbling back over the levee just as Mick was fading out—"it's a gas-gas-gas." They'd made a beer, Mad Dog, and chili burrito run to Wag-a-Sack and caught their breaths. They even brought me a burrito and a bunch of napkins. Whatta swell bunch.

Meanwhile, the mosquitoes had eaten me alive. I was a little calmer when they returned, holding up the (finally!) dead rabbit. "Hit a little low," I said, pointing at the hole under his eye. I threw him on top of Perry.

"Hey, man, watch it!" He jumped back, spilling Mad Dog all over his chest, just as the red flashing lights came over the levee.

"Holy shit!" Pelayo yelled. He grabbed my arm and turned to Chris. "Stomp it, man!"

"Get in!" Perry screamed while grabbing my other arm. Chris gunned it just as I grabbed the rollbar and jumped, but my foot slid on the wet fender. The gumbo mudders spun, and the Jeep swerved crazily, dragging me as I stumbled alongside. I held on with white knuckles while trying to lope along. Any minute I'll slip under the Jeep, I thought, where those gumbo mudders would mangle and splatter me like slow nutria on Highway 90. "Dead Skunk in the Middle of the Road" flashed in mind. "The blood and the guts, they're gonna make you swoon!" Finally, Pelayo grabbed my arms with one hand and my collar with the other. Perry reached down and grabbed my belt. "Get yer ass in here!" They heaved.

Ahhh! I finally made it, but landed with my head on Perry's crotch—OOOMPH! We roared off in another shower of mud and grass, with the law in hot pursuit. Now was the time for "The Midnight Rider" to really show its stuff. *"Ain't gonna let 'em catch me no . . . ain't gonna let 'em catch, the Midnight Rider,"* Greg Allman drawled.

Well, we weren't gonna let 'em catch us either. No freakin' way.

It looked touch and go for a few minutes as we roared atop the levee. They were gaining on us, and their bullhorn was blaring some threatening bullshit. Suddenly, Chris turned sharply, bashing my head smartly against the rollbar and almost sending Pelayo and Perry tumbling out of the Jeep as we zoomed down the levee.

"They're still comin'!" Perry yelled over the engine noise and crackling bullhorn. These cops were good, obvious pros at this kind of stuff. They had to be, on this beat. They seemed unfazed and followed expertly, close to our tail, all the way through the old sand pit. Perry was slapping Chris on the shoulder. "Let's stop. Come on, we'll never make it." Pelayo looked at me, nodding and grimacing, like he agreed with Perry.

"Get your goddamn hands off my neck!" Chris yelled, just as we hit the pasture. "Jump out if ya want! Me, I ain't spending the night in no jail!"

It was a very soggy pasture. We stalled for a second then started spinning and sliding. The cops almost jumped us right then. The bullhorn message was booming across loud and clear and ominous, from less than fifty yards.

"I'm gettin out!" Perry gasped. "I don't need a rap sheet, okay? Stop this thing! I mean it!" I looked back and the cops were right there. One was opening the door. They figured they had us. Chris was still gunning the engine and turning the wheel, grimacing crazily and cursing. He refused to look back. Perry was still shaking his shoulder. "Come on, Magoo"—Chris' nickname for a while. "Come on!"

"Jump out if ya want!" Chris finally yelled without turning around. "Go ahead! I ain't!"

I was torn. Didn't know what the hell to do. We were digging ourselves deeper with every second, literally and figuratively. Smacked with billy clubs, yanked by the hair, maybe a little shot of pepper spray—I could already feel it. Then, "resisting arrest, speeding, drunk and disorderly. Sign here, please. The clang of the bars and a night in a piss-ridden cell, surrounded by reeking winos with blood crusted on their heads. Thugs menacing us and shaking us down for money and cigarettes all night. No way. My brain flashed the ghastly scenes, and I was about to side with Perry when we suddenly lurched forward.

The tires seemed to be catching hold, gripping, like they had claws. I thought of those "Tiger Paws" commercials with the Tiger racing down the road . . . Some definite traction now. Pelayo looked over wide-eyed, with a hint of a smile. Perry stopped shaking Chris's shoulder and poked me in the ribs, nodding. "The Midnight Rider" was doing its stuff, getting into form. Soon the tires stopped spinning, and the Jeep was plowing through the slop like a champ.

"Yeah, you right!" Chris roared with a quick glance behind us. "Gumbo mudders! There are *no* substitutes!"

Our gumbo mudders were bigger than the cops'. After a few minutes, we could barely hear their bullhorn, and it looked like we might be literally "out of the woods." Then we came to a ditch.

"No!" Pelayo yelled. His face was frantic again, his eyes wild. "You gotta be crazy, we'll turn the goddamn thing over! Too steep man! We're outrunning them anyway! Just keep goin'. Then we'll get back on the river road." Sure enough, I shot a glance behind us and the cops had stalled.

"Got a good river sand bottom up here a bit," Chris said, pointing. "I remember wading across it when we were dove hunting one day. We'll hit it at an angle. You'll see." Pelayo set his jaw, grabbed the passenger bar, and nodded. Even Perry was game now. He hunkered down and grabbed the rollbar with a death grip. Same here. The adrenalin was pumping. We were getting cocky again.

"Ready?" Chris screamed while gripping the wheel and revving the engine. "We'll take it at an angle! Hold on!"

"Whooaa!" We swooped down the bank holding on to the rollbar for dear life. We hit the water with a huge splash. My head smacked the back of the passenger seat, and Pelayo almost flew out from the impact. We were soaked with filthy water and spattered with mud. I couldn't see through my mud-covered glasses. My hair dripped with stinking slop.

"It's too freakin' deep!" Pelayo yelled while wiping his face with his shirt. "Told ya. We had 'em beat, too!" His eyes were wild. "They'll run up on us now!"

The wheels spun madly, all of us hunched up, grimacing and gripping the wheel and rollbar with white knuckles, pushing and grunting like we could somehow help push the jeep along with our momentum.

"I'm gettin' out!" Perry finally snarled while looking around. "I'm makin' a run for it!"

WREENNN! WREEEEENNN! WREEEEN! Chris said nothing. He kept gunning the engine, sending up more water and mud. It felt like we were under a waterfall, or in the middle of a freakin' hurricane. I was waiting for the engine to explode like a bomb. The racket was deafening. Perry couldn't jump out if he wanted to.

Suddenly, we lurched ahead, snapping my neck back savagely, but at nineteen nobody gets whiplash. The tires must have hit the patch of river sand. WREE-OAAAN! WREEE-OAAAN! Chris kept gunning that sucker. In seconds, the front wheels were out of the water and up on the far bank. Now the back wheels came over the bank ledge and again my head smacked the seat in front of me. Amazing, the flexibility of the human spinal column at that age, and the amount of skull cushioning.

We blazed through the ditch and spun up the opposite bank with a shower of mud and slop filling the air behind us. Chris was right about the river sand. We hit the top of the bank, stopped, and looked behind us. The cops were completely stalled now, fuming I'm sure. Some low crackling was still audible from their bullhorn.

We sat there stupefied for a second, shaking our soaked heads like labs just in from a retrieve, wiping off some of the mud. Then the *Hot Rocks* eight-track clicked on. "That thing still working?" Pelayo laughed, just as the little harmonica intro to "Midnight Rambler" boomed out.

We looked around, laughing. That was one tough tape deck, soaked, battered, mud covered, and still booming away. No static even. And boy, was the timing perfect. *"Did ya hear about the Midnight Rambler . . . ?"* We high-fived and chimed in with Mick. *"He don't go in the light of the morning. He split the time the cockerell crows!"*

The "light of the morning" was still eight hours away. A very fast night here, but still young. We were pumped now, blazing along a firm pasture, the cool wind in our faces and making good time, our pursuers nowhere in sight. I reached for the bottle of Mad Dog somewhere on the floor for a celebratory swig. My hands were shaking crazily as I grabbed it. We were all laughing—but still nervous. These were erratic laughs with much gasping between cackles. I passed the good old Mad Dog 20-20 around. Everyone's hands seemed to be shaking. We could barely hold the damn bottle to our mouths. Chris stopped right before a gravel road so we could chug properly.

"AHH! WHOO!" Chris whooped. "Ready?" He stomped it again. We hit the road, sent gravel flying and bored out "The Midnight Rider" for about three miles to Buzzy's house. His garage was opened and we wheeled straight in. I jumped out, hit the button, and the garage door creaked and bumped its way closed.

I pounded the door, and Buzzy opened it almost instantly. He'd been in the kitchen. "What the—?" he laughed. "Y'all been swimming?" Then we heard the sirens and looked out the front window. We got to Buzzy's just in time. Two cop cars came blazing past the house, red lights flashing and sirens blaring as we watched from the window.

Finally, we closed the drapes and really broke up; laughing crazily—I mean drooling, high-fiving, and chugging more beer. "They finally got their fat asses off the stools at the doughnut shop!" Chris roared. "They won't even get outta the cars, watch!"

Yeah, we were wiseasses *now*. Always happened when you're finally safe, and nineteen. We had the world by the balls back then.

THE DISCO BABES WERE SMITTEN, HELPLESS.

An hour later, the dozen rabbits were gutted and in an ice chest, and we were boogeying up a storm in Fat City—Fletcher's Nightery to be precise. Must have been something primal about our moods that night. We'd stalked and hunted up some meat. We'd run roughshod over nature's obstacles. We'd eluded bloodthirsty predators. Some instinct told us females valued such prowess in the early Paleolithic era as much as in the disco era.

So we were *really* strutting that night, polypropylene shirts unbuttoned a little lower than usual (almost to the navel), medallions gleaming, our repartee surpassing its normal level of irresistibility and charm. No dithering that night. We paid the cover, pranced in, and immediately moved in for the kill.

A covey of disco babes pointed toward us and giggled from the edge of the dance floor. The strobe lights revealed them for foxes. A couple of them seemed to quiver while looking over at us, hunching over close to each other and covering their mouths in their trademark manner of expressing ardor.

"Ah," we looked at each other smirking. Our flashy attire, macho good looks, and bold demeanor had already done its work. How could they resist the Midnight Ramblers? We positively radiated with aphrodisiacal qualities that night—more than usual, that is.

The disco babes were smitten, helpless. The *coup de grace* would be a cinch—almost too easy for sporting beaux like us. Pelayo motioned with a flippant wave and a wink that he'd walk point on this mission. "Search and destroy," they called it. The search had been easy. Now the mere presence of these strutting, snappily clad magnificos had destroyed half the ladies' inhibitions. Time to consummate.

Pelayo pranced over and cocked his head. "Do y'all believe in love at first sight?" he drawled with his upper lip in serious Elvis mode. "Or do I walk by again?"

They rolled their eyes and pivoted their heads in sheer rapture.

The sensations must have been dizzying. More laughing and covering of mouths. Chris tottered over on his six-inch heels, bell-bottoms-billowing and collars flapping like seagull wings. "Excuse me," he said, winking. Then he flicked his tongue a few times. "But does my tongue taste funny to you?"

They swooned. A few actually doubled over, holding to each other for support as their knees buckled from the waves of passion that rocked them on their platform shoes. We charmed their phosphorescent disco socks right off.

At least, that's how *we* recall it. We met our wives (and we're all still married to the same ones, over twenty years later) under these conditions. Perhaps they recall it slightly differently? Perhaps they interpret this female body language differently?

Anyway, on a good night of bull-eyeing, we'd wind up with about a dozen rabbits, well short of a three man limit of twenty-four. It was the nighttime setting that doubled the pleasure, doubled the fun. Patti Smith said it best: *"Because the night belongs to us!"* or so it seemed when we were nineteen.

Neil Diamond knew it too: *"Thank the Lord for the nighttime, and forget the day."* Both Patti and Neil Diamond were singing about sex. We found it applied to rabbit hunting, too.

Yeah, bull-eyeing rabbits was *fun*. No two ways about it—and in some cases, it was actually legal. In Texas, for instance, right across the Sabine River from us, rabbits aren't classified as a "game" animal. They're like hogs. Take all you want, anytime you want, say the Texas wildlife authorities. We often took them up on the offer, like on college road trips to visit chums in Houston. Hell, we'd even spring for the non-resident hunting license. So it seemed stupid to revert back to daytime rabbit hunting when we returned home and passed that arbitrary border that separated the states. At nineteen, such things seem irrational or unfair. At that age, *many* things seem irrational and unfair. Jim Harrison hinted at the mindset when he wrote in his recent memoir, *Off to the Side,* "There is no one as abrasively judgmental as a nineteen-year-old."

Phil Caputo heard the same thing from his first commander in Nam.

Some flipped off "the system" by burning their draft cards. Some joined the Peace Corps. Some dropped acid and wrote poetry. We bull-eyed rabbits—to each his own.

In *Meditations on Hunting*, the always forthright Jose Ortega y Gasset wrote, "The hint of criminal suspicion which claws the hunter's conscience—without this ingredient, the spirit of the hunt disappears."

Ortega referred to our role in the premeditated violent death of an animal. The hunter is a "death dealer," as he put it. "Death is essential. Without it, there is no authentic hunting."

Combine that "hint of criminal suspicion," of wantonly killing an inoffensive animal, with the bona fide criminality of doing it at night and you double the pleasure, double the rush—or so it seemed when our testosterone counts were peaking. A penchant for mischief always lurks in the male. Civilization mostly throttled *our* fun, and it's only been ten thousand years since the "agricultural revolution," since "civilization," put the yoke on us, since we went from nomads and hunters to footservants and gardeners, since we went from wolves to poodles.

It's a damn wonder so few of us combat it, though the overwhelmingly male prison population in all civilized countries gives a clue. Monogamy, domesticity, obedience, repetition, tedium, nonviolence, ages of consent, and curfews—they all make war on the male's primal instincts. They read like a sentence from a judge: "For the crime of indulging your instincts and having fun for two and a half million years, you are now sentenced to . . . ."

Trips like this serve as a brief parole from such "cruel and unusual punishment." Now Officer Rizzo's trying to spoil it. Well, he's got his work cut out for him. We won't go easy.

Point is, twenty-five years after those lunatic bull-eyeing adventures, that little Wildlife and Fisheries emblem still spooks us, it sends a little jolt.

"Hell," Pelayo nodded while turning to Chris. "I wish I was

hallucinating again. Looks like Ratso's waiting for us. That prick is out to get us one way or another."

The bastard was trying to cover his trail, avoiding the main bayou, coming in the back way and hiding his boat, thinking we'd come in from the main bayou as usual, not thinking we'd take advantage of the high tide, too. "He's a slick one all right," Pelayo snorted.

"Wonder what that asshole's doing here?" Chris had finally regained his voice.

"He's staking us out," Pelayo laughed. "What else? He almost had us last trip with his bullshit about that shot he heard from our blind before legal shooting time. Now Commando Ratso's manning a clever ambush. He's gonna nab some poachers and get himself promoted out of this asshole of a place to Baton Rouge headquarters. He's got it all figured out. He knows sooner or later we'll slip up, and he wants to be around. Hell, with all these crazy laws on the books, we're bound to be breaking a few on every hunt. He wants to be the one to bring the hammer down."

"Yeah, Chris," I said. "We were talking to Mr. Haney, the other agent, during teal season down here. He's a helluva nice guy. Good agent, too. He told us about Rizzo, well, in so many words. You could tell they weren't exactly buddies."

Mr. Haney's name was actually McGeehee. He was from North Louisiana. His accent, mannerisms, and facial expressions were a ringer for Mr. Haney on *Green Acres*. At first we laughed, but like most agents, he was one hell of a nice guy. He waited till you were finished duck hunting before he came in to check limits, licenses, etc. He didn't motor through your very decoys during prime hunting hours and ruin the hunt, like Rizzo. When he sifted through the pile of ducks and asked who had shot what ducks, he did it almost apologetically, sheepishly, like the poor ticket agents at the airport asking those idiotic questions about, "has your luggage been out of your sight, blah, blah, blah."

"Come on, fellers," Haney would say when we complained about something particularly asinine. "Don't take it out on the fellers who enforce the law. Complain to the ones who *make* the laws, and *pass* them. It's you guys who elect them. I'm just doing my job." You had to like Haney. Great good sense resided in that unpolished skull.

Luckily (and amazingly), we were clean. Tom and On-the-Ball had the alligator in Chris's boat. They also had that the extra teal. We were two ducks from a limit when a huge flock of greenwing teal blazed in . . . .

BLAM! BLAM! BLAM–BLAM! Everyone shot, probably without aiming much, and three fell. Paul went out to retrieve them, and was preparing to stomp the extra one into the mud, when Tom bellowed "No!" and waved frantically. He wouldn't hear of it. He loves duck, teal especially. "Don't do that! Keep it! I'll take it!"

"Not worth it, Tom," Pelayo, who sat next to him in the pirogue blind, admonished him. "No way. Think about it. Ratso's after our ass anyway. He's dying to peg us with something. He won't be cutting us any slack at all, believe me. He'd love nothing better than to nab us with a duck over the limit. None of this 'it was an honest mistake' stuff is gonna cut it, either."

"I won't waste a duck," Tom said with a sharp nod. "Keep it. If we get pegged, *I'll* take the rap. We'll eat it tonight, anyway."

"Hey, On-the-Ball!" Pelayo cupped his hands around his mouth and yelled. Paul was still sloshing along the bank, hefting the big pintail from a patch of hyacinths. "Go ahead and keep the teal!" Pelayo told him while waving him in. "Bring it on in. Tom says he'll hide it. If we get nabbed, he'll take the rap."

Paul held out his arms, made a big shrug, and retrieved the teal from the patch of duck potato. He started splashing back with a fistful of duck by the neck.

Now it looked like folly. Those seven ounces of meat, half a chicken dinner at Popeye's, might have doomed us.

Minutes later, when clambering out of the pirogue into Chris's boat for the ride back to the campsite, Tom tripped. He splashed in the water face first and lost a contact lens. Paul had the fine-meshed live-bait net in the boat, and they started dragging through the muddy water for it. The water was barely two feet deep where he fell and didn't have any current. It didn't look totally hopeless.

Tom was blind as a bat without it. Only in one eye, true, but it was his right eye—his shooting eye. Distance perception was tough with one eye. He'd have a hell of a time with his wing shooting, so he was desperate for his lens.

But after fifteen minutes of dipping, and with darkness setting in, Pelayo, Chris, and I decided we'd head on to the campsite in Pelayo's boat and leave Paul and Tom to continue the dredging operation from Chris's boat, and then head back. We'd get the fire going, get dinner started, light up the place, etc. They'd follow up later. We hated to leave them, but we only had one net. Not much anyone else could do, anyway.

They said fine, popped open two beers, and waved us off with a shrug. Tom was his usual upbeat self. Takes a lot to faze that guy. Now they might be walking into a serious mess when they showed up.

"Holy shit," Chris gasped. His coughing fit finally expired and he was reaching eagerly for the flask from my grip. "We better go back and warn On-the-Ball and Tom. They show up here with that alligator, and I don't even wanna think about it. Worse, they're in *my* boat. Hell, I don't wanna lose it. "

"And don't forget the extra teal," I smirked as my throat finally cooled. "Two federal raps," I snorted. "They definitely don't need that! Ratso would gloat for years to come."

Just then a light came on the bank. The beam hit us, and sure enough, there was Ratso, in all his magnificence, resplendent in his Louisiana Wildlife and Fisheries uniform, badge gleaming in the moonlight. He was flagging us us in, with the exaggerated gestures of a rookie traffic cop.

We looked at each other disgustedly, rolling our eyes. Then Pelayo's face hardened. "Hey watch it, man!" he yelled resolutely at the light. "Ya trying to blind us or something! Turn that light off! I can't see!"

I punched Pelayo in the back. "Shut up!" I hissed. He was losing his cool. That always meant trouble. God knows, we didn't need any more. He nodded calmly and waved towards the bank. "Okay, that's better. Thanks." Pelayo turned back to Chris and I and bent down, talking low, a weird look on his face. "Look, if we turn around now, if we don't beach up and go up to the campsite, Ratso's gonna really get suspicious."

He had a point. He was far from losing his cool. Heck, he was thinking more clearly than Chris and me. We nodded. Chris arched his eyebrows and let out a low whistle as we prepared to disembark. The fat was in the fire. We'd crossed the Rubicon.

Then Officer Rizzo hit us with the beam again. Pelayo cursed, banged the console, and I saw his jaw muscles bunch. He had turned toward the bank when I grabbed his arm. He nodded in resignation and turned around. "Okay, okay."

We were idling to the corner of the island, and I could almost see inside Pelayo's head, maybe because I was thinking the same thing: "Gun it! Stomp it, and flee from this prick, like in our glorious kick-ass youth. But Pelayo was right.

Rizzo would call in reinforcements, and they'd chase us down, sooner if not later. They had speedboats, airboats, and helicopters. We'd be run down like rabid animals. "We got you surrounded! Resistance is stupid. Lay down your weapons and come out with your hands up! There will be no reprisals against your families. We promise!" We'd still try to make a run for it, and they'd break out the pepper spray, billy sticks, stun guns, and finally handcuffs—you never know with this guy.

All these things ran through my head as we rounded the corner of the island and beached the boat at the normal beaching spot, where Senior Agent Nicholas Rizzo, LDWF, considerately took our bow rope and made it fast to a willow. "How you fellows doin'?" he croaked.

Rizzo looked primed for action, swaggering with every step, .45 on his hip. Let this guy wash, shave, deck himself out in a clean creased uniform, and he still turns your stomach. There's something mangy about him that no amount of washing or cosmetics could mask.

Paul came up with the perfect moniker on our last hunt. Rizzo was hassling us about our boat-registration tag. It was "peeling," or "hard to read, maybe expired," some such bullshit. Our chum Glenn, who was on his first duck hunt, hadn't signed his duck stamp, either. Naturally, Rizzo wrote him up with a dramatic lecture and much fanfare.

"Ratso," Paul said as he finally pulled away in his skiff. "Ratso

Rizzo. Saw *Midnight Cowboy* on the AMC channel last week. That's him to a tee."

The name stuck. Though compared to him, Dustin Hoffman's character in *Midnight Cowboy* came across like Cary Grant or James Bond. When we'd first met Rizzo over ten years ago, Pelayo dubbed him Eraserhead. That day he was hassling us about keeping tabs on "who actually shot each duck in the pirogue," or some such bullshit—as if three people hunting together and shooting jointly into flocks of ducks can keep track of who's hitting what. We simply shot until we had a three-man limit, like I suspect most hunters do.

What a prick. Anyway, he took off his cap after counting our ducks, and damned if his head didn't look like a shoebox on end. We figured his cap had molded his hair, a classic case of hat-hair. He ran his filthy hand through his hair, and it got worse. Now it looked like an up-ended cinder block. The more we looked at it, even after he tried to smooth it down with his hand, the more we saw that it was his head, as much as his hair. Eraserhead was good. Ratso was better. To me, he always looked more like Mr. Roper on *Three's Company*, but Ratso it was.

The real Ratso Rizzo, disgusting as he was, had a certain perverse charm, if you recall. Now and then during the *Dukes of Hazzard*, you also felt for Boss Hogg. In *Taxi*, Danny DeVito's rascality occasionally waned for a few seconds and revealed a speck of humanity.

There was nothing like that with Senior Agent Nicholas Rizzo; just his weasel face, his chipped and blackened teeth ("I caught a sheepshead with better looking teeth," as Pelayo always said), and his spastic walk (from a hunting accident in his youth, they say). Hell, you usually feel sorry for a guy who limps. Not Rizzo. He managed to make it annoying. His very voice grated on your nerves; half croak and half whine, it had a nasal quality that made you want to strangle him, if only to shut him up. His eyes seemed always bloodshot, and his breath was chronically foul. He was a classic case of a little dipshit nobody liked, who finally found himself—by virtue of that little badge—in a position to talk down to people, to hassle them, to get back at society. Anyone who's lived in a communist country knows the type, and Rizzo was milking his position to the last drop. Lately, airport security seems to be attracting most of these types. And that's fine with those of us who hunt more than we fly.

Rizzo concentrated on hassling us weekenders from the city. He left the locals, the real outlaws, unmolested. Hell, they were all his buddies.

Pelayo and Chris grabbed the beer ice chest from the boat and started sloshing up to the tents, trying to ignore Rizzo, who moved aside courteously as they huffed by. I grabbed my gun case and got out onto the squishy mud, jerking the boat up another few feet with my spare hand.

"Just talked to your buddies down on Loomis Pass," Rizzo croaked as we walked past. "They been duck hunting. Say they'd lost a contact lens or something."

Pelayo and Chris dropped the ice chest and turned around. I flinched and grimaced but kept walking. My back was to Rizzo, so I rolled my eyes and bared my teeth heavily at Chris and Pelayo, who tried to look calm as I trudged by on the way to my pup tent. Their eyes gave them away.

"Well, that's it," we all thought. Paul and Tom are handcuffed at LDWF camp, maybe gagged and blindfolded, too. They might have the electrodes already attached to their balls.

The American alligator is still classified as a "threatened" species by the U.S. Fish and Wildlife Service, and onerous fines and penalties protect him. Rizzo would strut for a month if he busted us with one. I felt horrible. Tom and I had been the most adamant about keeping the damn thing. Pelayo wanted no part of it. Paul wanted to chop off the tail and be done with it. We could've wrapped it in foil and hid it with the food in the ice chest.

Tom insisted on keeping the whole thing. We'd grown quite fond of alligator meat. The legs and back had some luscious meat, too. I hated to see it go to waste. Now Paul or Tom or both were paying the heavy price.

Tom had grown quite fond of alligator meat himself. The first one he tasted was from a golf course pond. They get big, fat, and tasty in those. They have plenty to eat and little to fear, until that afternoon barbeque at our neighbor Spencer's.

CHAPTER TEN

AMBUSH BY AGENT RATSO

We were all taking it easy that afternoon, with mellow tunes on the boom box—Cat Stevens, James Taylor. Our friend Artie cranked it up a bit with some early Dylan. Pelayo was reading the paper in a hammock when he erupted in cackles. He'd just turned to some AP story about alligator problems in Florida. "Listen up, gang!" Pelayo roared. "This is in Florida, now. I quote: The drought is affecting alligator behavior. They're starting to prowl and are showing up in swimming pools, golf course ponds, and suburban canals. This has generated lots of calls to the Florida authorities about nuisance gators, which are usually relocated. Actually, alligators have no interest in contact with humans." The article naturally quoted an alligator "expert" from some university.

Turns out, my neighbor Artie was an alligator "expert," too, and not just on where to aim to cold-cock them with a twelve-gauge slug. His expertise extended much further, past the skinning process, all the way to the proper seasoning and cooking time. Escoffier, the grand old man of French cuisine, called fish "the most inexhaustible source of culinary inspiration." Artie might quibble with that.

"This Florida alligator 'expert' also informs us," Pelayo continued with a chuckle, "that crowding has severe *social* and *physiological* impact on alligators." Pelayo stressed the words while affecting a facial expression of extreme sympathy, like you might see on Oprah when she's interviewing an abused woman.

Aww. We sure hate to see that kind of thing here in Louisiana. We agree wholeheartedly with the good professor. The thought of poor alligators suffering "socially," and even worse, "physiologically," troubles us greatly. Our troubled consciences propel us to action rather than to vapid pontifications, from the sofa all the way to the gun rack for a remedy.

Spencer McKee, our host that evening, had recently moved to suburban New Orleans. His wife Megan's precious poodle, Princess, had disappeared near a golf course pond the week before.

Pelayo had just finished reading, and we were all laughing when a hysterical Megan and Shirley came running back down the trail. A few minutes earlier they'd embarked on a stroll through the green space by the golf course. "There's a huge alligator by the pond!" Shirley gasped. "He's on the bank!"

"Oh, Spencer!" Megan wailed. "Should we call the proper authorities and have him relocated?! Maybe it's the one who grabbed Princess!"

Artie and Pelayo sprung into action as one. They were a blur. "I got a shotgun in the trunk!" Artie howled over his shoulder while springing from the deck. "Slugs, too!" he said, while racing toward his car with a whoop.

"Spence!" Pelayo seized Spencer by the shoulders and screamed into his face. "The poor beast is probably suffering severe social and physiological impact! Where's your ax? And a rope!"

Artie was back in seconds, shoving shells into his shotgun as he leapt and galloped toward the action, followed by the rest of the guests. "No!" Pelayo shouted over his shoulder. "Y'all stay here, you sadists! Poor thing is physiologically impacted enough already! He doesn't need gawkers!" Artie was whooping with glee. He sounded like Slim Pickens riding that bomb at the end of *Dr. Strangelove*. It was over in minutes, and at no cost to taxpayers.

In Florida, they call authorities to relocate them. We "relocate" them, too.

BLAM! First, Artie relocates their brain with a well-placed slug. Then we relocate the carcass to the barbeque pit. In Florida, they call them nuisances. In Louisiana, we call them delicious. Tom tasted his first gator that night. So like I said, he backed me on keeping the one we blasted by the decoys. Now he might regret that decision—we all might.

We didn't want to hear what came next from Rizzo. It was bound to be bad news. He was getting ready to drop the other shoe on us. We could tell. So we said nothing in reply as he stood there with his shit-eating grin. The prick was hanging around for some reason. Pelayo and Chris dragged the ice chest by the tents and grabbed beers, then Chris lit his propane lantern and turned on the radio while Pelayo started pumping up his ancient Coleman lantern. I wanted a clean shirt from my duffel bag so I grabbed my tent zipper and noticed it was half open. I distinctly remembered zipping it closed that—morning, very important to keep out gnats and mosquitoes. Rizzo must have been rummaging around, the nosy prick.

I felt the bile rise. I wanted to scream something at him. "Hope you have a search warrant!" Or maybe "Did you find my weed?" Hell, what I really wanted was to bash in his ugly face.

I looked over at him briefly as I emerged from the tent. Rizzo looked over for a second and his eyes narrowed, but he said nothing.

He just stared with those dim eyes and half open mouth of his, like Mr. Roper. He knew that I knew that he'd been in my tent.

Then he walked over by Pelayo and pointed a finger at his chest, "I heard some shots this afternoon after legal sunset, Mr. Plywood," he croaked.

"The name's PE-LA-YO, Okay?" Pelayo said calmly.

Ratso ignored him. "Those shots sounded like they came right from where y'all were hunting," he said while looking around to the rest of us. Pelayo sighed heavily and shrugged, but said nothing. The bastard liked to literally get in your face, but he never made direct eye contact. Look him resolutely in the face, as Pelayo just did, and he always shifted his eyes. He was doing it now.

"We heard 'em too," Chris blurted. He snapped open a Bud and turned to fiddle with the radio. "Those were the guys hunting below Dennis Pass, the local boys from Boothville. I think we saw you checking them yesterday. Remember?"

Rizzo snapped his head towards Chris, mumbled something, and shifted his gaze again. Chris was making me nervous. "Shut up," I'm thinking to myself. Those were his local buddies from Boothville, all right. We all knew that. They had an illegal gill net in their boat, plain as day, and what looked like some deer legs poking from the stern. We saw them pulled over, talking with Rizzo yesterday, and it sure didn't look like a bust. They were chumming it up. They'd even waved at us as we slowed down to pass by. Calling Rizzo on it would get us nowhere; this backtalk just dug us in deeper.

Again, Rizzo knew we had his number, and he was groping for a rebuttal, but this could take hours. You could almost hear the tiny corroded wheels grinding and slipping inside that Eraserhead.

Pelayo finally turned away from the accusatory finger and started fiddling with his lantern. Thank God; I was getting worried. Pelayo's jaw muscles were bunching, he was tense, biting his tongue, as desperate to lash out at Rizzo as I was, as desperate to smash his face, crack his teeth, and dent his forehead.

Call it wisdom. Perhaps call it circumspection. Whatever. Age does that to you. But a part of me preferred our reaction to this type of shit when we were younger. Problem was, it always landed us in jail—New Orleans central lock-up twice for me, with Metairie and Baton Rouge lock-ups adding a little variety. I'd never stolen anything, damaged property, much less injured anyone. Not even a DWI. It was always my *mouth*. When you're that age, it's hard to sit still for the type of crap so many cops dish out. Worse, we had friends who were cops, and they confirmed how arbitrary their enforcement was.

Take our arrest for public obscenity after the LSU-Alabama game. To hear the charges, you'd a thought we mimicked Jim Morrison, Lance Rentzel, or even Pee Wee Herman. Instead, six of us had crammed into the Midnight Rider, took the top off, cranked up the radio, and went cruising around the campus waving LSU flags and bellowing along with whatever tune came on. Parliament came on:

Tear the roof off, we're gonna tear the roof off the mother, sucker! Tear the roof off the sucker!

Vanessa and Gina were standing on the back seat doing a mean bump as we all sang along. Spectators cheered from the sidewalks and balconies, from the windows of every frat and sorority house. We were having a good old time.

So here come the flashing lights. So here's a blast from the siren. The beers get crammed under the seats, and soon we're on the curb stuttering helplessly to the gracious public servants. A minute later, two of us have our heads slammed on the hood and sport handcuffs.

Now, was it *our* fault that these stupid cops didn't know their music? Why should we spend the night in a piss-ridden cell surrounded by vicious thugs who kept asking us for money and cigarettes because the cops didn't keep up with popular music? Why should reeking winos with blood crusted to their heads moan at us all night because some Barney Fife wannabes didn't know the words to the famous hit by Parliament?

"It's mother *sucker!*" Perry tried patiently to explain. "We weren't cursing!"

It's tear the roof off the *sucker*," I said calmly and respectfully, to no avail.

Some bystanders later claimed that we weren't really all that "patient" or "respectful." In fact, they almost got arrested themselves for laughing at what we said. Whatever. Vanessa's dad, a lawyer, paid the bail and got us out next morning.

After Chris's retort about his buddies being the late shooters, Rizzo's eyes started twitching. He folded his arms and leaned back against a willow, trying to look cool, even started rubbing his chin. He had no comeback. Those had indeed been his local buddies, and they'd been poaching fish. They'd probably bull-eyed a deer too. He knew we knew. He knew damn well it was them shooting after hours this evening, too. The sorry prick had to change the subject.

Here's the perfect point for Rizzo to drop the other shoe, I thought to myself, and braced psychologically for the horrible announcement: the big bust on Paul and Tom. The poor suckers are going upriver in handcuffs even now. They looked down the barrel of some heavy federal raps, probably lucky to get off without time.

We were tense. We hadn't followed up on his crack about seeing them. I didn't want to hear it. Poor Tom, with a federal rap sheet now, I thought. I'll offer to help with the fine, but he'll never agree. He'll lose hunting and fishing privileges for years now. *That's* the part that will kill him. I felt like crap. The vision rattled me deeply. It was too horrible. Pelayo and Chris were trying to smile, too, chugging on Buds and trying to look cool and loose, but their eyes gave them away, even as Pelayo fiddled with his lantern.

You could hear the lantern hissing from twenty feet away as he pumped away at the little handle. Finally he held up his lighter, poked it under the glass and flicked it—WHOOOOM!

Rizzo jumped back about twenty feet, "Hey, man!" he yelled while he staggered sideways and shielding his face. "Ya crazy or something?" Chris and Pelayo cackled. I was almost on the ground.

"Who's having all the fun?" Suddenly a voice boomed from

behind us. "Yeah, what's so dammed funny? We missin' somethin'?"

What the? It was On-the-Ball's voice! We turned around and sure enough. There they were. He and Tom were motoring into our raggedy campsite in Chris's Whaler, but from the front, the normal way down the main bayou. They hadn't taken advantage of the high tide to come in the back way. The racket from our radio must have hid the motor noise as they approached. Chris had cranked it up when "The Boys Are Back in Town" came on.

The three-chord classic by Thin Lizzy became our theme song in the spring of '77. The football games were over and these "boys" would come "back in town" to New Orleans from LSU every weekend. Every chord blasted us all back to some outrageous times. Every lyric seemed to hit the spot.

"*Friday night they'll be dressed to kill.*" Chris in his magenta bell bottoms, billowing magnificently under the strobe light, scattering the white smoke as he spun like a top on shoes that could double as stilts. Pelayo in his candy-apple metal flake shirt, collars flapping like giant wings as he jerked his arms maniacally, index finger pointing skyward à la Tony Manero. And me in my tangerine angel flights, the matching medallion bouncing wildly on my bare, sweat-damp chest, made enticing by unbuttoning my lime-green shirt well past the sternum.

When the boys "came back in town," we slayed them without mercy. When left again on Sunday—often from their beds—they clawed longingly at our bare midriffs, and pleaded, "Don't leave me this way . . . I can't survive!"

We wouldn't even look around. "Where's breakfast?" we'd snap on the way to the bathroom.

We always pranced in elegantly late, near midnight. They'd been sipping on amaretto sours and White Russians for a couple hours by then. Our task was made all the easier, almost unsportingly so. They looked over with furtive eyes. They smiled and pointed, nudging each other on the elbow and perhaps whispering wickedly in each other's ears. Perhaps we'd acknowledge them with a nod, but nothing too blatant. First to the bar, then leaning backward against it, bent knee, hand through the hair now and a hearty gulp.

Give them a profile shot now. Hard to believe, but sucking in the gut wasn't part of it then.

Finally, we moved in. They cooed and giggled at out approach. The lucky one covered her mouth and rolled her eyes dreamily, like a winner on *Family Feud,* as we extended our hands and nodded toward the dance floor. Casanova didn't waste words when a gesture would serve, nor did we.

They formed circles, smiling and clapping as we gyrated madly on the flashing floor. Then nature took over. Instinct took over. Their libidos were unleashed. Watching the feverish thrusts of our polyester-constricted pelvises was more than they could stand.

Shake-shake-shake . . . shake your booty.

You got that right, KC. By now, they'd be squealing and clapping madly, jerking in time to the throbbing bass notes. Their eyebrows danced suggestively. Their lips pursed passionately. Their eyes closed dreamily. Often, their faces flushed. They were helpless.

If you want my body, and you think I'm sexy, come on, sugar, let me know.

Rod Stewart's classic then took over.

Even crazier, we actually frequented a disco named Dino's. "Down at Dino's Bar and Grill." It actually had a grill next door, with colossal hamburgers that really hit the spot around dawn.

Anyway, twenty years later, the effect of "The Boys Are Back in Town" was damn near magical. Paul's boat was clearing the stand of willows and coming into full view of us. He was boogying and whooping, "Yeah, man!" He heard the song clearly. They had a lantern lit on the bow. Tom was at the wheel, and Paul stood on the bow, smiling. He held something in each hand and started chiming in on the song: "The drink will flow," and he held up his Bud, "and blood will spill!"He help up a pintail with the other. "Now that the boys are here again!" A little bayou karaoke.

We all whooped a greeting, except for Ratso, who was actually hidden from their view by a tent. Paul's timing with the beer and duck was perfect. He probably heard the song as they came up the bayou and set up the little act. That was the craziest part. They seemed pumped. They'd obviously been into the beer stash, probably found the contact lens, too.

Chris, Pelayo, and I all looked at each other with huge grins and wide eyes. There was no way they'd been busted by Rizzo. That kind of thing kills a buzz *instantly*, same as that flashing red light in the rearview. They sure as hell wouldn't be acting this way. Paul put down his beer and duck props and slashed away at his air-guitar with the last few power chords as the song faded. These were, quite literally, some happy campers.

They beached the boat right next to ours, and Paul hopped out. "Shoulda seen that stupid sonofabitch!" Paul was doubled over laughing as he climbed over the bow and jumped on the muddy bank. "That asshole Ratso pulls up flashing his little badge, and I'm sitting on the *very* ice chest with the alligator in it!" he roared. Then Paul started mimicking Rizzo's face, dim eyes and mouth half open. Then he started on Rizzo's bogalee accent: "All right fellas, let's . . . ." again he couldn't finish for laughing. He doubled over again in hysterics. "That Ratso's some kinda dense," he hooted.

The three of us bolted for Paul as one. Paul still hadn't seen Rizzo, who was hidden from his view by a tent, or his boat, which was around the *back* of the island. Fortunately, Rizzo had no idea we called him Ratso, so Paul's ravings didn't click, at least not yet.

Tom was cackling, too, as he climbed out of the boat. "I like to die when Ratso pulls up," he laughed. "And I see the alligator tail stickin' out the side of our ice chest, whoa-boy! And the extra teal was in my hip boot!" Tom was helpless with laughter. "I lunged over just in time to cover it! And *Eraserhead?*" he gasped. "Paul says y'all use to call that guy Eraserhead?"

Chris reached Tom and almost tackled him just as Pelayo grabbed Paul by the elbow and pressed his face an inch from his brother's nose. *"He's here!"* Pelayo hissed, grimacing violently and splattering Paul with beer-flavored spittle. Chris was nodding violently in front of Tom's face and jabbing his thumb into his own chest, pointing behind him, back toward the tents. His other hand grabbed Tom's arm like the jaws of a pit bull.

Paul flinched and tensed up, hunching his shoulders and looking around with a wide-eyed grimace. Tom looked over, bug-eyed. I looked over at both, nodding sharply, almost spraining my neck in the process. Finally Tom gaped and nodded slowly. Paul unhunched his shoulders and let out a low whistle.

"Ho–ly Sh–it!" Paul mouthed each syllable silently. He let out another low whistle and made some heavy eye and chin signals at Tom, who got the same forceful, but low volume, news from Chris, who was still cutting off the circulation in his arm. We made our point—Paul and Tom caught on quick.

"What's all the fun over here?" Rizzo finally stepped over. "Can I get in on the joke?"

"Just laughing at how Pelayo toppled in the water this morning" Paul said coolly. He was fully composed now. "He fell in from the bow of the boat," he pointed behind him. "And right next to an alligator, shoulda seen him come out the water. Jumped out almost like a mullet."

"Right." Rizzo smiled feebly and nodded. "Been seeing plenty gators out myself. Plenty big ones. Well, I checked y'all earlier. So I'll be goin' on back. Just wanted to see if y'all had shot any deer. Remember," he looked over seriously now, "you gotta check any deer in at the main camp the day you shoot them. Y'all forgot that last time."

"Right. Thanks for reminding us." I nodded. "But we just hunted duck today. Might get in a little deer hunting tomorrow. We'll be sure to check in any we get, don't worry. Take care now."

Rizzo had just motored off when I remembered: "My shell bucket! I left it on the bank where we parked for the duck hunt!"

"We'll get it tomorrow," Pelayo shrugged. "No big deal."

"We'll get it now!" I said while walking to the boat. "My wallet's in it. Come on."

"We can take my boat," Chris said while grabbing the Bacardi. "I've got plenty gas, more than y'all."

We motored back after finding my shell bucket exactly where I'd left it. We'd also stopped on the way back to the headquarters to "ooh" and "aahh" a couple of deer that were being checked in. We hadn't been gone an hour but now noticed we had new campsite neighbors on our little island. Tom and On-the-Ball sat around the campfire, but looked grim.

After tying up the boat and walking up, we learned they'd just walked back from a (very) brief visit to our new neighbors. Even On-the-Ball seemed shaken. "I don't know what's meaner or uglier," he said as we walked up. "Those hogs, those dogs, or those hunters." Tom nodded unsmiling assent.

"What a buncha pansies!" Pelayo snapped as he looked around. "What the hell's wrong with y'all?"

"Okay, Mr. Rambo." Paul pointed behind him. "Go see our new neighbors for yourself." He reached behind him for the beer Pelayo hoisted.

"I will," Pelayo rasped. "Saw they had some hog's legs poking out from the back of their boat. "I'd like to check it out."

"That one's alive," Tom laughed. "They *caught* the doggone thing! Chased it down with the dogs. You oughta *see* those dogs! I mean, I *never* . . ."

"Say they're part pit bull," Paul added. "For the killer instinct and the killer jaws. Part Doberman, for the size and a little more bloodlust."

"And part Catahoula for the nose, to track the hogs," Tom blurted. "Thank *God* they're in cages. The hog's all tied up. One of them says he tackled it while the dogs held him by the snout, and, well, hog-tied him. They say they're gonna release him 'by home.' Huge tusks on the sucker. He's a boar . . . about how big did the guy say?" He turned to Paul.

"Three hundred pounds," Paul answered. "That's what they estimate. I believe it, too. Damn thing's *huge*. Shoulders on him like a freakin' bull. Jet black, just like one, too."

"Well, let's go have a look." Pelayo looked over at Chris and I, and started rummaging in the cooler for another beer. "Still got plenty of duck gumbo here," Pelayo said, pointing to the black pot over the coals. "See you added the duck and everything, huh, On-the-Ball?"

"Sure did," Paul said as he came up with a dripping beer. "Threw in five grays and that bonus teal."

"Well then," Pelayo quipped. "Let's invite the new neighbors over, offer them some."

"Right!" Paul snapped. "Good neighbor policy and all that. Why not? Y'all go over there now. I'm sure they'll take you up on the offer. You'll see."

CHAPTER ELEVEN

MONGO AND GOOBER, OUR NEIGHBORS FROM HELL

"Wonder what the hell's eatin' them?" Chris asked, as we walked the one hundred yards or so down the muddy trail to the neighbor's campsite.

"Haven't had enough beers yet," Pelayo said.

Our new neighbors had three tents set up, two lanterns hanging from trees, and a roaring fire, but only one guy seemed to be around. "Looks like a nice hog y'all got in the boat," Pelayo beamed as he extended his hand to a big dude in muddy jeans, leaning on a willow by the fire. "I'm Pelayo. We're camped next door." He pointed behind him.

The guy extended something that looked more like a claw than a hand. I shook something that felt like hardened leather or sandpaper. I looked down and saw he was missing two fingers. The guy nodded feebly as we made the introductions, always staring into the fire. I noticed a tattoo ran from his exposed shoulder almost to his elbow. I stepped back a few feet and tried to look at it discreetly.

It was a hog's face, the same you see on that "Hog's Breath Saloon" emblem, but with exaggerated features, meaner eyes and snarl, bigger tusks, and a spiked collar like you see on cartoon bulldogs. The guy reminded me of somebody, some personality, but I couldn't place it.

I was standing there, deciding whether to compliment him on the tattoo, when Pelayo grabbed my shoulder and pointed with his chin, "Check 'em out."

"Wow," I nodded. From here we could see a meat pole set up between two willows behind a tent. Two hogs hung from it.

"Not bad!" Chris said as we walked over. "Where'd y'all get these?" No answer. Walking over, I noticed the dog cages. You couldn't see inside of them, and no sound came out, even as we walked by. No barks. No growls. Nothing menacing. I thought of Ernest Hemingway from *Death in the Afternoon*. "An animal bluffs in order to avoid combat," he wrote in that classic. These dogs *relished* combat, lived for it. So it made sense. They were mum.

The hanging pigs looked like pure Russian strain, long mean snout with tusks, huge shoulders, and silver-tipped hairs. "Nice," Pelayo said with pursed lips while nodding back at the guy. "They look like Russian boars. Y'all shot 'em with a bow? Shotgun? What?"

"Sheeeeee-iiiit," came a voice from behind. We turned and saw another guy sitting on an ice chest, next to the dog cages. He wore a camo cap backwards and his massive belly poked out from under a mud-smeared T-shirt. He'd been blocked from our view by the tent. He reached down beside him and lifted something. It was dark now and hard to make it out in the shadows. Then he lifted it higher and the campfire flames reflected from it.

It was a long, shiny bayonet. The guy held it up and turned it slowly in his hand while squinting over at us. "Come on," Pelayo laughed as he nudged Chris and me. "You serious? You killed these things with *that?*"

The guy looked back at his friend and smiled while nodding his chin at us, but it wasn't what you'd call a friendly smile. More of a leer. "How you like that, Jake?" he drawled. Suddenly he was on his feet, but wobbly. "They don't believe us. They think we're *liars.* They cain't believe you can kill a hog with—" his lips suddenly tightened—"*this!*" And *whack!* He jabbed the thing into the willow next to him.

"No, man," Pelayo said with a quick smile "Actually, I've heard of catching hogs, you know, with dogs and—"

"Sure, he killed it!" blurted Chris. I looked at him puzzled. He had a crazy grin. "He stabbed it with his steely knife, and he *did* kill the beast! Ha-ha!"

Pelayo chuckled. I forced a laugh. But remember Otis Day in *Animal House?* Remember his face after Boon entered the nightclub, waved, and shouted the classic: "My man Otis!"

Well, imagine a white face ten times as mean and with Otis's expression. The bayonet-man held the look for what seemed like a long time, probably five seconds. No, he didn't strike me as an Eagles fan. *Hotel California* was probably not in his CD collection. "What's that name ag-*gayne?*" Finally, he said something. He was cocking his head and looking directly at us.

"I'm Pe-la-yo," prof said with another quick smile.

"I'm Chris," Magilla (Chris's nickname from grammar school) said with a wave.

"And I'm Hum-ber-to."

"Pe-*who?* AHAAh-AHAA!" He looked over at his friend again, laughing, but again, not what you'd call a congenial laugh. The guy got a big kick out of the name. He took two wobbly steps toward us and it looked like something was wrong with his head. Maybe it was a shadow? He took another and stopped next to his hissing lantern. Nope, no shadow. Chris noticed too, and poked my ribs to notify.

The guy had a forehead like Conway Twitty, high with the same facial features, but one eye looked half closed and lower than the other. His nose had an exaggerated Meryl Streepish angle to it. And his forehead—well, it was obvious now in the light—was *concave*.

"Pe-*who?*" he yelled again while ripping off his cap and throwing his head back to laugh. He had the little widows peak like Conway, too, but with a big, dumb jaw and an underbite. "You say your name's Plywood, son? Or Plato? Pe-*who?* AHA–AHHH–HA!" He roared with mirth and kept repeating it, like he loved the sound. "And you there," he turned to me. "You Humperdinck? Horatio? Humdago? AHHA—AHAAA! What the hell you?" Finally, he stopped and leaned against the bayoneted tree, squinting again. "Where'n HAY-EL did y'all gets ya a name like THAY-AT?"

"He's a coonass!" yelled his partner, who had gone from leaning on that willow to sitting on an ice chest. Now he shot to his feet and immediately started wobbling, trying to focus on Pelayo. "That boy's a coonass!" He raised a hand gripping a Jack Daniel's bottle and pointed toward Pelayo, spilling a generous portion all over his boots. "Cayn't ya tell?" he wheezed. "He looks just like one!" His cheek distended grotesquely as he spoke, and I assumed he'd been wounded in a hog-battle like his chum, Conway. We hadn't seen that side of him as he leaned against the tree. Jesus, I thought. We're surrounded by mutants, like in *Total Recall*.

Suddenly, the guy looked down and spat out a huge wad of spit-drenched tobacco. His cheek collapsed. Ah.

"Mongo," I suddenly blurted. It came out on reflex, low volume. Chris kicked me, nodding, trying to suppress a laugh. That was it. He noticed, too. I finally remembered who the guy looked like: the "Mongo" character in *Blazing Saddles*, played by Alex Karras. The brute that punched out the horse. Who can forget Gene Wilder's classic line about him: "No, don't shoot him. That'll only make him mad." That certainly applied here. Didn't seem like they heard me, though.

Suddenly, Mongo started moved toward us, stumbling, gripping his bottle of blackjack with one hand and pointing at Pelayo with the other. His head was cocked sideways, and he was squinting. "You a coonass, son? Huh?" He was unsteady. Not weaving but wobbling, walking pigeon-toed in mud-caked, whiskey-splattered cowboy boots. "I asked ya a question, son!" His freckled face was bright pink and his eyes glassy. "Did ya hear me? Ya got shit in yer ears?"

Pelayo stood his ground and turned resolutely to face the lummox, no longer smiling. His face had hardened and looked like he was making a fist. I looked over at the bayonet-man, thinking he might restrain his chum, or offer a clue to what was going on. I can never tell when these people are serious or joking. The other guy offered no help; he was silent, looking on with a dim smile while bobbing his head slightly. He reminded me of the toothless one, holding his shotgun and chuckling while watching his chum in action during the famous *Deliverance* love scene. "Looks like a little hog, don't he? Come on boy, SQUEAL! WHEEEEEEE! WHEEEEEE!" But he looked nothing like him, much bigger.

Mongo finally stopped about ten feet in front of Pelayo and right next to the fire. We could see him clearly now, in all his magnificence. He was a big freckled ox, with a half-buttoned lumberjack shirt with the sleeves ripped off, the better to display that tattoo. What I thought was dirt on his neck turned out to be another tattoo, the spiked collar you see on those cartoon bull-dogs, around his own neck. His filthy blue jeans rode below a massive belly and exposed his ass-crack à la Dan Akroyd in refrigerator repairman mode.

The guy looked cross-eyed, but it was hard to tell with his pig-like face and the way he always squinted. He looked around with his head weaving, pivoting his neck, and stretching it like it might be sore, probably from lugging 350-pound hogs around on his shoulders all day. Looked like he had dried blood all over his shirt, but it might have been whiskey, or chili, or mud. Who knows? He turned and spat again, into the fire this time, then grimaced, like he was stretching his jaw muscles, exposing his tobacco-blackened teeth, all six of them. He looked back at Pelayo and squinted sharply. He was trying to smile, but his face wasn't working right. He leaned forward to where I thought he'd trip into the fire and gently hissed, "You a coonass?"

Pelayo resumed his tense smile. "No," he said. "Not really. We're . . . ."

"Hah! Yeah! I knew it!" Mongo leaned his head back, hoisted the the bottle, and chugged deeply. You could see his Adam's apple moving. He brought the bottle back down without even grimacing. I couldn't believe it. Looked like straight Jack Daniels, too.

He took another step toward Pelayo and roared, "Damn Right! I knew it! Dem coonasses . . . dem Cajuns gots all kinda crazy names!" Then he almost tripped over a log. He caught one of the tent cords on the way down and pulled it down with him. "Aw shee-it," he wheezed, while struggling on the ground like an upended turtle, the tent cord tangled around his arm. "I used to work oilfield," he blurted. "I knew me a bunch of dem coonasses!" he grunted at "bunch" and finally righted himself. Now he was leaning on his elbow and knees, about five feet from the campfire. His head swayed as he looked from the fire to us. For a second, it seemed the tension had eased. Heck, he knew a bunch of Cajuns? Maybe he had friends among them?

"*Bums*, most of 'em!" he snarled. Chris flinched. Pelayo's wife was born on Bayou Lafourche. Chris's own mom is from Lafayette. Here we go, I thought. Batten down the hatches. So much for the tension easing.

"Nothing but cheatin', lying BUMS!" he yelled. "Ever damn one of 'em! Aaagh." The lummox was trying to stand, but he toppled over headfirst this time, and his hand landed in the coals. He didn't jerk it out; it was so hardened and calloused he probably couldn't feel it.

Finally, "Aaghh! Aghh!"—he jerked it out and started rubbing it on his jeans. Now he was on his feet again, and we all stepped back a bit. His friend started laughing from behind us. "I tried to play that, whatcha call it?" The guy was still rubbing his soot-streaked claw-hand. "That card game. That card game dem coonasses . . . ?"

"Booray," Pelayo said while looking straight at him. He said it sharp and loud. The beer can he held was half-crushed from the pressure. Pelayo's other hand was balled now, the veins poked out, like the veins on his neck.

"BOORAY!" roared Mongo, exposing his hideous teeth again with the "ray" syllable. "Yeah, that's it! That goddamn Booray. HAYLE! They changed the damn rules after ever hand! Lost me a bundle! Had to open me up a can a whup-ass on one a dem boys . . . Booray! Booray!" Suddenly, he started stumbling in a circle, hoisting his blackjack and singed claw-hand in a touchdown signal, yelling "Booray, Booray!" He loved the sound of that, too. Good, I thought. At least it distracts him from our names.

"Actually, we're *not* Cajuns," Pelayo said, still looking squarely at the guy. No hint of a stutter either. If Pelayo was scared, he didn't show it. Myself, I could feel that icy clutch in the stomach. Last thing I wanted was a massive rumble with these brutes. Sure, in their condition we could probably stomp them into a coma in no time. Hell, they were halfway there. But in that condition and with that bayonet around and God knows what other weapons, the rumble might proceed well past the punching and stomping stage. I was in no mood for bayonet-swallowing or getting my teeth shattered by a dog-chain. They might even sick those dogs on us. I'd rather be in the Roman Colosseum with the lions. So no, I wanted to extricate ourselves, dammit. On-the-Ball had been right; why didn't we listen to him? And they'd probably been less drunk when he and Tom came over earlier. Some vacation: the gangstas on the freeway before we even leave the city. The lunatics on the dock. Now this.

"We're Cuban," Pelayo said. "Like from . . . ."

"Cubans!" The guy yelled from behind us. I turned around and he was holding the bayonet again, slapping it on his thigh. "Then why ain't you in Cuba? Huh?" You some kinda spy or sumthin, huh? Some kinda communist? Tell ya what. I cain't pronounce y'all's name so let's just say I'll call you Julio? You like that? Julio? Or maybe Fidel?"

"Call us whatever the *fuck* you want!" Chris suddenly bellowed from next to me. Holy shit, I thought, and tensed up, looking around. Chris and I've been close friends for thirty-five years, and I've heard that tone of voice from him once, maybe twice. It scared me. "And we'll call you—" Chris looked and pointed straight at the ox—"Mongo!" He turned around. His jaw muscles were quivering spastically, "And we'll call *you*," he lowered his chin, aimed his eyes straight at him, and pointed a rigid finger, "Goober! How's *that?*"

Mother of God, I thought. Action time. Here comes a banzai bayonet charge. I braced my legs, ready either to bolt or to kick the closest one in the balls as he charged. Chris was right, though. The guy was a fun-house mirror-version of that timeless Andy Griffith character. Same features, but all warped and out of shape.

"AHHHaa—AHHHaaaa!" Goober started cackling like a loon. No sign of a charge. "Heard that, Jake? Ya heard the boy? Goober! AHAAA—AHHHAA!" Another sound came through, outboards. We jerked around, and two boats were pulling up right in front, not fifty feet away. They shined a Q-beam on us for a second then started clambering out. "Jake! Ronnie! Come give us a hand," somebody yelled.

A tall guy in a camo jumpsuit was on us in an instant. He looked at Goober and motioned back with his thumb and head. "Go on! Go help unload!" Goober nodded meekly and started stumbling over. Mongo was trying to get on his feet but stumbled over headfirst again. The new guy nodded disgustedly, walked over, and grabbed him by the belt. He grimaced while hoisting him. "Get yer ass in that tent." He shoved him through the flap of the nearest one "Go to sleep. You're done for tonight, ya hear me? Done for!" He loped over to us just as two other guys walked over from the boats carrying ice chests. He extended a hand. "I'm Jesse. Y'all must be camping over there."

"Yeah, that's us," Chris said in a much more familiar tone of voice as he shook the guy's hand. Then the other two walked up. Pete and Mark, we learned while shaking hands. "Man, that's some nice hogs y'all got." Chris pointed at the meat-pole, his jaw relaxed now. "We came over to check 'em out." He frowned. "Your friend says he killed them with a bayonet, though?"

"Sure did," Jesse chuckled. "He sure did. I don't know what else he told you tonight. I can only imagine," he nodded and rolled his eyes. "But that part's true."

"Incredible." Pelayo smiled and nodded at the guy.

We spent the rest of the evening with the crew, even with Goober, whose real name was Ronnie, and who was silent for the rest of the night. Mongo never re-emerged. They were from Mississippi, and Hollywood scriptwriters Howard Stern and Paul Begala notwithstanding, this new bunch was much more representative of their friendly breed than Mongo, whom we learned was Jesse's nephew. "He gets a little crazy on whiskey," Jesse explained. "But he'll be all right tomorrow, you'll see. One hell of a hog hunter, though."

We shared our gumbo. They shared their whiskey. In the process, we got an earful about this lunatic sport of hog hunting. Chasing them down with packs of vicious dogs, wrestling and hog-tying them. Slaying them *mano a mano* with bayonets. The craziest shit you ever heard of. Turned out, they knew our only hog-hunting friend, Johnny Bonck of New Orleans. There aren't many hog hunters around, and it's a pretty tight fraternity.

Having a common friend really broke the ice. You know how that goes. Nothing engenders camaraderie like having common friends, except, of course, having common enemies.

"Y'all come with us tomorrow," Jesse offered midway through the evening. "An experience you won't forget. Hell, we'll let you do the honors," and he patted the knife on his belt.

"Think we'll take you up on that," Pelayo replied while looking around and hoisting his little cup of blackjack on the rocks. Chris and I nodded and toasted right back.

"But maybe not the 'honors,'" I added. "Hell, break us in first. I ain't going up against a wild boar with a hunting knife— not yet anyway."

After feeding the dogs, unloading the boats, and cutting more firewood, Goober finally stumbled into his tent. In minutes, we heard thunderous snoring, between gasping, almost strangulation sounds. "That's why my tent's waaaay over there," Jesse said, pointing behind him. "Ain't no sleeping anywhere close to that boy." Mark chuckled assent. "And I guess you saw Ronnie's head," Jesse added while tapping his forehead. "That boy's a crazy one when he gets after a big ole hog, whoo boy," he nodded. "And that day, we was after a *big* one, for sure. We was huntin' up near home. We'd already chased that damn hog . . . what?" He looked around to his friends. "Ten? Twelve times?"

"At *least*," Mark nodded, turning from the fire for a second.

"He killed three of our best dogs and ripped up just about all the others. He was coal black but with a little patch of white on his rump. He was mostly Russian, but had some feral hog in him, too. Not all that big, really. He was probably 'bout the size of the one we got in the boat." He turned to Mark again. "Don't ya think?"

"Yeah, I'd say about a 300-pounder," Mark replied. "Maybe a little more."

"But this ole hog was smart—and *mean*. We named the big sucker Diablo and knew pretty much where he lived."

"We sure did," Mark added after a little nip from his cup. "So usually we stayed away from the area. Why get more dogs killed, we figured? They ain't cheap, especially the good ones, and every time you went after Diablo, you pretty damn well figured you'd get one killed and a couple crippled."

"He's right," Jesse continued. "A good hog dog don't come easy. Well, we got us a big pack of dogs that day; our top ones, along with the best from some friends of ours from over y'all's way. Your friend Johnny was there too . . . I'm pretty sure . . . Where was dem fellers from, Mark? Ya remember?"

"They was from around New Orleans somewhere, some place called Chalmette, I think."

"Yeah, that was it," Jesse laughed. "What was it they called themselves? Some name? Some nickname? Dalmations? Somethin' . . . ?

"Chalmations!" Mark shouted.

"Yeah, that was it!" Jesse whooped. "Chalmations. Great buncha guys. Some serious hunters and serious partiers, too. We always had us a good ole time with dem Chalmation fellers. Anyway, ole Ronnie was on horseback that day. Up around home, sometimes we chase hogs on horseback. Depends on the terrain. Well, we hadn't been hunting half an hour or so, and we hear the track dogs at bay. A dog'll bark different when he's tracking, when he's on the trail, than when he's got the hog bayed, cornered, ya unnerstan'?" We all nodded. "So we heard that racket and knew they had one cornered somewhere, and somewhere close. That was one hell of a racket. Ronnie was the first on the scene."

"Hell," Mark added. "It figures. He was on a horse."

"Right," Jesse nodded. "Well, we finally ran up and the damn racket sounded like hell itself. Remember Mark? Barking and yelping and growling. Dem dogs was worked up good, but we already heard some squealing, too, and not from the hog. The squeals sounded like wounded dogs."

"Sure enough," Mark added. "We get there and one dog, ole Abner, well, he's already ripped open. He's laying on the ground, done bled to death."

"So Mark grabs another dog. He can see the dog has his flank ripped open and goes to work on him with the staple gun," Jesse added, then held up a hand and got up. "Here, wait a second." He ducked into a tent. Mark looked over, nodding, motioning with his hands for us to stay put.

"Here you go." Jesse came out holding a skin staple gun. "My wife works in a hospital," he said. "We get 'em cheap. They're disposable. Hell, we go through two dozen every season. Anyway, that's what we use to stitch up the dogs, and ourselves! I'll tell ya 'bout that later. Hell, it ain't just the dogs who get ripped. After we staple up a dog, he usually goes right back into action. They love it. Some say it's cruel, but hell, these dogs *live* for that fight. You cain't tear 'em away. But not that day."

"They was getting ripped up bad," Mark said. "And Abner was Ronnie's dog, too. But Ronnie's horse didn't want no part of that hog or that fight either. He was skittish, raring back. Ronnie could hardly control him. Almost got bucked off a couple times, but that boy knows how to handle a horse. He had a shotgun on a sling around his back, a sawed-off, loaded with buckshot for emergencies."

"He usually likes to catch the hogs," Jesse said. "He uses the shotgun mostly to save his dogs. When too many start getting killed or ripped up, he'll go ahead and shoot the hog. This was one a dem times, I tell ya. He was reaching behind him for the gun when Diablo charged another dog. Usually, a hog will stay his ground. He'll sit there at bay and wait for the dogs to make the first move, trying to slash 'em in the throat as they move in."

"Yeah, Diablo was a pro-active ole hog. He made the first move on dem dogs. He didn't make a sound when he made his break either. No squealing. No snapping the tusks. Not even much huffing or grunting—lotsa hogs do that you know, always snapping away. Diablo just took off, made a quick swipe with his snout, and ripped another dog through the eye and mouth and throat. That dog took off yelping like a banshee. It was one of Johnny's, if I recall. Well, he lost it. That dog died a few seconds later, after running about fifty yards. Another of Johnny's dogs, a hit dog this time—did I tell y'all about hit dogs?" He looked at each of us.

We shook our heads. "Okay, well," he continued after a whiskey nip. "These is the ones who make the hit." He grabbed his own neck with his free hand to demonstrate. "When that ole hog's brought to bay by the track or strike dogs. Did I tell y'all about the track dogs?"

We only had about half an inch in the whiskey bottle now. We all laughed and nodded. "Well, anyway the track dog-chase and bay the hog. The hit dogs usually come along on leashes with us hunters, following the chase of the track dogs. These hit dogs, ours anyway, are usually full-blood pit bulls. They ain't mutts like the others. They don't need a really good nose, or to be very big, or very fast. They need one thing."

"Jaws!" Mark yelled. He put his cup down and made big fists on either side of his jaw. "Dem big ole *jaws!* That's all they need. They the ones who rush in and grab that hog, clamping down with those triphammer jaws on his ears, or nose, or anywhere on his face to keep him anchored."

"And then, just hang on!" Jesse continued. "That's all they got to do. You wanna have a hit dog clamping down one on each side of the hogs head. That way the hog cain't move much."

"Or see you as you come up behind him," Mark nodded toward us.

"Right," Jesse said. "And when the hit dogs have that hog but good, that's when you come up behind him, grab his hind legs, and *flip* him." Jesse made the motions. "And tie him up."

"You guys are plumb freakin' *crazy!*" Pelayo laughed. Pelayo, Chris, and I looked at each other wide-eyed, laughing. We held out our cups, and Mark poured in another nip of blackjack.

"See this?" We looked over and Jesse was digging in his pocket. He pulled out and held up what looked like an oyster knife. "Even when you got the hog on the ground tied up, dem hit dogs'll still be holding on with dem jaws. These here are the only way to pry 'em open." Jesse made muscular motions, twisting and jerking with the oyster knife.

"Sounds easy, don't it?" Mark asked.

"The *hell* it does!" Chris laughed.

"Well, anyway, ole Diablo had other plans that day," said Jesse, picking up the story. "That hog makes a lunge and hits *another* dog, then he spins around—you'd be amazed how fast these big ole hogs can spin around, too—anyway, he spins around and cripples another of Johnny's dogs with another swipe with those tusks." Jesse placed his hooked fingers on either side of his nose for added effect. "With two more wounded dogs yelping like crazy, with Johnny and I trying to grab 'em to start stapling, with all this goin' on, I hear 'Whooaaa! Whooa!' From Ronnie. I look up and his horse is going crazy. Ronnie's barely hanging on. Looked like a rodeo rider."

"Diablo made a charge at Ronnie's horse!" Mark boomed. "We told you that Diablo was a smart one. Well, he knew who was causing his problems. He sensed it. Remember, Ronnie was the one with the shotgun, and he was getting ready to unload on him—to whack him but good with a load of double-O's."

"But now, with all the bucking, he dropped the shotgun," Jesse picked up. "And the horse finally turned around and gallopped off. Diablo was right behind him! I'd seen these bastards do some crazy shit, but this was a first!

"Even if Ronnie hadn't dropped the gun," Mark said, "it woulda taken a goddamn bazooka to stop that three-hundred-pound mountain of coal-black fury closing on him."

"He didn't have a chance," Jesse continued. "Ronnie was starting to wheel around on the saddle, trying to look behind him, but Diablo was already on him, under his terrified horse. Well, that boar just jerked up with his snout, slashed those tusks." Jesse held his fingers up and curled his lips for effect again.

"And ripped the horse's belly open like a butcher." I noticed I had a pretty firm grip on my whiskey cup at the time. Pelayo and

Chris, too. Jesse and Mark were on either side of us, so our heads were going back and forth like spectators at a tennis match.

"That poor ole horse's guts just spilled out," Mark nodded sadly. "They got tangled all up in his legs and he tripped."

"Ronnie sprung into the air like he was shot from a catapult," Jesse said grimly, "and smashed face-first into a red oak."

"Well, gentlemen . . . ." Pelayo got up, emptied his whiskey, and stretched his arms. "I'm sold. What time we headin' out tomorrow? I'm turnin' in."

CHAPTER TWELVE

WHISKEY, HOGS, AND TOPLESS BABES

Wild hogs are roundly loathed by all fish and game agencies, state and federal, north and south, east and west. Seems they're not "game animals" in the usual sense of the term. Instead, they're regarded as despoilers of game habitat, roilers of pristine mountain streams, stealers of food from the mouths of tonier animals—in brief, pests.

The official line is that hogs compete with true "game species" (like deer and turkeys) for food like acorns. So game and fish officialdom, almost to a man, want wild hogs eradicated, decimated, wiped out. In most states, the season on them is open year round—no limits, no nothing. In Texas, you can even bull-eye them and blast them with machine guns, with the local game warden's blessing. Incredible.

But nothing works. Pigs are too smart and prolific to wipe out, to even make a dent in their populations. They're among the most resourceful creatures on earth, thriving from Northern California scrub hills to the Smoky Mountains to the Everglades to south Texas brush country to the Virgin Islands and Hawaii. They thrive in twenty-six of our fifty states. Even better (or worse, depending on your viewpoint), they're omnivorous, like bears and raccoons. This means they eat anything, animal and vegetable, though the pork you buy at Safeway is all from grain-fed pigs—hence the bland flavor.

Free-ranging pigs will eat anything and everything, from roots to berries to rattlesnakes to baby rabbits to acorns. Recall one of the most hideous film clips from the Vietnam War: pigs eating roast suckling human in that burned out village. Yes, given half the chance, they'll turn the tables on us.

A sow might have three litters a year, each of ten piglets. In six months, *these* start breeding. Do the math. One sow can be responsible for one thousand pigs in five years. Wild pigs actually outbreed rabbits. They're virtually indestructible, individually and as species, a mammalian version of cockroaches. You gotta love them. Basically, they control themselves, based on food availability, like most animals. "I wish we could get rid of the damn things," says Louisiana's top game manager. "But it's impossible! They breed like rabbits and eat anything! But nothing eats them!"

In the wild, he means. Here in the *cochon-de-lait* capital of the world, we certainly do, but not nearly enough of them to dent the population. Wild swine are tough, adaptable, and ingenious. In 1969, the eye of Camille, the most murderous, powerful, and destructive hurricane of the century, passed right over the Mississippi Delta. Two-hundred-and-twenty-mile-per-hour winds lashed and leveled everything, along with a twenty-foot tidal wave that hit like an A-bomb and blasted everything with a huge wall of water. The deer, coyotes, and the few humans who stayed all drowned.

PIGS ARE A NOBLE QUARRY, INDEED

But these hogs survived. Rescue workers saw them huddled atop the oil and gas platforms that dot this marsh, waiting for the tides to fall. We'll be extinct before swine; cockroaches will be, too, probably.

Pigs are a noble quarry, indeed—historically the exclusive prey of knights and nobles. "The sport of kings" they traditionally called boar hunting in Europe. Alexander the Great and Caesar, Hannibal and King Juba, Charles Martel and William the Conqueror, Ghenghis Khan and El Cid—all these regarded boar hunting as superb preparation for a leader, a gentleman, and a warrior. Bravery, tenacity, agility, judiciousness—facing down this noble foe at close quarters instilled all the knightly virtues.

But not on this side of the Atlantic. Here, by some quirk, they're fit game only for the crudest of yahoos, which is strange when you look at the pig's role throughout western history.

"The wild boar is the greatest character of the wild," wrote Sir Robert Baden-Powell, Lord of Gilwell. This distinguished gentleman, born in London, founded the Boy Scout movement. He spent many years in far-flung outposts of the British empire at the turn of the last century. In his classic *Lessons from the Varsity of Life*, he wrote about his favorite sporting foe:

> The boar is the king of the jungle. He is the one beast that no other will face. When he comes down to the waterhole to drink, all others, including the tiger and buffalo and elephant, sneak away. They suddenly decide they're not very thirsty.

> No sport can touch pig-sticking for excitement or valuable training. The boar itself, mad with rage, rushes wholeheartedly into the scrap. Yes, it is a brutal sport—and yet I loved it, as I loved also the fine old fellow I fought against. He is the only animal that will go after you without first

being roused, because he is the only animal who is habitually crusty. He is always peeved about something or other. He is plucky and tough, as fast as a horse. If a native objects to his eating his crops, he knocks him down and disembowels him with his murderous tusks."

Pig-sticking was grand sport for British officers during the Raj in India. They mounted up and went after wild boars with lances, relishing every second, much like medieval knights.

If you'd care to consult your old poetry textbook, this is how Venus found Adonis:

'Tis true, 'tis true; thus was Adonis slain:
He ran upon the boar with his sharp spear
And nuzzling in his flank, the loving swine
Sheathed unaware the tusk in his soft groin.

The Greek myth also has it that several of Adonis's dogs were slain in the melee.

In his *Songs of the Doomed,* Hunter S. Thompson weighed in on the proper management of wild swine himself. It was a letter to his boss at the time, *San Francisco Examiner* owner Willie Hearst:

Dear Will,

If you can't arrange a state-of-the-art pig hunt at your place on the South Coast, I will arrange it on my own just south of Big Sur. We have killed many of those filthy black bastards down there, and I suspect we can kill many more. MANY. They are a menace, and they breed faster than rabbits . . . and I'll make sure you get at least one fine, fresh, blood-soaked trophy head right flat on the middle of your desk one bright morning . . . ."

Peter Hathaway Capstick wrote bestseller after bestseller about his exploits as an African white hunter, stalking and blasting the African big five: lion, leopard, elephant, buffalo, rhino. Hence his books' titles: *Death in the Tall Grass, Death in Silent Places, Death in the Dark Continent.* Well, here's what Capstick writes about the African bushpig, our local hog's African cousin: "The Bushpig is pure undiluted, industrial-strength *mean*, leave them strictly alone."

Right, play it safe, go after a lion or Cape buffalo instead. So here we were, surrounded by lunatics who not only eschewed his advice to "leave them strictly alone," but tackled (literally!) wild pigs with their bare hands!

Anyway, imagine how peeved a hog gets when he's roused from his nap by a yapping pack of dogs and a whooping gaggle of drunkards. Then chased through the slop for an hour or two. Then surrounded, bitten, and taunted. It's not exactly Sir Robert's or Sir Lancelot's version of the sport that we practice down here, but it's almost the identical quarry.

Pure Russian boars have been released (or escaped) all over America. The ones in the Mississippi Delta show the identical features of any you'll find in India or the Carpathian mountains of Central Europe. A friend of mine knows how they got here, too.

"I wanted a few pure Russian to train my dogs," he told me. "So I bought a few from a guy in Texas, expensive too, let me tell ya. I built a big pen for them behind my shop, with tall strong barbed wire fence and posts rammed deep in the ground. I trucked them into the enclosure, opened the back of the trailer, and they hit the ground running, I mean, literally. I mean they was *haulin' ass.*" He held two fingers over his head and shook them in the classic Louisiana gesture for "bookin'" or "haulin' ass." "Shoulda seen me and my buddy climb on the roof of that truck. You'da thought we were kangaroos the way we jumped up there, or spider monkeys.

"But those pigs were going *away* from us, not toward us. And *fast*, baby." He shook the fingers overhead again for effect. "And either they didn't see the fence or didn't give a shit about it. I'm tellin' ya these hogs didn't miss a step. I'm watching them from the roof of the truck and wondering: where's my fence? The fence I paid a coupla thousand to put up? That strong fence they use to corral Brahma bulls? I'm wonderin' about this, because I didn't even notice the pigs slow down. They hit that thing like a Panzer division, like big, black, hairy tanks, man. They trampled down that steel and barbed wire like it was straw and ran into the swamp. Me and my buddy just looked at each other wall-eyed. Hell, what could we do?

"That was thirty years ago, Hom-boy-da (Humberto in New Orleanian). I'm pretty sure that's where most of these pure Russian hogs we catch in southeast Louisiana marshes came from."

My friend, Doc Fontaine, is a big fan of wild-hog hunting, whether Russian, feral, or the usual blend. "The damn things are ten times as smart as any deer," he always tells me. "And ten times as tasty as any wild turkey. They're stronger and meaner than a black bear. And you're trying to tell me he's not a bona fide 'game' animal?

"Gimme a break! Shit, man, I made two African safaris and three to Alaska. All after dangerous game, so-called: lion, leopard, elephant, buffalo, and grizzly. I filled a trophy room—and never got a scratch. One of my trackers got trampled and stomped by a wounded buffalo. Another got hurled through the air by his horns like a rag doll. But I missed out on all the fun.

"Then I started hog-hunting here in the Delta, two hours from my house in New Orleans. Whoo-boy!" continued Doc. "I got charged and trampled on the first hunt! The bastard just ran right over me. I was blocking his escape, I guess. On my third hunt, I blocked another one's escape, but this one wanted vengeance, too, and he swiped me on the way out. I needed thirty-five stitches from that staple gun to close my thigh. I'm telling you I could see that beady-eyed little rascal looking at me before he charged. They have excellent lateral vision. They don't have to face you to see you. Those eyes are on the side of their heads. It wasn't no blind dash like a lot of people say about pigs. Lotsa people say pigs have bad eyesight—and it's true, it's not as good as a deer or a coyote's—but he's not Mr. Magoo either. Usually, when he's running straight at you, it's no mistake. No way, Jose. He wants to take you out, to teach you a lesson. I've hunted them too many times. I've seen it.

"So don't tell me about "dangerous" game, man!" Doc always gets worked up on this topic. "It's right here! These ornery bastards charge in a heartbeat. Nine times outta ten, a lion, buffalo, even a grizzly, runs away from trouble. Not these pigs. They're like Spanish bulls. They run straight *at* trouble, ready to slash, gore, and trample. So you'd better get to a tree *fast*. Or aim *good*.

"The marshes just east of New Orleans are full of hogs," he continued. "Like I said, there's no shutting him up on this topic. "But it's hard hunting them in there, almost impossible. There are no roads, no hard ground, and not enough deep waterways to follow by boat. That's why they got so many hogs and why they get so damn big. Well, we discovered a helicopter was the ticket to hunt them there. We'd drop down in the marsh and let the track dogs out, then lift off with the hit dogs still in the chopper and just follow the track dogs from the air. When they bayed, we'd drop in.

"I remember one day we landed in—my buddy who piloted the thing called it a hot landing zone. He was a Nam vet, a chopper pilot over there, a damn good one too. Three tours of duty. Anyway we land almost in the middle of the dogs and see they got a huge silvertip hog bayed. I hop out of the chopper when it's still a few feet off the ground, start walking over, and notice the damn hog looking straight at me. He ain't worried about the dogs, like they wasn't there. This sucker had a look that said, been there, done that. He's staring straight at *me*, for three seconds or so. I stopped, then he charged!

"I mean the instant he saw what I was, he was coming at me full blast! WHOOOOA! I had no gun with me, no nuthin', and it's the marsh, so there's no trees to climb. Podnuh, you better believe I wheeled around fast. The guys on the chopper said it looked like I spun around in mid-air. I just started haulin' some serious ass! I mean *bookin'*"—Doc shakes two fingers over the side of his head for effect— "back to the chopper! It's still hovering a few feet off the ground. I'm running, they're screaming, holding out their arms like to lift me in, just like in Nam at a real hot landing zone.

"Well, I dove in that chopper from about five feet away, and the guys grabbed me. They lifted me in and—BOOM—I felt the whole chopper shake. This was a smaller one. Well, that hog rammed head on into the landing bars, I mean BANG! We all looked down and that sucker was just sitting there looking up at us as we lifted off, like saying: 'You buncha wussies! Come back here!'

"Now, Humberto, how many animals you know will attack a goddamn helicopter? And with the rotors going, with all that racket? I remember that rhino attacking John Wayne's Range Rover in the movie *Hatari*, and I've heard of Spanish bulls attacking trains. But man, to have an animal like that to hunt, right here, right on our doorstep. Like Pete Townsend said, I call that a *bargain!*"

Doc exploded in guffaws at that *Survivor* episode where a contestant dispatched a wild pig in three seconds flat with a sharp stick. "That's Hollywood for ya!" he cackled. "I'll believe those titties on Pamela Anderson are real before I'll believe that pig-slaying scene. What a joke. Anyway, I've had more fun hunting hogs than anything else."

Maybe that's because some of these hunts took place from a helicopter with a mounted machine gun, while topless women served him whiskey. Others involved a tuna tower welded onto a customized Suburban, also with a mounted machine gun, roaring and bouncing over the south Texas brush country, while topless women served him whiskey.

"I probably shouldn't tell ya this, Humberto," he laughed. "But honest, I ain't never had so much fun in my *life*—not hunting whitewings in Mexico, where your gun barrel almost melts off, not hunting ducks and geese in Argentina with no limits and those guides to pick up all your birds, hand you shells, hand you another gun when the barrel feels like it's about to melt off, and hand you a cold *cerveza* between shooting. Hell, I had me a friend who was a little worried about going 'cause he didn't know any Spanish. Pronounce this, I told him: *cer-ve-za* (beer), *car-tu-cho* (shotgun shell), and he already knew *senorita*. So he was set. Had the time of his life and never spoke another word of Spanish.

"My favorite hog hunts took place in south Texas, Humberto," Doc said, rubbing his hands and with his eyebrows dancing. "I ain't gonna mention any names but those huge ranches down in the brush country. . . . Hell, there's no game wardens out there, no law really, except what the owners say is the law. The crazy thing was, everything we were doing was perfectly legal. I ain't kidding. Wild hogs, as you know, have no season or limits.

"We'd take off in that helicopter—it was a Bell, the kind they use to fly people out to the offshore rigs, ya know, but it's like a little Huey, the same kind this guy piloted in Nam . . . .Remember *Apocalypse Now?* Remember the Robert Duvall character? 'I love the smell of napalm in the morning!' Remember how he played 'Ride of the Valkyries' when they attacked? Well, this guy—can't name names, Humberto, I told you that—this oil man we hunted with down in Texas, he *loved* that movie. He was a Nam vet himself. He'd play—I'm serious Humberto, this guy was a RIOT, he liked music when we took off to attack hogs, too—but he played "Born to Be Wild." It was perfect! Think about it:

Lookin' for adventure
And whatever comes our way!" . . .
Fire all of your guns at once
And explode into space!

"And we sure did. Easy to spot hogs from the air. We'd be running pretty low; suddenly there they are! Okay, slow down! Think I got 'em: POW! POW! Hot casings flying out, trees falling! Dust and rocks kicking up! Pigs running all around in crazy circles— I'm sure they were squealing up a storm but there ain't no hearing from that helicopter, no way—watching 'em jump and twitch like Bonnie and Clyde at the end, like Sonny Corleone when they caught him in that toll booth and machine-gunned the living shit out of him; man I'm talking some *fun*! Oh, and I'll never forget this: one day we had tracers—like we weren't having *enough* fun already! Watching those things shoot from the barrel, watching 'em on the way down as they made the hit, that just doubled the fun. And what's blaring in the background when you finally empty a belt and take your finger off the trigger? (*I like smoke and lightning, heavy metal thunder!*)

"So you finish your burst, the song's blaring in the background louder than the damn machine gun had been, your arms are shaking, your head's spinning, you're grinnin' from ear to ear, you turn around and there's a topless woman handing you a whiskey on the rocks. Humberto! Is that livin' *or what?* Usually her nipples are swollen too. Don't let 'em fool ya. They get excited by that stuff. I'm not kidding. Something about that machine gun buckin' back and forth, back and forth, the power of the thing, watching the muscles bulge in your arms as you hold the thing. Don't let 'em fool you that they like those little Hollywood fags or those dizzy little fruitbags on *Friends* and stuff. Yeah sure, anytime you're getting two million bucks a picture or half a million an episode, you're gonna have women all over ya, but if ya ain't got that kind of money, be a machine-gunner.

"Okay, so you mowed down five or ten pigs. Now you knock back some whiskey and get on the radio and give the coordinates of the carnage to the Mexican guys in the Jeep below. They roll on over, pick 'em up, and get 'em ready for the next day's barbecue, where the topless women serve the drinks again.

"Like I said, Humberto. Everything was perfectly legal. Here we were with outright machine guns, but perfectly licensed. The guy who hunted with us was ex-CIA, he said. He was involved in that mess? That invasion your folks went on, Humberto?"

"The Bay of Pigs?"

"Yeah, that's it. He used to always talk about it. Anyway, somehow or another he got these machine guns, the tracers, the licenses for everything. We just had a ball with them, let me tell ya. He was gonna get us a couple of bazookas, too, for the hell of it, ya know? We wanted to see what that would do to 'em. Also some white phosphorus grenades, too. Shit man, blast them and barbecue 'em at the same time. But we never got around to it."

We should all be so lucky and well connected as my friend Doc Fontaine. One thing Pelayo, Chris, and I never do is pass up an invite to a fishing trip with this lunatic. The last one comes to mind . . . .

We drove down to Grand Isle and found Doc Fontaine's spanking new Sea Ray docked up right where he said in the marina. Pelayo was first out and onboard. Doc was nowhere in sight. Chris and I watched Pelayo go up and around to the bow as we started unloading.

Pelayo came back in seconds, his eyebrows dancing. He hunched his shoulders, cupped his mouth, and hissed, "Yow-za!"

His faced was creased with the weirdest look I'd ever seen, half smile and half grimace. "Fun but potential trouble," it seemed to say. He grabbed his heart in the old Fred Sanford "The big one! Coming to meet ya, Lizbeth! Comin' to meet ya, honey!" routine. "Go look for yourselves," he finally whispered while grabbing Chris' shoulder and pretending to steady himself.

Chris went first. I was right behind, watching his face for a cue as he stepped around the cabin, grabbed the handrail, and froze like a Brittany spaniel on point. "Hi, guys!" came a female voice. "Finally here. Heard lots about y'all. I'm Raven."

"I'm Val!" chirped another voice.

"Yes, Yes? Hi! Um-um," Chris stuttered. "Is Fontaine around?" I shoved him up and stepped up myself.

"Yowza" indeed! No wonder Chris was stuttering. They were lying on towels, tummy down, cheek to cheek. "There he is right there!" The blond one leaned on her elbow and pointed to the marina store behind us. The arm moved and revealed a breath-taking vista. The pointing motion set it into heart-stopping motion.

"Finally here!" Fontaine bellowed from behind us. He was coming down the stairs, carrying four or five grocery bags. "Some last minute supplies here," he yelled. "You guys owe me fifty bucks each! Great!" He beamed as he hopped on the dock, "See you met the first and second mates for the trip. They're experts! Old hands at this kinda stuff!"

"Act cool," I thought. "Act nonchalant. You're a sophisticated guy. You see these things all the time. Nothing to get frantic about. Take deep breaths. And for heavens sake, *talk*, respond, do *something*, you doofus! They'll think you're a deaf-mute, for heavens sake.

"Yes, hello!" I finally turned back to the girls and stuttered. "Sure-sure looks like we'll have good-good-good," she was turning over now "weather for sunbathing. Man it's per-perfect!"

No tan lines on these women. This form of sunbathing was normal for them so they could sure act cool. At least they had bottoms on, if you want to call them that. These were tangas. No tan lines down there either. I noticed Chris's knees starting to shake, like mine on a climbing stand when I've drawn on a deer and five minutes later he's still j-u-s-t b-a-r-e-l-y out of bow range. I didn't know what the heck to do or say.

Chris turned around to look at Fontaine and almost went overboard like a spastic. I grabbed his arm just in time. He looked up at me, and his face was just like Pelayo's a minute ago, like saying,

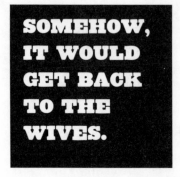

SOMEHOW, IT WOULD GET BACK TO THE WIVES.

"What the heck have we got ourselves into here?"

We were supposed to sleep on the boat two nights. Most of the best bull-red fishing is at night, at least in our experience. The sleeping quarters might get cramped on this trip, I thought. No way we could keep this a secret either. My brain was flashing scenes a mile a minute, like a music video. Some of the scenes were fun (of this trip), some hideous (when we got home).

Somehow, it would get back to the wives. Somebody would see us and report back. I was torn. Chris and I walked back to Pelayo. "Do we bail out now, and stay outta trouble?" Chris gasped with that crazy look still on his face.

"Yeah," Pelayo said. "Maybe we oughta get a hotel room. Maybe call Buzzy and see if we can stay at his camp? I'm not sure . . . ." He reached out just as Fontaine walked by and caught him by the arm in a bone-bruising grip. "You crazy sucker!" he hissed inches from his ear, dousing him with spittle. "Ya trying to get us killed? We weren't planning on this, man! The ole ladies are bound to find out."

"PAR-TY!" Suddenly a voice boomed from door of the marina store.

"Eddie!" Chris roared while looking up. "What the hell *you* doin' down here?"

"Yeah," Pelayo laughed. "We heard you were in jail!"

"Who's spreading these vicious rumors about me?" roared our old LSU dorm-mate (Stadium, naturally) Eddie Fleeks, while hoisting a bottle of Black Label in each hand. "I'm BACK!" he yelled as he hunched over. One bottle became a guitar and the other a pick. "I'm back in the saddle *again!*" He started high-stepping down the stairs.

"God help us now," Chris rolled his eyes, but he was smiling. We were all smiling. How could we forget Eddie's famous wedding reception? Whoo boy!

The reception started normally. "Strokin'" came on and the

dance floor filled. Smiling fathers in tuxes danced with giggling daughters in frilly pink dresses. Blue-haired aunts and grandmas smiled, clapped, and swayed from the sidelines. Their little darlings were cuter than buttons. When Ed Sullivan forbade Mick Jagger from singing "Let's Spend the Night Together" in 1967, these ladies probably said, "Good for him! Enough with these degenerate songs!"

Now they smiled and clapped along to the following lyrics:

I be strokin! I remember one time making love on the back seat of a car and the police came and shined his light on me and I said, I'm strokin' . . . .That's what I'm doing . . . I stroke it to the east, and I stroke it to the west, I stroke it to the woman that I love the best! But don't stroke so fast. If my stuff ain't tight enough, you can stick it up my . . . .

I always marvel at this. Has anyone ever listened to these lyrics? It didn't last long; soon "New York, New York" had them swaying, which was nice. Then, alas, that dreaded "Wedding Song" came on. *"Whenever two or more of you are gathered in his name, there is looooooove."* And all the females started dabbing their eyes.

That was Eddie's cue. He jumped on the stage and grabbed the mic. "Turn that shit off!" he raved, and stormed over to the DJ booth, where he started fumbling with the tapes. Eddie was half crocked when the limo picked us groomsmen up that morning. Hell, he was still crocked from the bachelor party the night before. Looked like he'd never completely sobered up.

He flipped some switch at the DJ booth and the telltale organ notes emerged. Those who knew the song by heart looked at each other, trying to decide between laughing or storming out of the hall. Then the lyrics started: *"You better watch what you say! You better watch what you do to me!"*

Yes, it was Tom Petty's "You Got Lucky, Babe." Eddie grabbed the mike and was acting it out onstage, pointing at his poor bride while groaning out each word with a teeth-baring grimace, á la Petty himself. *"Good love is hard to find! Good love is hard to find."* Eddie's lips were tight and his finger trembled as he pointed. *"You got lucky, babe! You got lucky, babe! When I found you!"*

His poor bride tried to smile at first, awkwardly. Finally, her lips started trembling, then she burst into tears, running into the arms of her mother and bridesmaids. None of us were exactly sentimental types, but good Lord, that poor girl. Eddie was outdoing himself here. The marriage lasted all of two months.

CHAPTER THIRTEEN

THE HELLPIG HUNT

Normally I'd be half-crazy with restlessness by now. An hour on a deerstand and my eyes usually start begging for different scenery. My muscles yearn for activity. My nervous system pleads for stimulation. My buttocks itch for a softer seat.

None of that today, because I'm perched in a scraggly willow on a mushy spoilbank in the Mississippi Delta. Hence, I'm in bliss. I'd decided to sneak in a quickie morning deerhunt before the hoghunt with the neighbors. They said we wouldn't be heading out 'till nine or so. I had plenty of time.

For a lover of wetlands there's nothing quite like this place. To my left; a canopy of lush green willows contrast against a lightening sky, under them a thick mat of elephant ears, glistening with dew. To my right; a vast shallow bay, lightly rippled by the breeze, stretches for a quarter mile until it meets a wall of Roseau cane that wraps around it's eastern edge. At an opening with the pass, duck potato, three square grass and knee-high willows sprout from a network of sandbars left by the high river last spring.

Since daybreak I've been watching pintail and gadwall dropping into the bay. Sometimes they circle to within a hundred yards of my perch on the way down, the sun, just topping the treetops, makes their late winter plumage glisten gorgeously.

The delightful racket of pintail whistling and gadwall gabbling isn't a sound normally associated with deer hunting. Neither is the banter of a few hundred geese conversing on their flight overhead. But down here you learn to expect it—indeed to yearn for it. It's part of the reason for going through the trouble of getting down here.

Add the sights associated with these sounds, the bays shimmering in the sun, the willows and elephant ears still green in January, the rafts and flights of ducks, the osprey crashing into the pond and struggling off with a mullet in his talons, the raccoon groping for a meal along the mudbank, the Roseate spoonbills winging overhead, the deer ambling—THE DEER??!!

Holy shit, it's a deer! A buck, no less! The sight finally jolted me from my reverie. He's ambling along between the marsh alders and elephant ears, about a hundred yards down the shoreline, and heading my way. He's probably making for that thick stand of Roseau cane just behind me, to bed down for the day. If so, and he if he stays on the trail, I'll get a twenty yard broadside shot. Good god, the shakes are starting.

Deer stick out in this habitat. This far south, they never get that grey winter coat. This one's still reddish-brown. And he's not a wall-hanger by any measure, looks like spindly forks on his head.

But so what? He looks fat and healthy, as befits this Delta habitat and it's year-round buffet. I can't make out his ribs. That's the best sign of succulent venison—if I get a shot, that is. And if I make it good. Lot's of "ifs" coming up.

My bow was hanging from a branch and I reached for it—but . . . s-l-o-w-l-y. There, got it. Now clamp the release on the string—but . . . s-l-o-w-l-y. No jerky movements. There, did it. Now turn slightly to get the perfect angle when he walks by—but again . . . s-l-o-w-l-y . . . PLENK!!

Now I did it! The damn bow (fiberglass!) taps the deerstand (metal!) as I tried to bring it into position. The deer stops! He's looking this way! He's rock still. Don't move Humberto. Don't even *breath*, for God's sake. Now he's bobbing his head! . . . Looks like I blew it . . . .

Wait a minute. Maybe not? Now he takes another step. Now he stops and looks behind him. He nips at the bush next to him. Hummmm. Looks like he's calming down.

VRRRRRMMMMMMM! What's that?! Don't tell me! Yes, it's a boat coming down the pass. Probably Ratso. Knowing that asshole, he'll probably stop when he sees my pirogue on the bank, and walk up to spoil my hunt. The buck's looking towards the pass now. His ears are up and pointed towards the noise.

I look over and see the boat. But it's not Ratso. It's Chris, Tom and On-The-Ball, heading out for their duck hunt. Hope they don't . . .

Ah, the deer turned back now. He's nipping the bush again. Shoulda known. These deer live with dozens of blazing boats every day of their lives. They don't associate an outboard's racket with danger. Much like their upland cousins who don't associate cars and trucks with danger—until they *stop* that is. Especially in Louisiana.

A recent incident explains why no deer "infestations" bedevil Louisiana motorists and yardkeepers. The Louisiana Department of Wildlife put a plastic deer with luminous eyes beside a well traveled bayou highway, planning to stake the place out that night and maybe nab some poachers.

When they came back a little later for the actual stake out, that deer was already . . . remember Bonnie and Clyde at the end of the movie? Remember Sonny Corleone when they trapped him in that toll booth?

Well, they got off easy compared to this deer. Plastic deer confetti is what the agents found. The thing had been blasted to smithereens by every caliber bullet and conceivable projectile. A few recognizable pieces of plastic even had arrows sticking out of it. We take our cuisine seriously down here.

So the game agents came back with another plastic deer, put it out and STAYED this time. If I recall from the news story, about half the vehicles—everything from pick-ups to limousines—stopped and had a go at the deer with armaments ranging from standard rifles to shotguns to pistols to crossbows. One guy charged it with a pocket knife, cheered on by his wife. Another guy was observed belly-crawling towards the deer clenching a tire iron!

The game agents said they almost needed respirators on this fascinating assignment. Their stomachs ached for days.

Anyway, this ain't no plastic deer still walking towards me. His ears are down and now he's back on the trail, about 60 yards out. At twenty, I'll take him. Just a few seconds to go here . . . My knees are starting to knock . I'm a basket case. Always happens when I see a deer.

At twenty five-yards I finally raise the bow—and D-R-A-W! There, perfect, to the corner of the mouth. The sight-pin dances over his chest, just behind the shoulder as I take a deep breath. I'm breathing in gasps. Calm down for heavens sake. You'll blow it. Another deep breath. The sight-pin finally stops jerking . . . stops wobbling . . . steadies. Right behind the shoulder now . . . .The deer's stopped and looking straight at me.

Release.

—RELEASE for God's sake, Humberto! He'll bolt . . . FLUNK! I squeeze the release—then WHACK!! The arrow hits and the deer's bolting off. Two bounds and he's lost in the brambles to my right. I'm shaking spastically now, a complete basket case—like David Byrne in that *Once In A Lifetime* video. My knees are almost knocking together.

But I didn't like the sound of that arrow hitting. That wasn't the nice wet, hollow "WHUNK" you hear when you slam an arrow through a deer's ribcage. No, this was more like? . . . Is that?

. . . Let's see. I peer closer.

YEP! There's my arrow, stuck in that big driftwood log. Looks like I blew it. No way that arrow would embed in hard wood like that, after exiting the deer—not this 60 lb bow. I humped down the tree frantically with the stand, ripping off half the skin on my wrists in the process, and walked over.

Sure enough, my arrow was imbedded in a huge, brush covered board that probably floated in with the last hurricane. No blood or hair anywhere. I shot over the damn deer. I blew it. But it's only . . . let's see? Ah! Only 8:15. Got plenty time to make that hog hunt with the new neighbors.

"That's a *dog!*" I gasped, after returning from my deer hunt.

"And a damn good one," Jesse nodded. "Here, you wanna bring him along?" He started handing me the leash. I reacted like he was trying to hand me a scorpion. "He's Wally," nodded Jesse, as I finally grabbed it. "Best hit dog we got. You're gonna be a hit-man on this hunt. Did Pelayo tell ya? Means you're gonna bring along the hit dog."

"Wonderful! But I mean, does he . . . can't *you* . . . ?" I was aghast.

"Don't worry," Jesse said. "He won't go after ya—unless we tell him to."

"AHHAAAA–AHAAA." Ronnie (Goober) got a big kick out of that. He was pouring a little whiskey into his coffee by the fire, and his bayonet hung on his belt.

We were going hog hunting with these people. Pelayo and I, that is. Chris elected to hunt ducks with On-the-Ball and Tom this morning. They'd been gone two hours already. No reason to get up with the stars to chase hogs, though. That's one advantage to this sport. Sure came in handy this morning, too. This dog they wanted me to bring on the boat was the most hideous creature I'd ever seen. Full-blood pit bull, they explained. He definitely had the jaws and little pig eyes of one, and the body, low and squat and powerful. "Pit bull" summed it up perfectly.

He looked like a walking tackling dummy, but with a huge ugly head. George Lucas couldn't dream up a creature this grotesque for his next *Star Wars*. I've never seen a dog I didn't want to pet. It's instinctive. I love them, all breeds. But *this* thing—if I saw something like that in my backyard, I'd shoot it on general principle, just to rid the world of something so vile-looking.

"I guess you're wondering why Wally don't have any ears," Jesse said looking over at me.

"Yeah," I replied. "That kinda hit me right off. And no tail either. Don't pit bulls usually have tails?"

"Usually, yes," replied Mark, who'd just emerged from his tent right behind me. "But you don't want anything on a hit dog for a hog to grab." Mark made a snapping motion with his hands around his ears for effect. "Any little thing that sticks out of his body, a hog will try to grab with his snout to get the dog close to him, so he can slit his throat with his tusks. We'd seen it happen too many times. So we figured we'd rather have an earless dog than a dead one. I'm sure Wally there agrees. Don't you, little feller?" And he bent down to pet and nuzzle the hideous thing. The creature licked his face and wiggled his butt as if he was a cute little beagle puppy.

I had to laugh at the sight, then a thundering yell from our campsite jerked my head around. *"Well I got up this morning—and I got myself a BE-er!"* Pelayo was doing his Jim Morrison again, "Roadhouse Blues," to be precise. He ambled down the trail, bobbing his head, singing between swigs, acting out the song. He stopped short when he saw Wally. "What the—?" He looked over laughing, beer spurting from his mouth.

"Well, makes sense," Pelayo snorted after I explained. "And what the hell," he said after a hearty chug. "Cheryl would freak out if she saw that dog."

"Shirley, too," I nodded.

"She'd probably call that *cruel*. Yeah, right. Yet she had our Pekingese "neutered." He mock-smiled and made little quote marks in the air and scissor motions near his groin. "But shit, man, if I was a dog," he suddenly roared. " I'd rather have my *ears* cut off than my balls!"

Ah yes, nothing like an early morning beer to make a man acutely philosophical. Bud and venison sausage, can't beat it for breakfast. I grew up in South Louisiana, so I'd been in some pretty weird hunting groups in my time, believe me. But here I look one way and see an earless pit bull nuzzling Mark, who now, without his hat, looks like Seinfeld's neighbor Kramer. And there's Jesse, who I can't look at without thinking of Mr. Ziffel on *Green Acres*. He's even got denim overalls on this morning, just like Arnold the pig's owner. Mongo and Goober provide the backdrop.

Jesse's getting the strike, or track, dogs in the boat with him. Those are a sight, too—airedale, pit bull, catahoula mutants. Craziest looking things you ever saw. They have the long hair of the airedale around the face, the head of the pit bull, and the body size, long legs, and coloration of the catahoula. They look like four-footed Chewbaccas that had been spray-painted camouflage by graffiti artists.

Mongo, wearing a battered straw cowboy hat this morning, is doing his little pigeon-toed shuffle toward the boat, looking sharp in his tattoo and bulldog collar. He passes us on the way, but makes no eye contact.

Pelayo and I got in the hit boat with Jesse and the hit dogs. Chases down here usually aren't long, not nearly as long as in pine uplands or even hardwood swamps. Due to the nature of the terrain, hogs usually come to bay fairly quickly in this Delta. There's not much high ground down here. The natural ridges alongside the main passes, the spoil banks created when canals are dug or the passes dredged for navigation, that's about it. These all sprout in veritable jungle.

The mild climate and fertility of the soil means any little tuft of ground down here sprouts in lush tangles of elderberry, willow, briars, rosseau cane, elephant ears, pea vine, marsh alders, and wild millet. You almost have to hack your way through with a machete, except for the deer and hog trails. Just hacking out a campsite takes some doing; fortunately, they last the whole season.

All the rest of the terrain in the Delta is water—shallow water, usually. These shallows convert to mudflats on the low tide (ask

Spence). So a hog chase is usually short down here, but messy and brutal, slogging through the slop, sinking to your knees, hacking and trampling through the thickets, sweating, panting, dodging cottonmouths. If the chases were any longer, you'd never bay a hog. You'd never get to it in time to save any dogs.

We'd gone about ten minutes down the pass when Mongo, Goober, and Mark started dropping off the strike dogs just ahead of us. "You pretty much know they're gonna strike in just a few minutes on this ridge." Jesse pointed ahead with one hand and edged the throttle up with the other. "We'll motor out ahead of them a bit now. Usually, we just follow along in the boat. Most times you'll see the hog rumbling along the top of the ridge as soon as you hear the dogs barking a strike. Then we'll try to follow as far as we can by boat, and get out when we hear the dogs barking bay."

Sounded like a cinch. We were actually on private land here, Jesse explained. "There's a few patches of it mixed up with the state and federal land. We've already had a few run-ins with that game warden, that Rizzo character."

"Ratso!" Pelayo yelled as he handed me a brewski. "Oh, yeah! We know Ratso *well*, don't worry!" Just then an osprey flapped overhead. Jesse looked up and pointed with his chin. The osprey had a mullet in its talons, but they hold them parallel to their body, like a torpedo plane carries its torpedo. He was only about fifty yards overhead and you could see the mullet wiggling, dripping water. He'd be ripped apart and eaten alive in a few seconds.

Ain't nature grand? I thought to myself. Like I said, nothing like an early morning beer for a clear view of the Big Picture. A flock of pintail over the osprey distracted us as they cupped up and started circling down. "Pintail Alley," smirked Pelayo. "We oughta hear Chris and them shoot any minute now."

But the next sound was barks. The strike dogs erupted in howls. "There's ole Rocky!" Jesse's eyes light up. "Just like him to strike first!" Then the two other hounds joined the chorus. "They got his trail now!" Jesse looked behind him, doing a thumb's up to Mark, Mongo, and Goober, who followed in the other boat behind us.

Mongo returned the gesture and actually seemed to *smile.*

Goober whipped out his bayonet and held it aloft with a two-handed grip, like a samurai, like King Arthur hoisting Excalibur, grinning crazily with that mangled face of his. Everyone nodded excitedly. "They got him now!" yelled Mark.

"There!" Jesse grabbed my shoulder just as I turned back, and pointed. "See him!" Ah yes, a huge black blob was plowing through the brambles like a tank. But it looked like it had a tail, a straight tail. "Sure that's a hog?"

"A big one—a *boar!*" Jesse roared back. His face was aglow. "Whatsa matter with you, boy? Ain't never seen a wild hog before?" Actually I had, and plenty, but usually from a deer stand. This offered a different profile. That's the first thing that hits you about truly wild pigs: that straight tail. When chased, they often hold it straight up, too, like this one.

He topped the ridge and disappeared over the backside. The dogs loped by a few seconds later, howling crazily. Hot on his tail, literally. Wally was going crazy on the end of the leash, yelping, tugging, shaking, and dying to get in on the action. I was holding that leash. Pelayo was holding the one with Huck, the other strike dog. He also lugged the little beer cooler in a backpack. Huck was going nuts, too. I looked down at the dogs and thought: I've seen these same excited faces, heard this same panting, observed this same spastic trembling, this drooling—on friends as we enter the Gold Club.

"Looks like here's where we get out, boys." Suddenly Jesse rammed the boat up on the muddy bank. Mark did the same behind us. They hopped out, stumbled up the ridge, and headed for the action. Another canal turned off at a right angle here, but it was silted up. No navigating it. That hog must have known that, because he took off along it's spoil bank, headed away from us now, headed for the thickest and wettest and remotest stuff around. We knew the area well. Deer like the area, too, especially late in the season after the pressure's on. We'd hunted deer there once before. We entered in pirogues during a high tide, then the tide fell. Getting out was a major hassle; especially with the spike and doe we'd arrowed. Never again, we said. Now we were being led back into it by a wily wild hog.

"YOW—YOW!" came the yelps from over the ridge. "Bay!"

yelled Jesse. "Sounds like they got him!" Goober was just topping the ridge. He looked back at Jesse and held up both fists, then he started waving us in.

"Let's go, guys!" Jesse was yelling as he grabbed Huck's leash from Pelayo and pushed me off the bow. "Let's go!" We started clambering up the spoil bank. I still had the leash with Wally, and the ugly little bastard was actually pulling me along, like a little tank, when: "YEE-YEE-YOW!"

"Goddamn, that dog's been cut!" Jesse cursed. "Hurry!"

"Rocky! Rocky! Get outta there!" Mongo was yelling. "Get outta there boy! Git!"

"YEE-YEE-YOW!" A hell of a battle was raging. Wally was barking up a storm. Huck, too. Then the barking changed. "He broke bay!" grimaced Jesse next to me, as he tugged back on Huck's leash. "Hell, shoulda known! Couldn't be *this* easy! Let's go!" And we stumbled forward.

We got to a little clearing surrounded by willows, and Mongo waved us over. "Over here!" He was holding Rocky by the neck as Goober worked on him with the staple gun and some iodine. The dog was frantic, shaking his head, whining, trying to slip from Mongo's grip. He had a six inch gash along his rib cage, yet he was frantic to get back into the fight.

"Told you guys," Jesse said, looking over at Pelayo and me. "Dem dogs live for this stuff!" Then he looked down at the dog. "Ain't that right, Rocky?"

Rocky looked over, whining, barking, drooling, squirming. He could hear his buddies yapping in the distance. He was desperate to join in. Mongo snapped the last staple, and he was off like a rocket, yapping away, like yelling: "Wait for me gang! Don't hog all the fun!"

"Here!" Mongo suddenly grabbed the leash roughly from my hand with his claw. He turned to Jesse. "Whattya say, Jesse? Let Huck and Wally go now?"

"Yeah, guess so," Jesse replied while bending down to unsnap from Huck's collar. "We'll all go faster that way." YOW-YOW-YOW! The hit dogs scrambled off instantly. Their stubby legs going a mile a minute.

A crazed, sweaty, mud-splattered scramble through stinking slop and brambles lasted another half hour. We'd traveled maybe a quarter mile, then the barking changed again. "Got him bayed!" panted Jesse, as he pulled his boot out of the mud next to a sweating, panting Pelayo. "Got him bayed *again!*"

It sounded no more than a hundred yards ahead. "YOW-YOW! YEEE-YEE!"

"Goddamnit!" yelled Jesse as he took off again. "Another one's cut!" Mongo, Mark, and Goober sounded like they were already at the bay. Pelayo and I raced after Jesse, the racket increasing in volume and ferocity with every step.

"Outta there, Rocky!" Mongo was yelling "Outta there boy! "YOW-YOW!" We hopped over a little slough, cleared another ridge top, and finally got to the action, and what action! That Rocky hadn't had enough. He was lunging into the fracas like a maniac. The hog was surrounded, huffing and snorting, spinning around as a dog grabbed his butt, never letting one get behind him. Amazing how agile the big bastard was. They'd nip his butt and he'd spin around as fast as a rabbit, lunging with his big head, swiping with his tusks, but fast, *lightning* fast.

WHACK! "YEE–YEE!" He got one that time. "Huck!" yelled Mongo. "Get outta there, boy!" Huck ('cause he don't give a fuck) came in fast for the hog's head, but the hog had just spun around and saw him. He jerked that massive snout, and Huck actually sailed through the air, legs spread. Christ, I thought. That dog's gotta be dead!

Instead he hit the ground, spun around, and charged again, just as Wally moved in from the other side and CHOMP! got hold of an ear. The hog snorted and started shaking his huge head like a terrier with a rat. Wally was lifted in the air, but his jaws hung on like a snapping turtle's. He flopped back and forth in the air like a stuffed animal toy.

Now Huck made his hit from the other side and grabbed an ear. Now Rocky and another track dog came up from behind and started nipping. I couldn't believe this shit! It was horrible! It was brutal! It was cruel! It was crazy! Let's admit it: it was—

as J.J. Walker might say—DY-no-MITE! Thrilling as hell! Back to the fang and claw!

Suddenly, the hog lunged, jerked violently, and Wally flew off his snout like a toy. Now the boar makes a mad dash, but with Huck still hanging on his ear. Huck bounced alongside the boar as it rumbled past a willow and—SMACK! Huck hit it with a blow like from a baseball bat. Finally, he fell off and sat there for a second. "That freakin' dog is dead," I thought.

Then, "YOW-YOW!" He's back up in a split second, giving chase right behind ugly Wally.

The hog runs thirty yards and turns around again, but now he's got a huge driftwood log behind him. No dogs can blindside him now. "This here's a smart one!" Jesse gasps from next to me, smiling, panting, and wiping his muddy brow. "Think we'll catch him live. Bring him back home to release, huh, Ronnie?" He looked over and Ronnie nodded assent.

"Hail yeah!" Goober whooped. "We could use some of his kind up near home! Looks pure Russian!"

Like a brave *toro* who gives a magnificent account of himself, a brave boar often gains a pardon on his execution. Sympathy has nothing to do with it. The boar hunters, like the prancing matador and the cheering aficionados in the stands, simply want the privilege of challenging and tormenting the magnificent animal again, and to let him spread his valuable seed. This calls for one guy coming up behind the hog as the dogs distract him by gripping his face in their trip-hammer jaws, grabbing his hind legs, and flipping him, then quickly tying his legs. They'll release him elsewhere to sire more broods, to spread his valiant genes to another herd in another swamp.

A thumbs-down for the hog means close-quarters stuff, no rifles, pistols, or even bows. In die-hard boar hunting circles, these qualify as long-distance weapons of pansies and faggots. Purists, true aficionados, like the dirty business at intimate quarters, the full fury of the desperate prey erupting in their face, his crazed squeals and popping tusks, the ghastly musk from his inflamed glands, his blood (and possibly theirs) gushing in crimson splendor.

"Blood has an unequaled orgiastic power," writes Jose Ortega Y

Gassett in his classic *Meditations on Hunting.* "When it is spilled it intoxicates, excites, and maddens both man and beast . . . .the Romans went to the Coliseum as they did to a tavern, and the public bullfight does the same . . . .Blood operates as a stupefying drug."

Not exactly fodder for the Oprah Book Club, but perfectly true. With a death sentence for the hog, the hunter rushes in from behind and flips the boar by his legs, or stabs him as he stands, low behind the shoulder, where the racing heart erupts in a geyser of blood, drenching the hunter and anointing him into this barbarous brotherhood—assuming the hit dogs hold fast on his head with their trip-hammer jaws and keep the hog from jerking around and slashing his human executioner across his face or neck, using his tusks like deadly daggers.

"Hell, Humberto," Jesse turned to me. "We was gonna let you do the honors with the bayonet. Remember drawing straws last night? But you don't mind if Jake catches him, do you?"

"No problema!" I shouted, elated. "None at all! Y'all go right ahead and catch him!"

Now, with his rear covered, the big boar had a little breathing room. He even looked more relaxed now. No more huffing or squealing as he turned around to face his tormentors. The dogs barked maniacally all around him, but the boar was silent. He just stood there, glowering at his barking captors.

No bluffing by this animal. That's what worried us. He was coal-black with a silver sheen to his coat. "Gotta go three hundred pounds!" Goober yelled. He grabbed a beer from his pocket and gulped a foamy swig. I was parched myself and motioned Pelayo over for one.

This pig was a veteran, definitely keeping his cool even as canine bedlam erupted around him. The dogs seemed to sense it, too. None rushed him this time. They were content to stand ten feet away and bark like banshees.

Finally, Huck, Jesse's prize dog, made his move. Unlike Wally, he had ears ("My wife grew attached to Huck," Jesse explained. She wouldn't let me.) He rushed in and tried to grab an ear. The boar made a swipe so quick you could barely catch it, lighting-quick.

"YEEEH-YEEH-YOW!—YOW!—YEEEH!" Huck got ripped good this time. He hit the ground, rolled, and we immediately saw the crimson gash, running clear from his neck to his haunch.

"HUCK!" Mongo growled. "You stupid little bastard!" Mongo was yelling as he ran over with the staple gun.

"Get him!" Jesse yelled. "Get him outta there!" Huck wasn't back up and jumping into the fight *this* time. He was moving slow. If the hog caught him again, he'd kill him for sure, but Wally distracted him. The plucky little bastard rushed in and clamped down on the hog's snout, but up close to the nose, too far up, too close to those tusks. The hog swung his head, and this time, Wally swung off, rolling in a flurry of brush and mud twenty feet away. The track dogs barked, but kept their distance. They couldn't get behind the hog.

"Huck!" Jesse was roaring mad, too. "You stupid sonofabitch! Come here, boy!" First Rocky gets his flank ripped, now Huck gets mangled, too. This was getting expensive.

"The truly brave bull gives no warning before he charges," Hemingway wrote, "except the fixing of his eye on his enemy."

Yes, it was the hog's beady little eyes that were starting to worry me. They'd turned from the dogs, they were focused on *us*.

The boar was looking past the maniacally barking dogs to the upright creatures that chugged beer while pondering his fate like a Roman emperor at the Coliseum. We were no more than sixty feet away, in an area pretty much cleared of brush by the spoil deposit from some recent dredging. Yes, he was a smart one. You could almost see the wheels turning in his big ugly head. "They're the instigators of this whole mess," he seemed to say with his beady eyes and twitching snout.

We were just starting to relax when he bolted, at us! "Pelayo!" Jesse yelled, but Pelayo hardly needed the warning. He saw the boar; how could he not? It was thirty feet in front of him, and closing *fast*, headed straight at him in a mad rush.

Pelayo sprung into action. Like I said before, not many trees down here. Next to a sawed-off shotgun loaded with .00 buck, a sturdy tree with low branches is a hog hunter's best friend. Pelayo had a lean willow just to his left, and he sprung for it like a goddamn gazelle. I'd never seen the boy move like that. He jumped, grabbed a low branch, and lifted himself up like a monkey, just ahead of the hog. I was stunned by Pelayo's agility this morning. Sometimes it takes him five minutes just to move from his La-Z-Boy to his refrigerator.

The dogs closed in on the hog again. Rocky grabbed him by the butt, and the hog spun around quick as a cat, swiping with that wicked snout, but missing this time, thank God. The hog made another swipe at Wally, who charged in from the left, missed, then stopped and backed up to the willow—Pelayo's willow. He stood there again, glowering at the canine bedlam around him. Looked like he picked the willow trunk as his back guard this time.

Pelayo was clutching frantically at the branches above him now. The damn hog was no more than three feet under him. Luckily, that's one thing hogs aren't good at: looking up. Their bone structure doesn't allow them to lift their heads very high. Pelayo appeared to want a little more elevation, though.

"Shoot the goddamn thing!" Pelayo yelled between gasps. "Shoot him! Stab him! Take him out!" At first, I thought Pelayo was laughing, then I looked closer. No, that crimson tone to his face was *not* from laughing. Those cue-ball eyes did not denote mirth. Those desperate screams were not of hilarity. "Shoot him!" Pelayo's voice was cracking. "Shooooot the goddamn thing!"

"We wanna take him alive!" yelled Mongo, who quickly looked over at Goober. Were they smiling at each other? Sure looked like it.

"Bullshit!" Pelayo raved. He was gasping and grunting, clutching maniacally at branches still higher above him, breaking them off in his frenzy, slipping, grunting, wheezing, "Shoot him! Blast him!"

Goober and Mongo appeared in no hurry. Hell, we had no guns anyway. Then the distance between Pelayo's ass and the hog's snout started shrinking. What are willows famous for? What does Stevie Nicks say in "Stand Back": "'Cause like a willow, I can . . . .'"

Bend, right? Well, this willow was true to its genus. The branch Pelayo had his legs wrapped around was about wrist size. He weighed 160, easy. Now he was bringing the whole top of the tree down with him . . . down . . . down . . . down. The higher he climbed, the lower he came. He looked behind him and saw he was about a foot above those tusks. "Shoot him!" he raved.

If he grabbed a little lower, the trunk would start straightening up, away from the hog tusks. Damn if Pelayo didn't sound just like our friend on the dock yesterday, the rotund fellow imploring Clem to "Cut the crap!" I detected a similar tone of urgency in Pelayo's voice.

A hell of a choice here. If Pelayo tried to climb higher, the tree would bend lower because of his weight on the upper, slimmer trunk. If he got lower, the tree would hold him but no more than two feet above the hog's snout. "On the tusks of a dilemma," you might say.

Suddenly, Wally rushed in out of nowhere and made his hit, chomping an ear. Must have hit a sensitive spot this time. The hog bawled like a banshee, kicked, and started snapping his tusks in rage, but Wally hung on, growling like a chain saw, tightening his muscle-bound jaws on that big, black head. This set off the other dogs; they closed in barking and nipping.

"Now we got him!" Jesse beamed. "That's it!" he roared at his pack. "Git 'im! Git 'im!"

"Wonder if they can hear this in Venice?" I looked over at Jesse.

"They can probably hear Pelayo," Jesse laughed. It was a hellish racket—mangled dogs, bloodlusting dogs, furious hog, terrified Pelayo—a din straight from Dante's third circle of hell. The boar jerked his huge head savagely from side to side, desperate to shake the pit bull fangs that gripped and ripped his face.

He turned, slashed with little Wally still attached, and the yelps erupted, "Yeeeh! Yeeeh! Yow-Yow!"

"Goddamnit!" Ronnie yelled. "We're gonna lose half the pack! Knew we shoulda brought the damn gun!" Now a track dog made a hit on the other ear, and Mongo rushed in without a word or warning. I couldn't believe it. He grabbed the hog's hind legs and flipped. Ronnie was right behind him. Boy, were they fast, like those rodeo riders who rope and tie up the calf. I was stunned. The whole thing was a blur. They had the damn thing trussed up in *seconds*. "YEEEE–HAAA!" They stood and raised their arms in triumph.

Jesse whooped himself and then moved over, pulling the oyster knife from his pocket, ready to start prying those jaws loose. Pelayo slid down from his precarious perch, almost on top of the newly trussed boar, looked at it for a second, then staggered over, actually high-fiving Mongo's claw on the way over to me. "Brewski time?" he gasped while nodding at me. I stifled a laugh. I could only nod.

We popped open the Buds and toasted. They were hot and well agitated. They foamed all over us. No matter. They tasted superb. Unreal. The whole thing was simply: Un-freakin'-real! I patted Pelayo's shoulder and guffawed. He doubled over himself, cackling crazily. We couldn't help it. The craziest shit we'd ever seen.

A camera crew from a local TV station went on a hog hunt with our friend Johnny last year but shucked it after the first chase. "This is barbarous!" blubbered the yuppie producer, who had a sausage biscuit for breakfast. "You people are *sick*. And *crazy!*"

"Perhaps," Johnny answered, "but seems to us, these hunts pay a boar the tribute he deserves."

Chill out and think for a second. Which swine exits more nobly? The poor sap in the slaughter pen? Or the one battling a pack of bloodlusting dogs and a gaggle of drunken, whooping yahoos after a two-hour chase? To ask the question is to answer it.

These delta boars go out like a bull in a ring. Like the fighting *toro*, he dies violently but nobly, face to face with a foe bent on his destruction but who chose weapons that shrink his odds. His miserable domestic cousin dies at a porcine Auschwitz—mechanically, anonymously, horribly, and obscenely. His death is ordered by a fat-assed bureaucrat from afar and carried out mechanically by a weary and joyless dolt.

The gloriously wild pig of the Mississippi Delta exits in a blast of trumpets and blaze of glory, like the defenders of Bastogne and Stalingrad, his death inflicted on the spot by visible adversaries in the heat of battle. This boar becomes Davy Crockett at the Alamo or Tom Hanks in the rubble of that Norman village, or a gladiator himself, dead in the end, true—but ah! What a grand finale! Brave, defiant, glowering at the enemy and lunging at him with his last blood-choked gasp, maybe taking a few down with him.

I'm sure the boars would agree. With us, not only does he go out in a blaze of martial glory, he also gets his picture taken in various poses. Then his carcass, lovingly marinated and draped over open coals, inspires another south Louisiana outburst of revelry and gluttony, another occasion to gather and imbibe. Long after any memory of his domestic cousins has been grunted out and flushed, his mounted head, adorning a den or hunting camp, provokes no end of convivial yarns and banter—and all in his honor.

Yes, compare this life and fate to that of the fat, feeble porker incarcerated for his short life in a stinking pen, castrated without anesthesia, whomped on the head by a bored drone, then churned into plastic-wrapped sausage so you, dear readers, can enjoy a hearty breakfast. No contest. And heck, this one actually lived, to do battle another day.

As for the dogs, they loved every action-packed second; they reveled in the primal brawl. That gelded and perfumed little poodle with the diamond collar on Malibu Beach will never know the thrill, will never be as true to his canine ancestry either. That's the dog I feel sorry for. His claws are clipped so he won't rip the sofa, his hair is cut so he'll look "cute," his testicles removed to curb his natural exuberance. He'll keep using his teeth and jaws for that mush they give him in a bowl. That's not what they're for. Ask Rocky, Wally, and Huck. They'd sooner walk into the ASPCA's gas chamber voluntarily than trade places with that poodle.

CHAPTER THIRTEEN

GAS ATTACK

Poor Tom, our official guest on this hunt, was new to the area. On the second evening, he decided to go off and duck-hunt (his all time favorite sport) alone. He hates to impose.

His screams woke us two hours later. We emerged hungover from the tents, cupped our ears, and followed the hysterical din. We found him a quarter mile away, just off the ridge, waist-deep in a quagmire. He was mud-caked, red-faced, and frantic, flailing the mud with his arms, screaming hoarsely, "Rope . . . throw a rope! Please!"

"Tom!" On-the-Ball cupped his hands around his mouth and shouted as Pelayo and I spurted out beer and collapsed cackling. "Listen to me! Calm down! Don't *fight* it. You'll sink *deeper*. Just pretend you're swimming. Yeah, like that."

Tom leaned over and started pushing with his arms, groaning piteously, grunting. He was indeed pulling his way out ever so *slowly*. Ugh-ugh, yes, that's it, ever so *slowly*, almost, almost . . . THERE! He made it.

"Now just slide out on your belly, Tom!" Paul yelled. "Like a turtle! That's it . . . attaboy. Perfect!" Oh, for a camera, but there was no time to run back to the boat and fetch it. Pelayo does have his gun, however, in case a hungry alligator mistakes Tom for an overgrown muskrat, or an amorous one mistakes him for a mate.

"Yeah, he looks like a big muskrat!" Pelayo cackled as Tom wallowed in the slop, grunting and belly-crawling his way back toward the ridge and us.

We escorted a very muddy and tired Tom back to the campsite. On the way he almost stepped on a cottonmouth. BLAM! A geyser of mud, twigs, and mangled moccasin head. "There!" Pelayo smirked as he shucked out the shell. "See how easy." Tom had backed into a spider web in the process and a huge and hideous banana spider was crawling on his shoulder.

"Hey, Tom." Paul pointed. "Lookit, you got a spider . . . ."

"AHHHH! AHHH!" Tom went berserk. A complete spastic— swatting, grimacing, growling.

"That's pretty good!" Pelayo laughed. "And here I'd always thought John Belushi did the best Joe Cocker imitation!"

A change of clothes, a can of sardines, and a few snorts of whiskey, and Tom was raring to get back to his blind, to get even with the ducks, and especially with the alligator who ate two of them when they fell beyond his reach. "I shot four," Tom moaned. "And the damn gator ate half of them!"

"Don't sweat it, Tom," Pelayo smirked. "Those don't count in your limit, you still got four to go, but it'll be dark in half an hour. Let's wait till tomorrow morning. I think we've done enough hog chasing. Let those lunatics go alone tomorrow. I'm hunting ducks, too."

"Same here," said Paul.

"And same here," I said while high-fiving all around.

So we plucked and iced the ducks we'd blasted that morning,

and popped the brewskis around the campfire.

Just at dark, a Texaco crewboat roared up and beached itself on our campsite. Jesus, we thought, the guy's drunk, or ripped on weed. More dope enters the country through these bayous than through the Florida Keys. Our marshes are wilder, shallower, and harder to navigate—hence harder to patrol, ideal for evading authorities. Ask Jean Lafitte. Ask the scores of drug smugglers and poachers who infest the place to this day.

The boat's cabin door opened, and a potbellied dude in grimy T-shirt and a hardhat leaped onto the bow. "Get outta here!" he shrieked, "NOW!"

Yep, just as we thought. We'd seen it often enough. The guy's looped. Paul hoisted his beer and started taunting him. "Shit, man!" he said. "We just got here!"

"Don't even break camp!" the guy raved, ignoring Paul. "Leave!" He was waving frantically. His partner was backing out, revving the engines to a thunderous roar. These guys were in a hurry and looked serious. Paul shut up and looked over shrugging. We stared, momentarily mute.

The guy looked up again just as his partner started revving the engine into forward. He cupped his hands around his mouth. "A rig blew by Southeast Pass!" he bellowed. "It's spewing hydrogen sulfide—deadly stuff! And the wind's blowing this way! The whole area is evacuating! We're the last out! Get going! I'm *serious!* Get going!" And they roared off.

We looked at each other, not knowing what the hell to do, except for Pelayo, who'd worked on a rig one summer and was already moving. "Let's get the hell outta here!" he gasped, while running clumsily to the boat in his hip boots. "I'm serious, man! That hydrogen sulfide's deadly!"

"Wait a minute!" Paul said with a weird gleam in his eye. "What rig? That Chevron rig we fish right off the coast?"

"Get moving, man!" Pelayo screeched at his younger brother. "Fast! " You couldn't blame Paul. He was a recent law-school graduate, scrimping for clients and eager to sniff out any trail that might lead to a serious tort case. This was a godsend, a windfall.

Sinking his teeth into an oil company, for heaven's sake. "Bhophal on the bayou," as they say down here. It's bound to happen, and here he was in the middle of it.

But Tom and I were in no mood to discuss class-action litigation just then. We sprung into action, scurrying to the tents only to retrieve our wallets. "Holy shit, man!" Tom gasped. "Gas attack! Let's go!" He'd been in Desert Storm as a reservist. We hopped in Pelayo's skiff and waited for On-the-Ball.

"Let's go!" Pelayo yelled, waving, as Paul dallied. "Okay, *fine!* We'll leave yer ass here! Ya ain't gonna sue anybody with your lungs puked out and brain foaming! That hydrogen sulfide's a killer, man!"

Paul finally scrambled over. I grabbed his arm in mid-air as he leaped from shore to the bow. We rumbled into the pitch dark and fog of the pass, heading back upriver to safety. Sure didn't look like it though. The night was moonless. The willows, canebrakes, sky, and water merged in a black void. A gas flare burned to the east, illuminating the low, scudding clouds, its eerie glow our only light, and now a little drizzle. Our path looked like the bowels of hell itself.

Paul plugged in the spotlight and waved the beam around. "That crew boat had radar!" he yelled.

"Turn that shit off!" Pelayo barked. The light made it worse, always does in the fog. "Can't see a freakin' thing! Cap it!"

"We shoulda followed the crewboat!" Paul screamed back into his face. Pelayo ignored him and turned sharply to dodge something, sending me heavily against Tom and him against an ice-chest, stomach first.

"See!" Pelayo blurted. "That's all we need, to bust the lower unit on a tree trunk—stranded out here, with deadly gas on the way. Turn the goddamned thing off!"

Paul did, plunging us back into drizzly darkness. "We shoulda told him to wait!" Paul kept shouting. "Just look! Look around, man!" He waved his arm to indicate the gloom and drizzle around us. "We'll never get outta here in this weather! We'll run aground for sure. Those chickenshit oil-company bastards! We'll sue 'em! If we get outta this alive!"

"That south wind's really kicking," Tom said, while holding his cap and regaining his wind with heavy breaths. "How far's that rig that blew up?"

"Hell if I know!" Pelayo barked. "Hell man, we might go into convulsions and start puking blood before we get a mile. That stuff might be on top of us! Those guys sure seemed in a hurry. We better start hauling ass." He gunned the throttle.

The stern plowed for a few seconds, then the bow started leveling out. Soon we were on a plane, roaring down the pass and virtually blind. The drizzle stung our faces, and I was getting tense. At any moment we could smash into a piling, plow into an anchored barge, or go careening into shore. We'd only survive the last, probably crippled by multiple fractures, and only until the gas moved in and finished us off, our groans replaced by bloody gurgles as the deadly gas invaded our lungs and ruptured the capillaries, snuffing us out.

Scavenging raccoons would find us soon enough. The area swarms with them. They'd cover our shattered bodies like ravenous rats, gnawing at the choicest morsels first—the most tender and juicy—our lips, eyeballs, and genitalia. They'd snarl and spit at each other for hours, lunging for juicy bites of our tongue and scrotum, gorging on this succulent and unexpected feast.

Finally, they'd waddle away to grab some nookie and sleep it off. The tide would rise, and the crabs and minnows would start on the ragged edges left by the raccoons. The rescue people would probably puke as they jammed us into body bags for the ride upriver.

Of course the front could pass, the wind could shift, and we'd escape the horrible death by gas. We'd lie crippled in the mud after the smash-up, moaning piteously, unable to swat at the mosquitoes that cover our faces. We'd send up a little cloud every time we blinked, until our eyelids swelled closed—and still they'd sting. We'd lie exposed to the cold rain and lightning as the front passed, thunder booming all around. Our metal boat, fifteen feet atop a willow after the crash, would attract a blast of lighting that would burn off our clothes, hair, and eyebrows. Some passing hunters, finally find us. "Holy shit!" we'd hear through our delirium. "How'd that boat get up there!"

The wives would get the news on the cell phone at Brennan's, during a champagne brunch, where they go mourn when we leave for extended weekends. "What? Oh, yes, yes!" she'd snap at the Coast Guard guy. "Yes, it's probably them. No, we can't come down right now. Just send the goddamn papers. We'll sign whatever you need. Yes, yes, of course."

The ghastly vision rattled me deeply. "Slow down!" Paul screeched, jolting me back to reality. The motor was revved to the max and I could barely hear him from two feet away. His red face and jerky head motions conveyed the urgency of the message. He grabbed his brother's shoulders, moved his head closer: "Slow down!"

Now I heard him, but Pelayo shook him off as the boat swerved sharply, plastering Tom and I against the pointed rod holders on the console. Suddenly, Paul lunged for the steering wheel and throttle.

Pelayo bashed him on the temple with a powerful elbow jab, shrieking: "Let go!" in a tone that scared me. "Let go!" He jabbed him again. I'd never seen him like this. His face was scary. Paul staggered sideways from the blows, pawing at his head and almost tumbling overboard but landed on his hip. Tom was wide-eyed, shaken.

"You're gonna kill us!" Paul raged from his knees. He seemed to be crying but more in rage than in pain. "You're gonna kill us, you stupid sonofabitch!" he blubbered lunged for Pelayo's knees, trying to tackle him. "Grab the wheel, Humberto!" Paul looked up and screamed. "Grab it, Tom! *Please!* This stupid sucker's gonna kill us!"

I was stumped myself. What was better? To go flying into a grove of willows at fifty miles an hour with Pelayo at the wheel? Or to let Paul have it? He'd slow down and we'd die of convulsions and foaming lungs, like in an Auschwitz gas chamber. Looked grim either way. I was starting to tremble, my teeth shattering like castanets, from cold or wet or fright or whatever.

Pelayo suddenly jerked his head and grimaced. "AH! AHH!" he yelled, while karate-chopping his brother's arms which were groping for his knees. Paul started yelling again just as, WRRRRUUUN! We ran up on a mudflat with a hideous roar. The prop showered us with slop as we bounced and tumbled inside the skiff like pinballs.

"Now ya did it!" Paul's voice sounded strange, muffled. I looked up while rubbing my throbbing knee and saw he was in a heap under a decoy sack, rubbing his head. "You stupid bastard! We'll never get outta here in time!"

"Shut up!" Pelayo yelled as he went over the side with Tom and started pushing. "Shut the hell up, and help push, you lazy prick!" He was grunting, gasping, and spewing spittle with every syllable. "This tides falling—and *fast*. Won't be a high till ten, tomorrow morning. We'll be history by then. Maybe they'll find our bodies floating downstream, if the alligators don't find them first. We better work fast!"

I jumped into the three inches of water, leaned my shoulder into the stern and felt my boots sinking in the mud to my ankles with the effort. "Together!" Pelayo gasped. "On the count of three. Okay . . . one, two, GO!" We growled, shoved, and the boat budged maybe an inch.

"We're stu-uck, ma-an," I stammered. My teeth were going crazy. My whole head bobbed with tremors. I could barely talk. "Stu-uck bad!"

Pelayo started to laugh at my rattling teeth, then shouted, "Look!" He pointed at Paul, still huddled in the bow. "No wonder! Get outta there!" he barked. "And help push! Can ya believe this sucker?"

Tom moved to make room but stumbled in a hole and to his waist. Pelayo grabbed him by the arm. "Great!" he yelled. "Hypothermia, now! That's all we need! Better get outta those clothes. You'll freeze going upriver."

"And change into *what?*" Tom asked. "And who's goin' upriver?" Then he shrieked, "I already smell it! It's here—the gas!"

"Hit the deck!" Pelayo yelled. "Put your nose against the floor, against the water. Just get *low!* That gas is lighter than oxygen! It floats above it. It's our only hope!"

I jammed my face to the water, my nose actually in it, and freezing, holding my breath. Pelayo was next to me, squatting. "I feel dizzy," Tom whispered hoarsely. "I'm serious. My head's . . . ."

"Me, too," I stammered. Then I heard a thump and splash. Paul was scrambling over the side of the boat when he stumbled over Tom and went into the drink.

I looked up, and he was shaking his head and spitting out water. Good, he wasn't dead. He was silent for a second, lying prone in the shallow water. He jerked his arm out, pointing at the motor. "That's the exhaust, you idiot!" he gasped. "Look!" he pointed again at the outboard while kneeling in the water.

Smoke was wafting from the exhaust hole. Tom's face had landed a foot from it. "What's hydrogen sulfide smell like anyway?" I stuttered while cupping my nose.

"Like rotten eggs," Pelayo grunted.

"I think it's the exhaust, guys," Tom groaned, "Sorry . . . but wait a minute! Listen! That a boat?"

"Sounds like a helicopter," Paul said, tilting his head. "It's up above the clouds . . . maybe a plane."

"Naw, man," Pelayo said, brightening up. "That *does* sound like a boat." Just then the green and red running lights appeared as a boat made the turn from behind us. Our own running lights had gone out at the impact, so he couldn't see us.

We exploded into shrieks, "Hey hey!" Pelayo waved, as if the boat could see us in this dark. My own eyes had adjusted to the dark by now, and it was possible, but unlikely. "He's probably the last boat out here!" Pelayo blurted. "Get the spotlight, fast! A flashlight, the flares! Anything!"

Tom scrambled over the bow for Paul's spotlight. Pelayo leaned in, groping under the console, "The flare gun!" he gasped. "The goddamned flare gun! Where is it?"

Paul had his fingers in his mouth and was whistling like a banshee. I was still roaring, "HELP! HEEELLLLP!" I turned back to the scrambling crew, "Hurry, damn it! He's gonna pass us. He can't hear us!"

He was probably the last boat out here. Our last hope—how else to get towed off this mud bar? "Hey, HEEELLLPP!" I was hoarse from screaming, and my throat burned.

Then a *pop!* behind me, as I stumbled forward covering my head. Christ! I thought. "Now what, somebody shooting at us?"

Pelayo had found the flare gun and sent one up. What a gorgeous sight, but it disappeared into the fog above us in short order.

Did they see it? The green-red speck of their running lights was still blazing past us. Is it slowing down? Just a little? Oh please.

"They're turning!" Tom yelled. You talk about a pretty sight, those little lights, bouncing in their own wake now as they came toward us from about a quarter mile.

"WHOOOO!" We started whooping and high-fiving, even Paul and Pelayo. That was nice to see. We splashed around stupidly in the shallows and Pelayo started rummaging around the boat again.

He lifted a flat bottle of something that I couldn't make out in the dark. "Whatcha got now?" I asked.

"Mad Dog!" he whooped, right before jamming it to his mouth. "WHEEEEW!" he blew out "Time to celebrate! Here, On-the-Ball!" He passed it off to Paul, who guzzled and whooped himself, then to Tom. Finally, I got it.

"Where'd ya get this crap?" I asked. "Jesus, I can't believe it." MD (Mogen David) 20/20, "Mad Dog" for short. "It's been a while," I said while wiping the mouth. Then I took a deep breath and chugged. "WHOOOO!" I howled as it seared my throat.

"Now watch them get stuck!" I suddenly yelled.

"Yeah, man," Paul said. "That's all we need now." He started walking slowly out, feeling for the edge of the mud bar, so they wouldn't share our fate.

We outran the gas and made it to Venice that fascinating night. It turned out there wasn't nearly enough gas released from the rig for any "deadliness" anyway, or even sickliness, much less a new Jag and Bourbon Street loft for On-the-Ball, and college tuition for all our kids. What a drag. We never let Tom live down his gaffe.

Indeed, we cackled till teary-faced while changing into some dry clothes we'd left in the truck at the marina. It was late by now, and the marina workers were knocking off. We were huddled by the truck with the Mad Dog, guzzling and laughing, when one walked by. "Hey, dudes," he waved. "Lingerie show . . . goin'?"

"Where?" I asked after a throat-searing gulp.

"Black Gold Lounge," he replied, pointing. "Right up the highway."

"Sounds like a winner to me," I said, looking around. Everyone nodded back. We'd been looking at the crude sign in front of the metal pre-fab building that was once a pipe storage shed for two duck seasons now, and always remarking: "Gonna have to check that out one day," as we headed wearily home. Well, here it was. No excuse this time.

We entered the Black Gold Lounge still cackling about the gas attack. The place was crammed with burly oilfield workers in jumpsuits, shaggy commercial fishermen in ripped shirts and white boots, and a little knot of marlin fishermen near the stage, most in Ralph Lauren polo shirts and fancy jeans. They were already whooping and grabbing and pinching.

Looked like a very combustible mix, especially considering the horrendous weather, which had kept everyone—commercial and recreational—inshore for two days. Serious cabin fever here. No trophies to brag about. Moods were uniformly foul, no doubt. They'd probably been drinking since noon. One of the dandies was already hustling over. Paul looked at me frowning, "Isn't that . . . ?"

"Pelayo!" The dandy extended his hand while bulling through the crowd. He wore a fancy striped pullover and Rolex. "Humberto!" he beamed.

"Max!" we yelled back." Lookat ya, man!" Pelayo said. "Didn't even recognize ya. We thought you were in prison."

I saw his eyes flinch for a second, but he recovered. Max Palermo was looking sharp. An old chum, we'd all been serious running buddies at LSU. Lived in the same apartment building, Tiger Plaza. *Animal House* (just out at the time) was a monastery compared to Tiger Plaza. The place was condemned by city authorities the year after we moved out, but ah, the memories.

Max was now a disbarred attorney, we'd heard, who lived on his forty-foot Hatteras at the end of the world marina. He'd been down here since his ugly divorce a year ago from Priscilla, my wife's sister, as it turns out, who fleeced him savagely in the settlement. "Some lawyer," we all said. He got cleaned out.

"Lotus." Max jerked his head around and waved. The female Cambodian bartender looked over. "Four double Turkeys on the rocks! Right here!" He pointed at us. "And get my friends a table!"

"What's this Turkey crap?" Pelayo snorted. "Bacardi, man,

Bacardi. How quickly you forget."

"Oh, yeah!" Max laughed in our faces. "Right! Lotus!" He called back. "Make those Bacardi, doubles." His breath was heavy with scotch and marijuana, his nostrils inflamed.

WE HAD FUN ALL RIGHT

"Keep mine a Turkey, Mama-san," Tom grinned. He'd visited her country briefly in 1970 atop a tank at Henry Kissinger's invitation. Mama-san smiled and nodded. She seemed to understand. She looked old enough and tough enough to remember. Maybe it was the Screaming Eagle patch on Tom's bush jacket.

"Saw who else is here?" Max said, nodding behind him. Pelayo and I squinted toward the corner where the guys in the fancy pants and polo shirts huddled. One was in white shorts, sitting on a table rotating his head. A smiling bleach blonde in a sheer black nightie worked on his neck and shoulders from behind.

"Naw!" Pelayo laughed. "Don't tell me—Al!" he yelled, a little too loud for my comfort, especially as he was right next to a brooding mullet fisherman, who jerked his head and grimaced at the shout. "Ain't this some shit!" Pelayo kept booming. Mullet-guy flinched again, spilling part of his beer on Tom. "You crazy sonofabitch!" Pelayo continued, waving toward Al, finally catching his attention. The mullet guy gave a loud snort, looked around pointing at Pelayo (who didn't see him), and finally shuffled off, shaking his head. It's not bad enough that these bastards ruined my livelihood, he seemed to say. Now they come in here and screw this place up.

"Ain't this some shit!" Pelayo was still calling and waving. His face was florid. We'd looked doomed there for a while. We usually keep a quart of rum in the boat's "medical supplies" under the console. Anyway, the Mad Dog's effects were beginning to manifest. "Hey what the hell is this, anyway?" Pelayo boomed.

"A reunion by any other name," laughed Max.

Aladdin (Al) Comeaux had been Max's roommate at Tiger Plaza. Pelayo and him had been tight for a while, but we hadn't seen him in several years. He went to LSU Law School also. We palled around awhile after college and even after our weddings, but then our friendships flickered. Our wives loathed each other with burning passion, constantly sniping at each other at parties, constantly rumor-mongering about the others, accusing them of attending orgies and wife-swapping parties with mounds of dope. Eventually, we drifted apart to new circles of friends.

Then with Al's divorce, the coast cleared somewhat, and we started socializing again. After Max's divorce, things got even better. We—the ole Tiger Plaza gang—started hitting tittybars in the French Quarter every Thursday night for a while there, telling the wives we'd started a Ducks Unlimited chapter and were earnestly fund-raising. They kissed us and waved us off merrily every Thursday after dinner, that wetlands might be preserved and the glorious hunting heritage preserved for our darling children. "Have fun," they chirped.

We had fun all right . If only DU banquets and raffles raised half as much as we shoved into those G-strings. But that fell apart too. As usual, Max had to push it, take it to the edge. Lap dances weren't enough for him. He always wanted to set up the "Upstairs Room" with some girls for the "special." Pelayo, Chris and I always had a problem with that.

Anyway, between our rejoicing at being alive and the unexpected college reunion we really whooped it up that night. Towards midnight Pelayo grabbed my shoulder and pointed towards the corner where a portly gent sat with a pole-dancer on each lap. "Lookit that sucker!" Pelayo laughed in my ear.

I peered closer . . . and sure enough! It was Clem.